Designing
Professional Development
for Teachers of
Science and Mathematics

Designing Professional Development for Teachers of Science and Mathematics

Susan Loucks-Horsley
Peter W. Hewson
Nancy Love
Katherine E. Stiles

CORWIN PRESS, INC.
A Sage Publications Company
Thousand Oaks, California

This book is a project of the National Institute for Science Education (NISE) and was supported through a subcontract between the University of Wisconsin–Madison and the National Center for Improving Science Education at The NETWORK, Inc. The NISE is supported by the National Science Foundation under Cooperative Agreement No. RED-9452971. Any opinions, findings, and conclusions or recommendations expressed in this publication are those of the authors and do not necessarily reflect the views of the National Science Foundation.

For information:

Corwin Press, Inc.
A Sage Publications Company
2455 Teller Road
Thousand Oaks, California 91320
E-mail: order@corwin.sagepub.com

SAGE Publications Ltd.
6 Bonhill Street
London EC2A 4PU
United Kingdom

SAGE Publications India Pvt. Ltd.
M-32 Market
Greater Kailash I
New Delhi 110 048 India

Printed in the United States of America

Library of Congress Cataloging-in-Publication Data

Designing professional development for teachers of science and
   mathematics / by Susan Loucks-Horsley [et al.].
     p. cm.
Includes bibliographical references and index.
ISBN 0-8039-6661-X (cloth: acid-free paper). — ISBN
0-8039-6662-8 (pbk.: acid-free paper)
1. Science teachers—In-service training—United States—
Congresses. 2. Mathematics teachers—In-service training—United
States—Congresses. I. Loucks-Horsley, Susan.
Q183.3.A1D47 1998
507′.1′55—dc21   97-33794

This book is printed on acid-free paper.

98 99 00 01 02 10 9 8 7 6 5 4 3 2

Editorial Assistant: Kristen L. Gibson
Production Editor: Diana E. Axelsen
Production Assistant: Lynn Miyata
Typesetter/Designer: Christina M. Hill
Indexer: Virgil Diodato
Cover Designer: Marcia M. Rosenburg
Print Buyer: Anna Chin

Contents

Preface

First teacher:

With all of these new frameworks and standards, I feel I don't know what's going on anymore. I need a workshop!

Second teacher:

I know so much more than I'm able to do with my students! What I need now is not another inservice program but some time and support to work with other teachers on using these new ideas in our classrooms.

First superintendent:

My teachers don't know what they need to know to teach mathematics. We need an expert from outside to come in and train them.

Second superintendent:

We can't keep paying for these high-priced consultants to come in who don't know our schools or our students. We need to develop our own experts in the district.

District mathematics coordinator:

We need to stop offering so many one-time workshops. Teachers need more opportunities to learn over time, with attention to both the new approaches and how to use them in their classrooms.

District science coordinator:	*At last week's conference, I participated in a stimulating discussion of a science teaching case. I think I'll bring in the facilitator to offer the same thing to our teachers.*
University mathematics educator:	*The teachers in my summer institute were so enthusiastic when they left. I need to know the best way to support them in the coming year.*
University scientist:	*The teachers in my summer course got so involved in the labs on DNA! It's a shame that few of them think they can use what they learned in their curriculum this year.*

The previous statements are common among educators today. They underline the great importance and value placed on opportunities for teachers and other educators to learn what they need to participate fully in the mathematics and science education reforms currently sweeping the country. Most teachers are keenly aware of what they need to learn, and superintendents, district staff, and university-based educators search for the best ways to support teachers' learning. As revealed in the previous comments, however, there is a wide diversity of opinion about how best to perform professional development and how to involve the many individuals whose expertise and support are needed if learning is to occur and make a difference in classrooms.

The purpose of this book is to engage individuals involved in professional development in careful examination of how professional development needs to change to meet the challenges ahead and how to make it an indispensable fixture in our educational systems of the future.

Challenges of Professional Development

There are few who debate the need for ongoing professional development. The call is frequently heard from every level of education and beyond. Professional development is one of the national education goals (National Education Goals Panel, 1995). The demand has increased markedly because of the release of the *National Science Education Standards* (National Research Council, 1996) and the anticipation of a revision of the National Council of Teachers of Mathematics' *Curriculum and Evaluation Standards for School Mathematics* (1989) and *Professional Standards for Teaching Mathematics* (1991). It also increased because of the call by the governors and business leaders at their March 1996 summit for state-created world-class standards in critical content areas and because of the president's January 1997 State of the Union address. Millions of dollars are being spent by individual teachers, schools and districts, states, federal agencies, foundations, businesses, and industry in an effort to upgrade the skills and knowledge of teachers to prepare students for the next century.

As we anticipate the arrival of the 21st century, several challenges require more extensive and effective approaches to professional development (Hixson & Tinzmann, 1990). The first challenge is *diversity*—the need to educate an increasingly diverse student population with different histories and cultural perspectives, experiences and expectations, and styles and approaches to learning and organizing information than those of students in our schools today. Another challenge is *enhanced goals*—the change required by new goals for schooling: goals proposed in national standards that focus more on deep understanding, inquiry, and problem solving than on acquisition of facts; application of knowledge across subject areas; collaboration among learners; and alternatives to traditional assessment that measure progress of individuals in relation to new learning goals while providing accountability for the effectiveness of teaching and schools. A final challenge involves *new organizations*—the necessity for teachers and other educators to not only function well in but also actually create new organizations—schools that are centers of learning in their communities, with different clientele and new learning goals. In such settings, collaboration is critical, teachers become colearners, and building cultures and environments for learning replaces the traditional ideas of classroom teaching.

These challenges require that teachers know their subjects in-depth and know how to teach them to diverse learners. Teachers must design learning environments that are sufficiently flexible to accommodate varying needs of learners and that utilize the full array of tools currently available and new tools as they emerge. Furthermore, teachers need to view themselves and behave as members of a community working together for the benefit of its youth. The knowledge, skills, abilities, and attitudes required by this new vision of education and the roles of educators are simultaneously broad and deep. Like their students, educators must become lifelong learners, with the understanding that there will always be important things to learn.

Clearly, the traditional ways in which professional development has occurred are inadequate. The current state of professional development includes (a) significant numbers of teachers who have few or no professional development opportunities; (b) a large percentage of the opportunities in the form of workshops, courses, and institutes that may not be appropriate to the learning goals or provide sufficient support over time for teachers to apply what is learned in classrooms; (c) a focus on individual development, one teacher at a time, without attention to organization (e.g., department, school, and district) development; and (d) some pockets of innovation but with minimal means for greater impact both within their own system and beyond. Students will fall far short of the national standards in science and mathematics if their teachers' learning opportunities are so restricted.

Designing and implementing meaningful, effective professional development initiatives for mathematics and science education is complex. It is fraught with barriers and pitfalls. There exists, however, a strong knowledge base and, indeed, a great deal of consensus about what constitutes effective professional development, which is revealed when examining the national standards for science, mathematics, and professional development (Loucks-Horsley, Stiles, & Hewson, 1996). Therefore, why is there a gap between knowledge and practice? One major reason is the lack of rich descriptions of effective programs constructed in various contexts addressing common challenges in unique ways. Nowhere is there an accumulation of the knowledge of effective professional development strategies and structures for teachers of mathematics and science, nor is there any one place where guidance about how these teachers can best be assisted in their professional growth can be found. There are many reasons for this. First, research and theory building in professional development have been driven not by subject matter concerns but rather by those concerns generally regarding adult growth and development. There is a large body of literature on adult learning and staff development; it is not, however, connected to the disciplines of mathematics and science, and many of the mathematics and science educators who design and conduct professional development programs for teachers do not know this literature. Second, although there is consensus about the general characteristics of effective professional development, there is much less known about how to put those principles into practice. This is largely due to the fact that professional developers are so busy designing and conducting professional development that they have not had the time nor inclination to write about their work. Like teachers, they are often too busy working to reflect and write.

Purpose and Evolution of the Book

This book is intended to fill the gap discussed previously—to bring together in one place a thick description and rich discussion of the practices and issues of professional development for mathematics and science education. It is at once a "primer" on principles of effective professional development and a conversation among experienced professional developers about ways in which they address the many barriers to creating programs that emulate those principles. The book examines the thinking of designers, illuminating their purposes, strategies, triumphs, and failures.

The idea behind this book—and the professional development project at the National Institute for Science Education that produced it—evolved as experienced professional developers examined their practice. The purpose of the book as originally conceived was to offer a few distinct and robust models of professional development—ones that provided alternatives to traditional formats such as inservice workshops. We began by examining the "models" in use by each of our collaborators. In doing so, we realized that, rather than offering distinctly different approaches, each program or initiative was a unique combination of professional development strategies whose choice was influenced by the professional learning goals and the particular context—and those strategies changed over time as learning occurred, goals and context changed, and various issues developed. We determined that professional development, like teaching, is about decision making—designing optimal learning opportunities tailored to the unique situation. Rather than offering a few models for professional developers to adopt or adapt, we instead provide guidance in the form of a design framework. Drawing on research, the literature, and the "wisdom" of experienced professional developers, we offer multiple "best practices" to assist professional developers in designing and strengthening their programs.

More specifically, this book is designed to

- Identify characteristics of effective professional development for teachers of mathematics and science

- Describe different strategies that have those characteristics, creating images of professional learning opportunities that include and then go beyond the more common inservice workshops and institutes

- Offer a design framework to assist professional developers in combining strategies uniquely tailored for their contexts and their particular goals in improving science and mathematics teaching and learning

- Provide examples of how elements of the design framework were used to create real-life professional development initiatives for teachers of mathematics and science

- Discuss critical issues that cut across professional development programs and initiatives and ways these issues have been addressed

- Provide references and resources for further exploration and inquiry

Two notes are in order before we proceed. First, throughout this book, we have made an effort to depict professional development as a critical activity for all educators. Because teachers are closest to where learning occurs and the vast majority of professional development opportunities are focused on teaching and learning, our strategies and examples often depict teachers learning. This is in no way meant to imply that learning is not required for other educators, nor should they be excluded from any of these learning opportunities.

Second, the terms used in this book must be discussed. We use the term *professional development* to mean the opportunities offered to educators to develop new knowledge, skills, approaches, and dispositions to improve their effectiveness in their classrooms and organizations. We avoid the terms *staff development* and *inservice education*. *Staff development*, to some people, connotes mandated participation, and *inservice education* connotes after-school workshops to others. Using the word *professional* signifies a commitment to continuous learning, which is a requirement of professionals. We have chosen to define *professional development* broadly and so make limited use of other terms that may be misconstrued. Similarly, we do not equate professional development with the word *training*, which is one of many strategies for learning and teaching. Finally, we have chosen to narrow our scope and focus on only that part of professional development that occurs after the teacher has begun teaching. Therefore, we do not use the term *teacher education*, which often connotes the preparation phase.

Uniqueness of the Book

Although there is a great deal of material available about professional development, including theory, research, program descriptions, and evaluations, it is only now that professional development specifically for mathematics and science education is being addressed in the literature. The information in this book was gleaned from a wide variety of sources, including the general professional development literature and information in science and mathematics education and generic education journals; websites; unpublished "fugitive" documents that few beyond the authors knew existed, including program evaluations; and project descriptions and stories, most of which were not written, by dozens of professional developers. Accumulating and making sense of this material has been a challenge, and it is also a unique contribution of this book: It offers "one-stop shopping" for busy practitioners who have limited time to search in this wide variety of places.

A second feature of this book is its intent to go beyond descriptions of characteristics of professional development programs and offer rich images of what is possible. These images are presented in two ways. We present images in the form of vignettes, which are not always real situations but rather composites of what the authors have learned or a vision of what could be. The images are also in the form of cases or case illustrations—descriptions of real programs or program features that illustrate ideas as they play out in the world. In no way do we pretend that this book is a "how-to" guide, but it does provide a bridge between theory and such a step-by-step manual. It also suggests where to go for specific guidance.

Finally, the focus on mathematics and science makes this book unique. Characteristics of these two disciplines directly correspond to the new directions professional development is taking. The paradigm shift in professional development (Loucks-Horsley, 1995; Sparks, 1994) suggests a change in emphasis from transmission of knowledge to experiential learning; from reliance on existing research findings to examining one's own teaching practice; from individual-focused to collaborative learning; and from mimicking best practice to problem-focused learning. Note that the new paradigm does not reject transmission of knowledge, reliance on research, individual learning, and so on but rather the heavy emphasis that is traditionally placed on these in the design of learning experiences. These shifts are the very backbone of the reforms in science and mathematics education because they mirror the practice of these disciplines. Furthermore, the important connections between professional learning and student learning are clear: We are talking not only about the process of professional learning but also about the way in which such learning mirrors and extends to a deep and new understanding on the part of students. Looking at best practice in mathematics and science professional development reminds us and reinforces for us the most important ideas in the reforms.

Audience for the Book

The primary audience for this book is composed of professional developers—those who design, conduct, and support professional development for practicing teachers of mathematics and science. Our focus is at the inservice level. These professional developers are found in schools (as teacher leaders, advisers, mentors, administrators, and members of leadership teams); school district offices (as curriculum supervisors, coordinators, and staff developers); intermediate and state agencies; colleges and universities in faculties of education, science, and mathematics; professional associations, such as the National Science Teachers Association and the National Council for Teachers of Mathematics, and their affiliated leadership organizations; state and federally funded projects and initiatives, such as those focused on teacher enhancement, systemic reform, and materials development, funded by the National Science Foundation, the U.S. Department of Education's Eisenhower program, and individual states; independent training and development firms; museums and other informal education organizations; and research labs and other organizations. There are several secondary audiences for the book, including funders, sponsors, evaluators, policymakers, and mathematics and science teachers in their roles as consumers of professional development. All should find this book useful because it depicts best practices and how critical issues can be dealt with in different contexts.

Book Organization

Chapter 1 uses vignettes of classrooms and professional development experiences to illustrate what this book is about. The vignettes illustrate the kinds of teaching and learning that must go on in classrooms and the kinds of professional development experiences that must occur for teachers if the vision for reform embodied in the national science and mathematics standards is to be realized. Beginning with these images, not as strategies to replicate but rather as a way to communicate a sense of where we need to be, demonstrates our commitment to a new paradigm across the board.

Chapter 2 introduces the design orientation of the book. This chapter discusses why, with the wide variety of professional development goals and contexts in which they are pursued, it is more fruitful to think of professional development as a dynamic decision-making process rather than as a static set of models, no matter how compelling. The design framework, which can be used to design new programs or analyze and improve existing programs, is described: Inputs of knowledge about effective teaching, learning, and professional development, alternative strategies for professional development, and the nature of the disciplines of mathematics and science are combined in unique ways, given the goals, audience, and context of a particular professional development initiative. Each of these components of the framework is discussed in a later chapter. A case of professional development is used to illustrate the design process.

Chapter 3 describes what is currently known about learning, teaching, professional development, and the change process in mathematics and science—knowledge that can form the foundation for a professional development initiative.

Chapter 4 describes 15 strategies that provide learning opportunities for mathematics and science educators. Each strategy is described by its

underlying assumptions, key elements, and implementation requirements. Specific examples are given.

Chapter 5 discusses several dimensions of a context that influence
the design and nature of professional development, including the nature
of the students and teachers (their needs, backgrounds, abilities, motiva-
tions, etc.); policies that constrain or support professional learning; current practices in teaching and professional development; available resources; and the nature of the culture of the school and district. How
differences in these dimensions influence design and implementation of
professional development is illustrated using a variety of examples in
different contexts.

Chapter 6 discusses issues that need to be addressed in professional
development initiatives if they are to be effective and successful over
time. Nine issues are defined and illustrated (what they are and why they
are an issue), the existing literature is cited, and different strategies for
addressing each issue are discussed.

Chapter 7 uses the initiatives of experienced professional developers
to illustrate the process of design: who is involved and how a plan including the unique combination of strategies is developed, implemented,
monitored, and adjusted.

Chapter 8 captures voices from the field. Like teaching, professional
development is an evolving area of concern. There are no formulas for
success and effective practice changes as goals, demands, and knowledge change. Thus, even within the medium of a published book, it is
necessary to emphasize the importance of the ongoing conversation
about professional learning, hearing different perspectives, and adjust-
ing our approaches to be responsive to the needs and demands of a wide
variety of educators and noneducators. This chapter captures the ideas
of people in very different roles, including teachers, students, professional developers, policymakers, and the general public, with regard to
what is important in professional development.

The resource chapters contain detailed descriptions of five professional development programs or initiatives that were designed and conducted by the book's collaborators. These cases are referred to throughout the book; the resources chapters provide in-depth details for those
interested in knowing more about the cases.

How to Use the Book

There are a variety of ways in which this book can be used. The design
framework itself, introduced in Chapter 2 and discussed with illustrations in Chapter 7, can be used by professional developers to design new
programs or improve current programs. Beginning with these two chap-

ters will immerse the reader immediately into the dynamic world of decision making about professional development. An alternative is to read the chapters sequentially, in which case different inputs into professional development programs are introduced one by one—the knowledge base, strategies, context, and critical issues—combining increasingly more considerations about professional development design before the actual planning and implementation process is described in Chapter 7. Another alternative, one that may be more immediately helpful to professional development planners, is to review the section in Chapter 3 on the knowledge base in professional development and then to turn to Chapter 4, which describes each of the 15 strategies and suggests circumstances in which they might best be used. Because professional development is a complex and dynamic process, we believe that each chapter has something new to offer the reader, but the order in which chapters are read is not critical.

Values Shared by the Authors

Early in framing this book, we realized that what we were creating was based very much on our shared beliefs, and that a book by another set of authors might read quite differently. Therefore, we decided it was important to be explicit about our beliefs as a form of "truth in packaging." Readers who share these beliefs should find the contents quite compatible; we hope that those who do not will be challenged to consider an alternative perspective and direction and its value in their work. The values that underlie this book include the following:

1. *Professional development experiences must have students and their learning at their core—by that we mean all students.* Science and mathematics education reforms and the national standards on which they are based share a common commitment to learning for all and not just the privileged or talented few. This implies not only a whole new perspective on the content that students should learn but also the teaching and learning strategies that need to be employed by their teachers (especially ways of knowing what students know). We believe that, given the scarcity of resources, including time, for teacher learning, all those resources must be focused on learning and developing the best means for reaching all students.

2. *Excellent science and mathematics teachers have a very special and unique kind of knowledge that must be developed through their professional learning experiences.* Pedagogical content knowledge—that is, knowing how to teach specific scientific and mathematical concepts and

principles to young people at different developmental levels—is the unique province of teachers and must be the focus of professional development. Knowledge of content, although critical, is not enough, nor is knowledge of general pedagogy. There is something more to professional development for science and mathematics teachers than generic professional development opportunities are able to offer.

3. Principles that guide the reform of student learning should also guide professional learning for educators. Professional development opportunities need to "walk their talk." People teach as they are taught. Therefore, engaging in active learning, focusing on fewer ideas more deeply, and learning collaboratively are all principles that must characterize learning opportunities for adults.

4. The content of professional learning must come from both inside and outside the learner and from both research and practice. Traditionally, knowledge that is officially due respect has come from external sources such as research or the consultant from at least 50 miles away. Recently, the wisdom that teachers themselves have gained over time has received more attention, often to the neglect of external knowledge. We believe that internal and external knowledge and knowledge from practice as well as from research are all valid and important. It is the artful professional development design that combines these most effectively.

5. Professional development must both align with and support system-based changes that promote student learning. Professional development has long suffered from separation from other critical components of education, with the common result that new strategies and ideas are not implemented. Although professional development cannot be expected to cure all the ills of the system, it can support changes in such areas as standards, assessment, and curriculum, creating a culture and capacity for continuous improvement that is so critical to facing current and future challenges.

With these values explicit, the reader is invited to enter some classrooms and professional learning opportunities that begin to depict a new direction for professional development for mathematics and science educators.

Acknowledgments

From its conception, this book has been a complex undertaking. It represents a year of collaboration by a variety of people from vastly different "communities": practitioners and researchers; scientists, mathematicians, and educators; people working in elementary, high school, and higher-education settings; and people with school, district, state, and national perspectives. Our challenge has been to avoid simply gathering and describing efforts to support professional learning, but to examine and understand, search for common themes and struggles, and write a book that represents the collective "wisdom" of the field. Our success in this undertaking rests in large part on the contributions of hundreds of voices.

We are grateful to our collaborators, Hubert Dyasi, Susan Friel, Judy Mumme, Cary Sneider, and Karen Worth, who are exceptional professional developers who shared their learnings, their struggles, and their enthusiasm for their work. Their stories weave through this book and illustrate the main ideas we formulated together.

For their careful reviews and substantive contributions, we thank Joan Ferrini-Mundy, Iris Weiss, Deborah Schifter, Josefina Arce, Ed Silver, Ned Levine, Mark St. John, and Vernon Sells. For their help in completing and producing drafts of the book, we especially thank Susan Mundry, Joyce Kaser, Bo DeLong, Don Horsley, Mary Kay Stein, Peg Smith, Uwe Hilgert, Jill Forney, Diane Enright, Michelle Mercer, and Steve Lewis.

We are grateful for the vision and guidance of the leadership of the National Institute for Science Education—Andy Porter, Terry Millar, and Denice Denton—and the National Center for Improving Science Education—Senta Raizen and Ted Britton. We are grateful for support from the National Science Foundation, especially that of Susan Snyder, Margaret Cozzins, Larry Suter, and Daryl Chubin.

We thank the dozens of professional developers who enthusiastically contributed descriptions and analyses of their programs and initiatives, many of which we have used as examples and cited as resources. The fact that we have used only a small number of the contributions is a testament to the energy and commitment of professional developers nationwide. Finally, we thank the many educators who thoughtfully contributed their voices to those represented in our concluding chapter.

Susan Loucks-Horsley
Peter W. Hewson
Nancy Love
Katherine E. Stiles

About the Authors

....

Susan Loucks-Horsley is director of the Professional Development Project of the National Institute for Science Education (NISE), director of Professional Development and Outreach at the National Research Council's (NRC's) Center for Science, Mathematics, and Engineering Education, and program director for Science and Mathematics at WestEd. Her work at NISE examines effective practice in professional development, both inservice and preservice. At the NRC, her primary work is promoting, supporting, and monitoring the progress of standards-based education, especially the *National Science Education Standards*. At WestEd, she works with projects evaluating and assisting in mathematics and science education reform. She is senior author of *Continuing to Learn: A Guidebook for Teacher Development, An Action Guide for School Improvement, Elementary School Science for the 90s*, reports from the National Center for Improving Science Education on teacher development and support, and numerous chapters and articles on related topics. While at the University of Texas at Austin Research and Development Center for Teacher Education, she helped develop the Concerns-Based Adoption Model, which describes how individuals experience change. She received her PhD from the University of Texas at Austin.

Peter W. Hewson is Professor of Science Education at the University of Wisconsin at Madison. He is a principal investigator in the National Center for Improving Student Learning and Achievement in Mathematics and Science. He has also served as codirector of the Professional Development Project of the National Institute for Science Education and as principal investigator on several federally funded multiyear projects in science education. He is interested in how students learn science; the ways in which one should teach science to take account of students' knowledge and ways of learning; how teachers learn how to teach science; and the implications these topics have for the initial and continuing education of prospective and practicing teachers. He has been particularly involved in the development of conceptual change approaches to science teaching and teacher education and has published numerous articles on these and related topics. He received his PhD in theoretical nuclear physics at Oxford University.

Nancy Love is a staff developer and researcher for the Regional Alliance for Mathematics and Science Education Reform at Technical Education Resource Centers in Cambridge, Massachusetts. She is developing a handbook for schools on systemic reform in mathematics and science education. A seasoned staff developer, she has worked with hundreds of schools nationwide in professional development design, implementation of effective instructional and organizational practices, and change management. She served on the staff of the National Institute for Science Education Professional Development Project, as state facilitator for the National Diffusion Network, and as director of Cooperative Learning Services at The NETWORK, Inc., in Andover, Massachusetts.

Katherine E. Stiles is a team member of the Professional Development Project of the National Institute for Science Education (NISE), research associate at WestEd, and professional development specialist at the National Research Council's Center for Science, Mathematics, and Engineering Education. Her work at NISE examines effective practice in professional development, both inservice and preservice. At WestEd, she works with projects evaluating and assisting in mathematics and science education reform. At NRC, her primary work is promoting the progress of standards-based education through her participation as a team member of the *National Science Education Standards* Dissemination Project. She is author of several elementary science curriculum guides produced through the National Science Resources Center in Washington, D.C., for the *Science and Technology for Children* curriculum project and coauthor of a NISE brief titled "Principles of Effective Professional Development for Mathematics and Science Education: A Synthesis of Standards." She received her master's degree from Indiana University.

Images of Learning and Development

1

....

The reform of mathematics and science education rests firmly on a commitment to change the form of teaching and learning that is currently the norm in our nation's classrooms. The new vision of mathematics and science teaching is one in which all students engage in inquiry into significant questions in science and mathematics in supportive, collegial communities. To achieve this vision, teachers need new knowledge, skills, behaviors, and dispositions. They need to have ownership in the new vision and feel competent and comfortable to create appropriate learning environments for their students. This includes feeling secure in their knowledge of the content they will help their students learn.

For this to happen, teachers need opportunities for professional growth—ones in which they learn what they need to know to achieve this new vision in ways that model how they can work with their students. Because it is difficult if not impossible to teach in ways in which one has not learned, teachers also need opportunities to inquire into significant questions in science and mathematics—as well as into questions in learning and pedagogy—in supportive, collegial communities.

What do classrooms in which the new vision of science and mathematics teaching and learning is playing out look like? Also, what do professional development opportunities in which teachers learn in that way and learn to teach in that way look like? These questions are the focus of this chapter. We hope that creating images of alternatives to current practice in both teaching and professional development will contribute to progress toward the vision of reform.

The first two vignettes illustrate many of the elements of reform as demonstrated in classrooms. The following three vignettes move the action to professional development experiences in which teachers are learning some of the content and strategies they need to make these kinds of classrooms a reality.

Vignette 1: Fair Games[1]

Mr. Luu has been working on probability for a few days with his class of sixth graders. Because his textbook is old, there is little about probability in the book. He has been drawing from a variety of sources as well as making up things himself, based on what he hears in the students' comments. He began by asking students to decide whether a coin-tossing game he presented was fair or not. He found out that although most of the students did consider the possible outcomes, they did not analyze the ways those outcomes could be obtained. For example, they thought that when you toss two coins, it is equally likely to get two heads, two tails, or heads-and-tails. He also learned that many of his students were inclined to decide if a game was fair by playing it and seeing if the players tied: If someone won, then the game might be biased in their favor, they thought.

He decides to present them with two dice-tossing games—the sum game and the product game.

SUM GAME

Two players: Choose one player to be "even" and the other to be "odd."
Throw two dice.
Add the numbers on the two faces.
If the sum is even, the even player gets 1 point.
If the sum is odd, the odd player gets 1 point.

PRODUCT GAME

Two players: Choose one to be the even player and the other to be odd.
Throw two dice.
Multiply the numbers on the two faces.
If the product is even, the even player gets 1 point.
If the product is odd, the odd player gets 1 point.

After explaining how each game is played, Mr. Luu challenges the students to figure out if the games are fair or not. He begins by holding a discussion about what it means for something to be "fair." Then he pre-

sents the rules for each game, telling the students simply that they are to report back on whether or not either of the games is fair or not and to include an explanation for their judgment.

The students pair off and work on the problem. Some play each of the games first, recording their results, as a means of investigating the question. Others try to analyze the games based on the possible outcomes. Mr. Luu walks around and listens to what the students are saying and poses questions:

"What did you say were all the possible totals you could get? How did you know?"

"Why did you decide you needed to throw the dice exactly 36 times?"

After they have played the game or worked on their analyses for a while, Mr. Luu directs the students to stop, open their notebooks, and to write in their notebooks what they think about the fairness of the two games.

Next, Mr. Luu opens a whole-class discussion about the games. On the basis of what he saw when he was observing, he calls on Kevin and Rania. Rania beams. She explains that they figured out that the sum game is an unfair game "and we didn't even have to play it at all to be sure."

Kevin provides their proof: "There are six even sums possible—2, 4, 6, 8, 10, and 12—but only five odd ones—3, 5, 7, 9, and 11. So the game is unfair to the person who gets points for the odd sums."

"What do the rest of you think?" asks Mr. Luu, gazing over the group. Several shake their heads. A few others nod.

"Marcus?" he invites. Marcus's hand was not up, but his face looks up at Mr. Luu. "It don't make sense to me, Mr. Luu. I think that there's more ways to get some of them numbers, like 3—there's two ways to get a 3. But there's only one way to get a 2."

"Huh?" Several children are openly puzzled by this statement.

"Marcus, can you explain what you mean by saying that 3 can be made two ways?" asks Mr. Luu.

"Well, you could get a 1 on one die and a 2 on the other, or you could get a 2 on the first die and 1 on the other. That's two different ways," he explains quietly.

"But how are those different? One plus two equals the same thing as two plus one!" objects a small girl.

"What do you think, Than?" probes Mr. Luu.

Than remains silent. Mr. Luu waits a long time. Finally, Than says, "But they are two different dices, so it is not same."

"Hmmm," remarks Mr. Luu. "Where are other people on this?"

After three or four more comments on both sides of the issue, time is almost up. Mr. Luu assigns the students, for homework, to repeat the coin-tossing game they had investigated last week, to record their results, and to decide if it is fair when three people play it:

COIN-TOSSING GAME

Three players: One player is "two heads," one player is "two tails," and one player is "mixed."
Toss two coins.
If the result is two heads, the "heads" player gets 1 point.
If the result is two tails, the "tails" player gets 1 point.
If the result is one head and one tail, the "mixed" player gets 1 point.

Mr. Luu thinks that this game may help them with their thinking about the dice games. He asks them to play the game, to record their results, and to decide if it is fair when three people play it. They are to write about their experiments and explain their conclusion. Mr. Luu suspects that now, if they find out that the mixed result person gets about twice as many points as either of the others, they will be able to figure out what is going on and eventually agree with Marcus and Than.

Vignette 2: Straight Line Motion[2]

Sister Gertrude's fifth grade classroom had been working for several weeks on how and why things move. She had given them a circus of 22 examples to consider: a book at rest on a table, a parachute dropping, a toy airplane circling on a string, and so on. They had spent time in small groups working on a particular example, observing the motion, and trying to decide what forces were present. A group would present their conclusions to the other students. In time, the class had satisfied themselves, among other things, that when a book was at rest on a table top, they needed two forces to explain it: gravity pulling down and the table pushing up with equal magnitude.

Sister asked for a volunteer to explain another example, and Don presented to the class his explanation of the forces acting on a toy parachute falling from the ceiling to the floor. He had drawn a dot on the white board representing the parachute and two arrows of equal and opposite magnitude representing forces acting on the parachute. For Don, the parachute was falling in a straight line at a consistent speed, a steady pace. [A physicist would term this constant velocity.*]*

Don:　　I did the parachute and I think that there are [two] equal forces because it's going in a pretty straight line and consistent speed and those two arrows are. One's gravity and the other one is friction.

This statement was followed by a very rapid sequence of questions from a variety of students trying to understand why Don found this idea plausible. All of the students speaking at this time were very confident in asking their questions, and there was a feeling in the classroom that Don's idea was about to be refuted. Most were clear that a book at rest required two equal, opposing forces, and that an object speeding up needed an unbalanced force. Don's explanation did not fit into either category, and they thought that it should.

Kitt: Why do you have equal arrows? I don't think it would be moving if they had equal arrows.

Don: Well if [one arrow was] smaller they would be speeding up.

Kitt: Well . . .

Kitt's response strongly suggests she thought it was speeding up.

Kirsty, assisted by the teacher (T), decided to follow up on the two equal arrows in opposite directions in Don's diagram.

Kirsty: I'm not sure if this has a lot to do with this but if that parachute was at rest, what would the arrows look like? You don't think that's not at rest?

Don: Well . . . [it's not] at rest.

Kirsty: No, I mean if it was.

T: She's just saying, in your mind, imagine this thing at rest. How would you label it?

Don: Probably nothing [different].

T: Nothing [different]?

Kirsty had not bought Don's explanation, and after a while she continued with her argument about things at rest.

Kirsty: Yeah. How would you label it if it was at rest? Pretend it's sitting on this table, on a station, pretend it was just sitting there. How would you label it at rest? You don't think that's what at rest is [two equal and opposite arrows]?

Don: Well, gravity [is one force] and the table is a force.

Kitt: So it would be exactly like this [two equal and opposite arrows] . . . OK wouldn't it be going at a consistent speed?

Rob: It is! [said emphatically]

Kitt's reentry to the conversation showed she had reconsidered her earlier position, and things had also clicked for Rob. Don then explicitly stated the commonality he saw between objects at rest and those moving at a consistent speed.

Don: *At rest is also at a consistent speed.*

Stu: *So you have two [ideas] for the same sets of arrows?*

Don: *If a thing is at rest it's still going in a straight line at consistent speed.*

This was a significant breakthrough for Don and his fellow students: They recognized that the consistent speed and equal forces explanation was conceptually a more powerful bond than the visually obvious difference between a book at rest and a moving parachute.

Several things must be noted regarding these vignettes. First, the tasks presented by the teachers are familiar ones to the students, who have played with dice and tossed coins and with moving objects, such as toy airplanes and parachutes. Therefore, the tasks allow students to mobilize their prior knowledge and to tap into what they already know about probability and forces. The students are set up to build on what they know or challenge it (or have it challenged) in some way. Note that the teachers understand deeply the concepts they are teaching; therefore, it is possible for them to know where students are to begin with and to build constructively to new understandings.

Second, there is an extraordinary level of engagement by students. They are thinking deeply about the curriculum tasks of the classroom. They are expected and are able to explain what they are doing and why they are doing it. They listen to and expect to understand what their peers are saying. They do not automatically accept what they hear. The solutions to the tasks that they arrive at clearly matter to them.

Third, the tasks in which the students are engaged are constructed around significant concepts in mathematics and science. These tasks require them to think scientifically and mathematically by making conjectures and hypotheses and marshaling different forms of evidence to support or refute them. The nature of the solutions provided is deeper than a fixed set of symbols or words to be reproduced exactly.

Fourth, students are communicating constantly with each other and with the teacher, learning by constructing and sharing explanations and having their explanations challenged and elaborated by others. Students are not restricted to consider only the ideas of the teacher and textbook authors. They are unlikely to develop images of mathematics and science as something done in isolation or facts to be memorized and regurgitated. Their understanding of science and mathematics deepens and develops through communication and community.

Fifth, the teachers in these vignettes are playing a very different role than that in typical classrooms. They have chosen curriculum tasks that are important and challenging but not impossible for their students. They have established a classroom environment that enables students to express themselves, to disagree with their peers (and their teacher), and to feel safe in doing so. The teachers continually monitor classroom interactions, deciding when and how to intervene. They use their in-depth understanding of the concept they are teaching to help students make sense of their observations and analyze carefully what is going on.

As we discuss later in the book, there is reason to believe that the science and mathematics teaching envisioned in these vignettes leads to students who understand these disciplines (whether or not they intend to pursue careers that depend on them), are confident in their own abilities, and are motivated to study further because they see the value of their education. Furthermore, this vision is not a restricted one. It is not confined to a minority of students privileged by a social or a genetic inheritance or both, and it does not happen only in a few classrooms in which superteachers create miracles out of reach of others in the profession. On the contrary, it illustrates that all students, regardless of their gender or race or class or culture, are intrinsically curious about and capable of finding meaning in their world. All teachers have these high goals for their students, and they are capable of the quality of teaching needed to achieve them.

Teachers play an essential part in achieving this vision in the classroom. Although there are many factors in educational environments that hobble good teachers, without major change in typical teaching the vision of a reformed education will evaporate. This is the central theme of this book: the essential need for professional development of teachers of science and mathematics that enables them with the knowledge and strategies they need and empowers them to make the vision a reality in their classrooms.

How does such professional development look "in action?" The next three vignettes illustrate the nature of the professional development we advocate in this book.

Vignette 3: Science Alive

Science Alive is a 3-week institute for teachers sponsored by the Pacific Northwest Laboratory in Richland, Washington. Its purpose is to enhance teachers' content knowledge and instructional strategies in environmental sciences, with a special emphasis on global environmental change. It emphasizes the use of "scenarios" that immerse learners in problems that require them to use a wide variety of investigative skills and integrate knowledge from a number of scientific disciplines. During the 3 weeks, teachers participate in four scenarios, work with several science curricula that take a similar approach to learning, learn how to use community resources, and develop their own lessons.

Today is the field component of the environmental geology scenario. Teachers load into two field vehicles, with one geologist per vehicle, and arrive at the scene of a dump site. They learn that the farmer who owns and farms these fields has chosen this location, a ravine that drains down toward the road, to dump many kinds of waste from diapers to leftover herbicide. The question posed to the teachers is, what is the impact of this kind of dumping? They will address this question after a thorough tour of the area, learn about the geology and topography as they feel the need for information, and have an opportunity to work in the laboratory, doing any tests they feel would be useful.

A geologist asks: "What do you think you would need to know to address the question?" The teachers suggest many questions they have about the soil, water, underlying rock, nature of the waste material, and so on. All then reload in the vehicles to begin to get the "lay of the land."

The geologists have prepared for the teachers a nine-page guide, "Environmental Geology: Travel Log for Ringold/White Bluffs Site Survey." Each teacher has a journal, and the geologists have brought lots of materials along with them, including several road and topographic maps, air photos, soil and water sampling containers, Brunton compasses, hand lenses, dilute HCl, a Munsell soil color chart, and a fire extinguisher and shovel.

They begin 38 miles from the dump site and learn, through several stops and reading through the guide, about the economy of the area, the rock deposits, and the water diverted for agriculture from the Grand Coulee Dam. They mark several locations on their map: the water tower, the WPPS nuclear power plant, and so on. They stop near a culvert and are given a handout with a cross section of the area. A geologist asks: "Why is the water seeping out between the two formations?" The teachers discuss possible explanations, then the geologist talks about the difference in "hydraulic conductivity" between the two formations. They go on to another road cut through the same formation and a geologist asks the teachers to predict how water applied at the surface might move through the deposits. The teachers discuss this and make some jottings in their journals. More questions are asked by the teachers, and the geologists provide information—not too detailed—and they ask as many questions as they answer.

After several more stops, locatings on the maps, and observations about the nature of the rocks and water runoff patterns, the group begins to observe differences in the soils around the formations. A teacher suggests it would be useful to begin to take soil samples. A geologist produces the Munsell color chart, and they check for soil color and test for calcium carbonate content with the dilute HCl. There are more stops and soil sampling and discussions about what they are observing.

They have reached the dump site again, and from a distance the geologists ask them to describe the general topography of the land and compare it to the contour lines on the topographic map. What vegetation changes do they observe? What do these changes suggest about water movement in the area? What kind of sediment would they predict to occur in this location?

The teachers scatter around the dump site, and many of them take both soil and water samples, marking clearly on the map where they were taken from. The geologists suggest that to address the primary question of the impact of the waste dumping, the teachers might want to do several activities. These activities are listed at the back of the guide: (a) site characterization activities (e.g., What is the area underlying the waste debris? What is the slope? What is the direction and distance to the Columbia River?); (b) soil characterization activities (e.g., collect samples from various places and look for evidence of chemical or water movement off site); and (c) water chemistry and movement (e.g., observe vegetation patterns and take water samples from various locations).

As the day ends, the teachers and geologists reload into the vehicles for the trip back home. The discussions include implications for the nuclear waste site nearby, the accessibility of these activities to their students, and the variety of considerations real scientists must make to understand the natural world. Tomorrow will be spent in the laboratory, with small groups testing water and soil samples and working with their descriptions, their maps, and their calculations to address the primary question (as well as many other questions that have arisen during the course of the day). Their activities will be interspersed with input from the geologists and a laboratory chemist helping them understand the scientific ideas behind their observations, analyses, and conclusions.

Vignette 4: Computers in Geometry Class[3]

A group of high school mathematics teachers has been meeting twice a month at their school for a seminar with mathematicians and mathematics educators from a nearby university. These teachers have been using computers in their geometry classes for the past year and a half, and the seminar provides them with opportunities to discuss what is happening in their classrooms as they think about new ways of teaching and learning.

The computer software allows students and their teachers to construct geometric shapes and to make measurements of lengths and angles and computations based on these measurements, thus providing an environment for open-ended exploration and discovery of patterns and relationships.

Although the teachers have been excited about their use of computers in geometry, many have voiced frustration in trying to make decisions about appropriate tasks for their students. Some teachers have been most comfortable focusing student attention on specific relationships, while others are dissatisfied with activities structured to lead students toward a particular "discovery." At times, many teachers have felt their own knowledge of geometry inadequate to deal with questions and conjectures that arise from open-ended explorations.

Gloria described a task she assigned her class early in the year:

> I wanted my students to learn that the sum of the angle measures in a triangle is 180 degrees, so I had them construct a lot of triangles on the computer and record the angle measures. The software made it possible to collect a lot of data quickly and make a generalization. I thought my students would remember the relationship better if they discovered it themselves.

Rich talked about the same task:

> I was really reluctant to use that activity because it didn't seem like exploration. It made me feel that I would be directing the students toward a single result and not really taking advantage of the technology. But when Gloria told me about some of the things her students came up with, I thought it might lead in some interesting directions. I was amazed at what happened. My students didn't just see what I thought they would see; many of them went off in all sorts of directions exploring other shapes. One even asked about a circle! I wasn't quite sure where to go with that question, but it certainly seemed intriguing—and it took us into lots of other ideas when we discussed it in the seminar.

Constanza remembered a lesson that was especially important to her:

> One of my students had constructed a shape on the computer screen that he said looked three-dimensional. We took off on a discussion of geometric models and representations of shapes, something I hadn't really expected them to get into in that lesson. As we were talking about two- and three-dimensional shapes, Jan asked about a line. Well, a lot of the students thought that was boring, but then Raoul held

up a paper clip and said he thought it was two-dimensional. And another student said that if you bent the paper clip it would be three-dimensional.

That sent off a bunch of conjectures, with students coming up with good reasons for why the bent paper clip could be considered one-, two-, or three-dimensions. There was a lot more there than I had anticipated, and I thought it would be a great topic for discussion in the seminar. It made us think a lot about representations and how we describe and define geometric shapes.

The seminar has been a place where teachers can share their struggles with colleagues and university faculty and develop meaningful activities for their students. For many of the teachers, one of the most valuable aspects of the seminar has been the opportunity to extend their own understanding of geometry.

Vignette 5: Plants[4]

Andy Sanchez is a member of a study group that the teachers at his school recently formed to improve their teaching of science. When the district coordinator, Irene Patton, invited the school to form this group, she indicated that they would be drawing on scientists and science educators from the local university, and teachers from other schools, when the teachers' deliberations called for it. Irene would sit in on the sessions, but the teachers were on their own to find the direction that made sense to them.

At the first meeting, Andy brings a new book he picked up in their resource center titled The Case for Constructivist Classrooms. He says he has noticed a lot of reference to the idea of "constructivism" recently, and he resonates with what he thinks it is about. He would like to join with others who want to learn more about it. In fact, given that he is nearly ready to introduce a unit of plants to his fifth graders, a unit he has never used before, and that he does not know much about plants, he is interested in trying to do things "constructively." Maybe he can learn at the same time as his students.

Other teachers express interest, and Irene asks if she could suggest a first step. She suggests that teachers work together in teams with others who are soon to introduce a similar topic (in most cases, this turns out to be two or three teachers who teach the same grade level). Interestingly, all the teachers will soon, or in the future, teach some kind of unit on plants. They discuss and agree that they first should learn what the students know about the topic; then they should learn about the topic themselves; and then they should plan how to teach it to their students.

The teachers agree to spend the next week interviewing their students and then come back next week and share what they have learned. They ask Irene to see if a "friendly" scientist would be available to join them. Andy and the two other fifth-grade teachers decide to ask their students to describe how they think plants make food and get them to draw their ideas. Other teacher teams agree on other things on which to focus their students.

The teachers follow through in their classrooms during the week. Andy's students draw pictures and diagrams about relationships between plants and the sun and the rain and the soil, and they explain their drawings and Andy takes notes. He carefully records his data as well as keeps a journal of his reactions and feelings about the information-gathering process.

At the next week's session, the teachers are joined by a botanist and Irene (who is herself a former high school biology teacher) to share and make sense of their data. Andy and his team report that they are quite astonished at the range of ideas expressed by their fifth graders. One of Andy's students told him that plant food meant the green stuff his father mixes in water and puts on the plants in the house and garden once every 2 weeks. This student "knew" that plants need to be fed just like people do. Another student knew that the sun makes food for plants, which the plants can then give to animals. On probing, the child admitted that he was not quite sure how this works. One girl said she knew how plants make food because she planted carrots and beans in a little garden beside her house last year and then she ate the carrots and the beans. She was not sure, however, how the seeds turned into the vegetables. She guessed it has something to do with the dirt.

The teachers are fascinated by what they are learning from their students. It forces them to examine their own understanding of plants. What do they really know? How and where did they get this knowledge? Andy's team is sure photosynthesis is a key process related to plants and their food. What could they remember about photosynthesis from their high school biology course, however? They remember some cycle (one teacher calls it the Krebs cycle), and that it was a nightmare memorizing it for a big test. What were all those arrows exiting a circular path, like roads branching from a rotary? What was the point of it all anyway?

At that point, the teachers agree that it is time for them to learn more about plant physiology, and the botanist invites them to spend two consecutive Saturdays in the lab with him where they can pursue a "course" designed for adult learning. Once the teachers have a better grasp on the subject matter, they will need to discuss what is developmentally appropriate for each grade level of student and how they can address the students' questions in lively and engaging ways. They know from what they have done so far that they will need a teacher experienced with dif-

ferent ages of students and a strong science background to help them with that task. They ask Irene to begin to search for this other resource. Most teachers enthusiastically agree to participate.

In the first professional development vignette, the geology field trip, the teachers are students again, but this is different from anything else they experienced when they were in grade school and college. The way in which they are learning is different: The teachers are investigating an open question that seems simple and clear but that requires a complex, involved answer. They interact with one another and the instructors with interest and frustration; there is nothing repetitive in what they are doing. The science these teachers are doing is different: They are gathering information, making hypotheses, and arguing about the interplay of various factors. There is no book with the correct answers in the back, but there is opportunity to learn science content from experts on the spot, when it is appropriate. The teaching they are experiencing is different: Their instructors ask as many questions as they answer; many of those questions seem to have many possible answers; and the instructors have set the context for their activity and provided extensive resources for the teachers to use, but they have not shown them what to do.

In the second vignette, the mathematics study group, the teachers are teaching, but they are also studying their practice in collaboration with colleagues and peers. By sharing their successes and failures with each other, they get new ideas to try out, encouragement to keep going when things do not seem to be working, a richer understanding of the students they teach and the geometry they want them to learn, and a greater sense of their involvement in a professional practice and in improving their own competency. What a difference from the isolation of closing their classroom doors on the world outside!

In the third vignette, preparing to teach their young students about plants, the teachers are again collaborating with their peers, this time to construct new understandings about constructivist learning and the kinds of teaching it implies. They are conducting an investigation into their students' understanding of important science concepts and, in so doing, raising questions about their own understanding of the same ideas. At their own initiative, they combine their expertise about how children learn with the expertise of a scientist and teacher of older children; they pursue deeper understanding of science to design more effective learning experiences for their students.

These three vignettes provide a glimpse into the many faces of effective professional development, mirroring the beliefs of the book's authors identified in the Preface. If science and mathematics teachers are to become the teachers envisioned in the vignettes, they need to experience for themselves the science and mathematics learning they will want their students to do. Hearing about it in a vicarious manner is no substitute. Next, professional development takes time, it requires teachers to be reflective about their practice, and it is greatly facilitated by open discourse with professional colleagues. Professional development that is confined to short, discrete events is a wasted effort. Each vignette is part of an ongoing sequence of learning opportunities. Also, professional development happens in a community of learning; just as students deepen their knowledge of science and mathematics through communication, so too do their teachers learn through formulating, sharing, and challenging what they and their colleagues think they know in order to learn. Finally, professional development needs to address school systems because of the powerful ways in which they can influence teaching. This can occur indirectly through the structures and policies that can help or hinder a teacher's efforts and directly through the nature of professional development that is offered. School systems have a key role in developing leadership in their teachers.

These scenes from classrooms and professional development experiences suggest, but in no way detail, what effective professional development is and needs to be. Chapter 2 presents a way to think about the many considerations needed to design such professional development for teachers and other science and mathematics educators. Chapter 3 picks up this thread, surveying the research, literature, and best practice to identify a set of principles on which to build effective professional development initiatives.

Notes

1. Vignette 1 is from *Professional Standards for Teaching Mathematics,* pp. 40-42, © 1991 by the National Council of Teachers of Mathematics. Used with permission.

2. Vignette 2 is adapted from Beeth (1993).

3. Vignette 4 is from *Professional Standards for Teaching Mathematics,* pp. 141-142, © 1991 by the National Council of Teachers of Mathematics. Used with permission.

4. Vignette 5 is adapted from Raizen and Michelsohn (1994).

A Framework for Designing 2 Professional Development

....

The director of science of the Cambridge Public Schools, five kindergarten through sixth-grade science staff development teachers, and a consultant from the Center for Science at the Education Development Center (EDC) are huddled around a table in the science director's office. They are formulating ideas for expanding the work they have already started in developing an elementary science framework. They want to expand the "pockets of innovation" now in evidence to a more systematic, districtwide implementation of inquiry-based elementary science. The team is convinced that effective professional development will be key to the success of their plan, and they are very well aware of what has not worked in the past. They intend to present their ideas for a teacher enhancement program to the National Science Foundation for funding. Proposal writing is giving them the opportunity to dream a little. They are debating how they might do things differently and better. "With the potential of additional resources, what would be the best approach to professional development for us?"

This chapter describes a framework to help guide and inform the design work of professional developers such as the Cambridge team. The framework emerged from our conversations with outstanding professional developers about their programs for both mathematics and science teachers. They felt very strongly that what they had to offer were not "models" that others could admire and adopt. Their programs were more complex than that, combining elements of different models and evolving and changing over time. They emerged out of and were uniquely suited to their own particular goals and context.

Equally complex was the process they used to develop their programs. As professional development "designers," they consciously drew on research and "practitioner wisdom" and were guided by their own passionate beliefs about the nature of mathematics and science and student and adult learning. They had a repertoire of strategies from which to choose. They grappled with challenging, critical issues related to the "big picture" of mathematics and science education reform. They studied their own unique contexts and thought carefully about what approach would be best for a particular time and place. Drawing on all these elements, they carefully crafted their goals and plans. Once implemented, their designs never stopped evolving. As they learned from their mistakes, as teachers developed, and as their contexts shifted, their programs changed as well. For these designers, professional development was not about importing models or following formulas. It was a process of thoughtful, conscious decision making.

It is this process of decision making that we have attempted to capture, albeit greatly simplified, in Figure 2.1. At the center of the framework is a generic planning sequence incorporating goal setting, planning, doing, and reflecting. The circles represent important inputs into both goal setting and planning that can help professional developers make informed decisions. They cue designers to consider the extensive knowledge bases that can inform their work (knowledge and beliefs), to understand the unique features of their own context, to draw on a wide repertoire of professional development strategies, and to wrestle with critical issues that mathematics and science education reformers are most likely to encounter, regardless of their contexts. Finally, the graphic is punctuated with multiple feedback loops from the "reflect" stage to illustrate how design continues to evolve as practitioners learn from doing. Reflection can influence every input, which in turn influences the creation of a new and better design.

The framework describes professional development design at its very best—an ideal to strive toward rather than an accurate depiction of how it happens or a prescription for how it should happen. Given limited resources, especially time, professional developers will rarely have the luxury of giving their full attention to every input in the model. The professional developers who helped to develop the framework extracted its components from what they actually did and what they wished they had done better. With the benefit of hindsight, they helped to construct a tool that alerts planners to important bases to cover and pitfalls to avoid. For programs just being designed, planners can take advantage of the knowledge and experience of others who have gone down the same path. If programs are already under way, the framework can stimulate

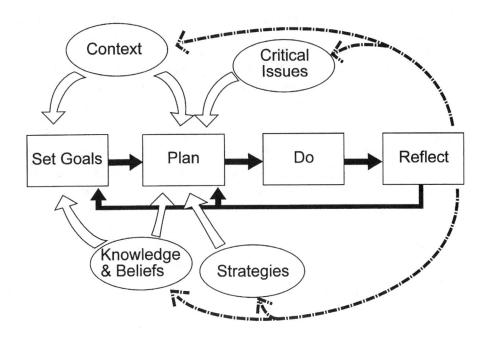

Figure 2.1. Professional Development Design Process for
Mathematics and Science Education Reform

reflection and refinement. No matter where planners are in their process,
they can hone in on the parts of the framework that best serve their purposes, knowing that no planning process is perfect and that even the
"best-laid plans" are subject to the whims and serendipity of change.

Knowledge and Beliefs

*The Cambridge team is not starting from scratch as they contemplate the
design of their professional development program. Collectively, they bring
a wealth of knowledge and experience to the table—and they intend to use
it! The science staff development teachers on the team have been practicing inquiry-based science in the classroom for years. Some members have
been involved in urban school change and science education reform since
the 1960s. They know the research on effective professional development
and change and have been living it for 30 years. Everyone is steeped in
standards work, from the EDC consultant, who was involved in developing
national science education standards, to the Cambridge staff, who had
drawn heavily on national and state standards to develop their own curriculum frameworks.*

On the basis of their knowledge and experience, the team brings something else to the table: a set of shared beliefs. They all believe in inquiry science and have a common picture of what that means. They give more than lip service to all students learning. They care passionately about it and are ready to face the barriers to it. They know why they are there—to see their vision of science learning come to life in their schools. They feel a sense of urgency to make change stick for the sake of the students.

Despite their impatience and their expertise, one of the first decisions the team makes is to find out more about successful science systemic change efforts. They want to know who is doing what, where, and what is working. They are determined not to reinvent the wheel or go down the wrong road.

No professional development planning effort need start at point zero. Much is known about effective professional development for mathematics and science education based on years of research and practice. Taking advantage of this knowledge can help planners jump start their efforts, put them on solid footing, and avoid unnecessary and costly mistakes.

Five distinct but related knowledge bases inform the work of planners such as the Cambridge team: (a) what we know about learners and learning in general, (b) what is known about teachers and teaching, (c) the nature of the disciplines of mathematics and science, (d) the principles of effective professional development, and (e) the knowledge base about change and the change process. In Chapter 3, we argue that there is a growing consensus about what is known in each of these domains and we summarize key principles. That is not to say that these principles constitute the final word, but rather that there is a substantial body of evidence to support them. Skillful professional development designers tap this reservoir of knowledge to inform the initial planning and whenever they face dilemmas that research has addressed.

When professional developers embrace pieces of knowledge as their own, these become their beliefs. Beliefs are the ideas people are committed to—sometimes called core values. Many researchers have found that organizations that are strongly committed to a clear set of beliefs and that act consistently with them experience the greatest success (Deal & Kennedy, 1982; Peters & Waterman, 1982). As designers clarify and articulate their beliefs, these beliefs become the "conscience" of the program. They shape goals, drive decisions, create discomfort when violated, and stimulate ongoing critique. In our design framework, we have delineated beliefs as a critical input into goal setting and planning and urge planners to take the time to coalesce around a set of shared values.

Strategies

Just because they share a vision, it does not mean that the planning team members in Cambridge always agree. At a subsequent planning meeting, members are in the throes of a debate about strategies. Some are arguing for a curriculum implementation approach, in which teachers throughout the system are given a common set of materials and the training to implement them. Others are dead set against a uniform curriculum. They think it will stifle creativity and turn teachers off. One member makes an impassioned plea against workshops that rely on outside experts. She is advocating for teacher-led, school-based study groups, in which participants study the standards and decide for themselves what materials to use.

Another important source and input for the designer to consider is a repertoire of strategies. The Cambridge team is able to engage in a debate about strategies because team members are familiar with different approaches. They are in a much better position to come up with a strategy or combination of strategies to suit their purposes than designers who have only one move—the workshop. That is not to say that workshops cannot be effective. They can if they are implemented well. The problem comes about when doing a workshop becomes a knee-jerk reaction and not a conscious choice from among alternatives.

Chapter 4 describes 15 different strategies for planners to consider. They are included in this book because they are robust examples of professional development in mathematics and science and are consistent with the principles discussed in Chapter 3. With each strategy, a set of conditions for success and implementation requirements are provided to assist planners in matching strategies to their own contexts. Combinations of strategies can be phased in over time, as noted in some of the cases presented. For instance, a program may begin with a series of workshops that then spawn teacher support groups.

Context

The Cambridge team has spent the past hour poring over the curriculum surveys they sent out last month. They are not surprised to discover that every grade has a different structure.

There is not much continuity from grade to grade, and the quantity and quality of science being taught are uneven. Some teachers in K-6 are not teaching science at all.

The survey results refuel the strategy debate. "We've got to be realistic," one member argues.

"I think phasing in a few units a year makes the most sense, given where we are now. Eventually, teachers may develop their own, but now that is premature," one member asserts.

Another responds, "But you know how independent our schools are. Any strategy that is going to work has got to be school-based." "Or at least have a lot of activity based at the school site," chimes in a third.

There is no prescription for which strategies are right for which situations—no "paint by numbers kit" for professional development. Skillful planners have one foot planted firmly in theory (knowledge and beliefs and strategies) and the other in reality. As the Cambridge team designs their program, they are influenced by their vision of what science teaching, learning, and professional development should look like, but they also know they are in Cambridge and need to design a program that makes sense for their own context. Each of the cases discussed in this book, from Cambridge, Massachusetts, to the state of California, illustrates how different contexts influence the creation of very different programs. The design process entails filtering all the other inputs—knowledge and beliefs, strategies, and critical issues—through one's own context to arrive at the most appropriate approach for a given setting.

Context is complex, composed of many interconnected and dynamic influences. Some contextual factors, such as the autonomy of the schools in Cambridge, were readily apparent to the professional developers, were talked about, and drove their designs from the outset. Others required more study and analysis, such as the state of practice in Cambridge. Still others were overlooked entirely, in some cases to the program's peril. Chapter 5 discusses several different factors that planners found were most important to consider: who the students and teachers are; the state of practice, including curriculum, instruction, assessment, and learning environment; the policies in place; available resources, such as time, money, the expertise of the available professional developers, and community support; and organizational culture and structure. (These factors are also mirrored in the research and literature.) Chapter 5 includes questions to consider to help planners get a fix on each of these dimensions.

Critical Issues

Laughter rings out from the team meeting today as members reminisce about the many change efforts in their district that have come and gone. The business at hand, however, is very serious. They are thinking hard about how to build a structure that will permanently sustain this program. Well aware that the grant money will eventually run out, they are determined not to allow this initiative to be another casualty. Someone has proposed that they put the bulk of the grant resources into developing a small science leadership cadre. The trade-off is huge. More for leadership development means less for direct teacher development. They wonder if it is the right way to go.

As we examined professional development programs throughout the country, we discovered some common issues that designers were facing. These issues seemed to be critical to the success of programs everywhere, regardless of the context (although context will heavily influence how they take shape). The issues are equity and diversity, professional culture, leadership, capacity building for sustainability, scaling up, public support, effective use of standards and frameworks, time for professional development, and evaluation and assessment. Proactive planners anticipate these issues and begin grappling with them in the initial design phase. The manner in which they are addressed becomes an important ingredient in program goals and plans.

The critical issues defy easy solutions. They are the "tough nuts" that professional developers work to crack over the life of a program. Chapter 6 examines these issues in all of their complexity—summarizing research, offering examples of best practice, and posing enduring, unresolved questions.

Set Goals, Plan, Do, and Reflect: The Implementation Process

The components of the framework described previously—knowledge and beliefs, strategies, context, and critical issues—are important influences on the professional development design process. While taking these into account, the design process has a life of its own. It sometimes follows a logical sequence from goal setting to planning, to doing, to reflecting. It often does not. Eventually, however, in some fashion, the implementation of a professional development program, from its initial conception to its postmortem, unfolds over time. A brief look at each of the phases of the implementation follows.

Create a Structure

The director of science in the Cambridge public schools, five K through sixth-grade science staff development teachers, and a consultant from EDC are huddled around a round table in the science director's office.

Before beginning, designers need a structure for planning and decision making. Creating that structure involves asking the following questions: Who sits at the table? Who makes the decisions? Who has input into the decisions? What do decision makers need to know and be able to do to effectively carry out their role? How do decisions get made? and How will designers communicate with stakeholders and build support for the plan? In Cambridge, for example, it was very important to the design process that teachers be brought in from the very beginning. The Cambridge team also employed an outside expert and established a collaborative decision-making process.

Set Goals

- *To improve science learning for all K through ninth-grade students in the Cambridge public schools*
- *To implement an inquiry-based modular science curriculum across the district*
- *To build teacher leadership and expertise within the system*
- *To develop a structure that would permanently sustain the science program*

With a structure for decision making in place, designers go to work setting goals for the professional development program. If professional development is to be linked to student achievement, two kinds of goals are relevant: goals for students and goals for teachers. As designers set goals for student learning, they tap into knowledge about teaching and learning and the nature of mathematics and science treated explicitly in the national and some state standards. For example, in Cambridge, planners developed a conceptual framework for students for elementary science based on state and national standards, which eventually led to the selection of the curriculum they are implementing. In addition, setting goals for students involves analyzing students' needs and confronting disparities in achievement between boys and girls or among racial or cultural groups.

Goals for teachers flow directly out of goals for students. If students are going to develop a set of understandings, skills, and predispositions, then what do teachers need to know and be able to do to realize those outcomes for students? Goals for teachers are also informed by referring to the standards and data about teacher performance, needs, and supports available. In the previous example, planners in Cambridge considered what knowledge and skills, professional development, and structural support teachers needed to successfully implement the new science curriculum.

Plan

Once goals are set, planners begin to sketch out their design. All the other inputs described previously—critical issues, context, knowledge and beliefs, and strategies—come into play in the planning phase. This is when planners scan their context, unearthing important factors to consider as they tailor their program to their own circumstances. This is when they may decide to do more research and study about learning, teaching, mathematics or science, professional development, and change. It is the time to revisit and clarify the beliefs that underlie the program. Critical issues arise as planners consider how to confront dilemmas such as scaling up or evaluation or leadership. Finally, during planning, professional developers think strategically about which strategy or combination of strategies to employ, much like a skillful teacher selects from a repertoire of instructional strategies. Considering all these elements, they craft a program design that is subjected to the ultimate test—doing.

Do

Having made the best decisions they can, designers move from the "sketching" to "painting"—the actual implementation of their plan. In this phase, they draw on their skills as change facilitators and knowledge about implementation and the change process (e.g., Fullan, 1991; Hord, Rutherford, Huling-Austin, & Hall, 1987; Loucks-Horsley et al., 1990). For fundamental change to happen, teachers need to experiment with new behavior and gain new understandings, and that takes time. They will move through predictable developmental stages in how they feel and how they are using new approaches. Frequently, things get worse before they get better, as teachers experience what Fullan (1991) calls the "implementation dip." Also, despite professional developers' best efforts to "manage" change, it is, by nature, unpredictable. Often, the best that can be done is to expect the unexpected and problem solve along the way. Taking these and other important principles of change into consideration can help prevent the all too common failure of professional development programs at this stage in the process.

Reflect

Despite the best laid plans, it is impossible to predict how the initial design will work. As the action unfolds, designers discover what works and what does not work. Like artists stepping back from the canvas and examining their work from different perspectives, professional developers continuously monitor their plan using a variety of data sources. They ask questions such as "Is this working?" "Are we moving toward our goals of improved student learning in mathematics and science?" "Are we meeting participants' needs?" "Is our program, in fact, a good match with our context?" "What conditions, if any, have changed and how should we respond?" Sometimes their reflection is enhanced by interested "visitors" (sometimes called "critical friends") who sensitize professional developers to important aspects of their programs from different perspectives.

On the basis of this feedback, planners go back to the drawing board. It is rare that an entire program is carried out exactly as planned. As the examples in this book will illustrate, the most successful programs do not begin with a flawless design. They begin with a sound idea that then goes through many revisions and continues to evolve. Programs change over time both because planners figure out a better way and because conditions change, sometimes as a direct result of the professional development program. For example, as teacher leaders in Cambridge became more self-assured and experienced, they started wanting fewer workshops and more self-directed study groups. Professional development changed the culture, which in turn created the conditions for a different strategy. There is a live interplay between context and implementation that is illustrated in the feedback loop in Figure 2.1 from "reflect" to "context."

None of the inputs, in fact, remains static over time. The knowledge base is constantly growing. Like the professional developers featured in this book, as professional developers learn from their experiences, they become active contributors to the knowledge base. Also, as their needs and interests change, they look to research for new ideas. Beliefs change too. Seeing the impact of their work, professional developers begin to think differently about students, teachers, their disciplines, professional development, and change. Critical issues are just as dynamic. Experience may lead designers to consider new issues or gain deeper understandings of the ones they have grappled with. Far from linear or lock-step, implementing professional development is recursive and sometimes messy, demanding flexibility and continuous learning throughout the process.

A Disclaimer and a Pitch

The design framework presented previously is not perfect. It creates artificial distinctions among components such as critical issues and context, which are far more interconnected than separate circles depict. It simplifies an enormously complex process. Also, it may miss important feedback loops and connections. With that disclaimer, allow us to advocate strongly for the use of a design framework such as this to guide professional development. Yes, it is imperfect. Yes, it demands tremendous time and energy. We are convinced, however, that only through thoughtful and careful design, based on sound principles and strategies, can professional development be elevated from its current state of mediocrity.

Chapters 3 through 6 unbundle the design framework, describing each of its major components in more depth. Chapter 7 puts it all back together by illustrating how the framework has been applied to the design of effective professional development in five different settings.

3 The Knowledge That Supports Professional Development

....

Chapter 1 contains rich images of learning and teaching that reflect what we hope to see in science and mathematics classrooms everywhere. Professional developers grapple with identifying and implementing reforms that promote and sustain ongoing development of teachers to reach this vision of learning and teaching. To help them achieve this, Chapter 2 introduces and describes the professional development design process, one element of which is the knowledge base supporting professional development. Our purpose in this chapter is to outline this knowledge base in the areas of learning, teaching, the nature of science and mathematics, professional development, and the change process. It represents what we currently know or think we know that supports the kind of professional development advocated in this book. Therefore, it is one of the most important inputs to the planning process.

In this book, we use the term *knowledge base* to refer to two different kinds of information. On the one hand, the term *knowledge* generally refers to something sure, solid, dependable, and certain. It also has the connotation of truth: something that is genuine and in accordance with reality or accepted principles or for which there is sound evidence to support. Knowledge is distinct from opinion—that is, from a point of view that is not necessarily supported by evidence. On the other hand, we recognize that restricting ourselves only to information that we know with certainty is an unrealizable ideal because we need to act now. This is particularly true when knowledge is evolving rapidly, as is currently the case in education. Therefore, we also recognize that part of the knowledge base includes *beliefs,* or what we think we know (Ball, 1996). Beliefs are more than opinions: They may be less than ideal truth, but we are committed to them.

When using the term *knowledge base* in this book, we include knowledge and beliefs but not, however, everything that anyone knows or believes about professional development. Rather, it is the knowledge substantiated in the research, in the literature, and in the "wisdom of practice" of experienced professional developers to which we are committed and on which we act when we design professional development.

Learners and Learning

Five general concepts frame what we currently know about learners and learning. These concepts are the following:

- Learners possess a diverse set of alternative conceptions about natural phenomena and mathematical ideas that influence their future learning.

- Learners acquire new knowledge by constructing it for themselves.

- The construction of knowledge is a process of change that includes addition, creation, modification, refinement, restructuring, and rejection.

- The new knowledge learners construct for themselves has its origins in a diverse set of experiences.

- All students, regardless of race, culture, and gender, are capable of understanding and doing science and mathematics.

What learners know influences their learning. There is an extensive body of research that has documented what learners of science and mathematics know (Pfundt & Duit, 1994). This research demonstrates that learners' knowledge has several significant features. Learners' conceptions are important foundations for future learning. When consistent with conceptions that are currently accepted by mathematics and science communities, this "prior" or "informal" knowledge is a strong base on which to build new understandings. Sometimes, however, learners' conceptions are inconsistent with accepted, extant knowledge. Interestingly, they sometimes parallel explanations found in the history of science and mathematics. They are often tenacious and resistant to change using conventional teaching strategies. They interact with knowledge presented in formal instruction, resulting in a variety of learning outcomes—some desired by the teacher and others unintended.

The overall effect of these features is to give learners' existing knowledge a much more important role in teaching than it has in conventional practices, which pay attention to it only to the degree that it matches curricular goals and objectives (Wandersee, Mintzes, & Novak, 1994).

Learning is influenced by many aspects of learners' existing knowledge. In addition to the concepts of science, mathematics, and other disciplines they know, their expectations, attitudes, and beliefs about themselves and about knowledge, learning, schooling, and the community in which they live are also important. When individuals are learning effectively, they are deeply engaged in what they are doing and expect that it will make sense to them. They do not expect learning to be easy and instantaneous, but they have confidence that understanding will come from persistence, interaction with ideas and natural phenomena, dialogue with peers and teachers, attention to other possible ideas, and a willingness to change their view on the basis of compelling new evidence.

Learners construct new knowledge. We recognize that learning is a process in which learners construct their own knowledge (Cobb, 1994; Driver, Asoko, Leach, Mortimer, & Scott, 1994). The conventional view is that knowledge is received from others when learners listen to what they say. We now accept, however, that learning is more complex (although there are times when listening stimulates learning). Learning is a process that learners need to do for themselves rather than one that is done to them by others. This does not imply that others are not influential in the process but recognizes the active role that learners need to play to learn. When learners try to understand new information, they use their existing knowledge and their own ways of learning. The process of learning involves the construction of links between new ideas and what learners already know to create meaning.

Another important aspect of learning is the process of personal reflection. Good learners are able to monitor their own ideas and thought processes, compare and contrast them with those of others, and provide reasons why they accept one point of view rather than another. Current literature also supports the idea that learning is mediated by the social environment in which learners interact with their peers, teachers, parents, and others. It is from this milieu that learners acquire (very often implicitly) the norms, expectations, and values that influence whether, how, and what they learn (Silver, Kilpatrick, & Schlesinger, 1990).

In summary, learning is an intensely personal activity that is embedded in and enabled by social interaction. In other words, the second concept builds off the first by recognizing the interactions between what learners already know and what they see and hear. Together, these two concepts challenge the current perspective at work in many schools to-day—that people acquire concepts by receiving and memorizing information from other people who know more than they do, that students will learn what their teachers know by listening to what they say, and that the presence of other students is incidental to learning (Schifter, 1996a).

Knowledge is constructed through a process of change. There are different ways in which learners evolve from their current state of knowledge—ways that depend on the interaction between new and existing knowledge. There can be change when new ideas fit naturally with existing ideas and are added to them; when a learner creates a new idea out of existing knowledge; when new ideas extend and challenge existing knowledge, leading to its minor modification or wholesale restructuring; and when the learner sees that new ideas are powerful but irreconcilable with existing knowledge, which leads to the rejection of the existing knowledge.

What type of change occurs for learners depends on different conditions that apply both to any new ideas being considered and to the status quo. With respect to what is new, initial questions relate to its intelligibility. This means finding answers to questions such as the following: What is it? Do I know what it means? Can I represent it? and Can I find images that epitomize it? Once a new perspective becomes intelligible to a learner, he or she can consider its plausibility and its fruitfulness. Plausibility results from positive answers to questions such as the following: Do I believe it? Is it possible that the world could really work like that? and Does it fit with other things I believe to be true? Finally, an idea is fruitful if a person can reply affirmatively to questions such as the following: Does it achieve anything for me? Does it solve problems I have been grappling with? and Does it suggest approaches I had not thought of (Posner, Strike, Hewson, & Gertzog, 1982)?

With respect to the status quo of existing knowledge, the question is whether the person who holds the knowledge has any reason to be dissatisfied with it. Even if learners find that a proposed change has a high status for them—that is, it is intelligible, plausible, and fruitful to them—they may not consider it worth the trouble and effort to adopt (because change is difficult and time-consuming) unless they have reason to be dissatisfied with the status quo of their current knowledge. If what they currently know has high status for them (if not for others), they may not be prepared to adopt a new idea (Hewson & Thorley, 1989). In other words, learning is a process of construction that not only involves additions to knowledge but also may, on occasion, involve remodeling of existing knowledge.

New knowledge comes from experience. Different types of experiences contribute to the construction of learners' knowledge. Learning arises in different ways as the learners experiment with natural phenomena, grapple with problematic situations, interact with other people directly through conversation or indirectly through resources (books, videos, etc.), and reflect on their own thoughts and ideas. In other words, these diverse types of experiences include direct observation of and experience with phenomena and ideas that could lead to the process of inquiry. They include input from authorities, such as textbooks, teachers' explanations, instructional materials, mathematicians, scientists, and so on. They arise as learners live within their own culture (particularly that of their peers) and use their native language. In other words, recognizing that learning is an act of personal construction of knowledge does not imply that learning is self-contained; on the contrary, it is greatly influenced by others. In many cases, the process happens so smoothly that we lose sight of the construction process and can easily talk of learning as the reception of external knowledge. When learning does not happen smoothly, however, it is necessary to interpret learning by recognizing the complexity of the interaction between existing knowledge and new information, the learners' input into and direction of the interaction, and the different outcomes that can result (Wandersee et al., 1994).

All students have the potential to learn science and mathematics in the ways described previously. Although particular circumstances have an important influence on the quality of education in any given school classroom, the rich knowledge base on learners and learning indicates that all learners have conceptions about the world, are curious about some phenomena, and can inquire into them and make meaning of them as they have done since they were born. All students, regardless of race, culture, and gender, are capable of understanding and doing science and mathematics.

Teachers and Teaching

Three general concepts frame what is currently known about teachers and teaching. Together, these concepts support a view of teaching that, even though it is far from typical in science and mathematics classrooms, is one we believe all teachers can make their own. It is a view of teaching that coherently builds on the concepts of learners and learning outlined previously. In particular, this view contrasts strongly with the view underlying teaching in typical classrooms in which teachers outline procedures they expect students to follow, provide authoritative explanations they expect students to memorize, and evaluate students' work only to see if information has been reproduced correctly (Schifter, 1996a). The concepts are the following:

- The purpose of teaching is to facilitate learning.
- Teachers are professionals with specialized knowledge.
- The practice of teaching is complex.

The purpose of teaching is to facilitate learning. This may seem so obvious that there is no need to state it. We reiterate it, however, because of its importance and because it has implications not explicitly included in its statement. For us, teaching is a set of tasks and activities carried out by a teacher who has the intention that these tasks will bring about learning. The tasks of learning are carried out by learners who have the intention of concluding these tasks by knowing something that they did not know before. The tasks of teaching need to express or embody the intended knowledge and need to be related to the current state of the learners in such a way that it is possible for the learners to learn the intended content (Fenstermacher, 1986; Hewson & Hewson, 1988; Hirst, 1971). What this means is that learning lies at the heart of any conception of teaching; the corollary is that a conception of teaching that does not include learning is a contradiction in terms. On the one hand, teachers need to match who the learners are and what they know with the intended curriculum in ways that make this a task that is reasonable for learners to be able to achieve. Assuming it is solely the learners' responsibility to make the necessary connections between where they are and where the teacher intends them to go cannot be a part of what it means to teach. On the other hand, this concept of teaching does not imply that teaching causes learning to occur and that, without learning, teaching did not happen. Regardless of how good a teacher is and how appropriate the tasks of teaching are to both the learner and the content to be learned, if the learner does not intend to learn there will be no learning.

Teachers are professionals with specialized knowledge required by their profession. Professional practice is complex and uncertain, and it uses an expert knowledge base (Schön, 1983, 1988). Professionals are constantly being called on to make decisions in unique circumstances without certain knowledge. Past experience and a base of expert knowledge do not provide a set of fixed rules to follow but rather provide heuristics that will guide decision making. To make decisions that are informed rather than reactive, a key characteristic of professional practice is reflection on past and current actions. There is expert knowledge inherent in such practice (Schön, 1983, 1988). The perspective of teachers as professionals is in contrast to a view of teachers as skilled technicians and of teaching as the expert application of bodies of disciplinary knowledge produced by others, which implies that knowledge of teaching does not constitute its own body of knowledge. On the contrary, teachers as professionals have a large body of knowledge that is worthy of respect. This includes knowledge of the content of their discipline, of the students they teach, of the forms of instruction and assessment strategies they use, and of the larger context in which they teach (Coble & Koballa, 1996; National Research Council [NRC], 1996). Equally important is their pedagogical content knowledge: what teachers know of the ways in which these different types of knowledge interact with one another and how they can be used to support one another in leading to effective teaching (Shulman, 1986). Teachers' pedagogical content knowledge includes understanding that some mathematical ideas and science concepts are more difficult for students to learn than others, more fundamental than others, more easily modeled than others, and less well understood than others. That teaching is a knowledge-based activity contributes to its status as a profession.

As professionals, teachers realize that their learning about teaching does not stop when they are credentialed. Rather, they expect to continue learning throughout their teaching career and to be able to improve their practice significantly with appropriate professional development learning opportunities. They recognize that they practice in uncertain circumstances, that much of their knowledge is embedded in their practice rather than in codified bodies of knowledge, and that their extensive, complex knowledge, particularly with respect to their understanding of how learners learn, profoundly influences how they teach. Teachers are members of the larger school community that is characterized by certain norms and behaviors (National Council of Teachers of Mathematics [NCTM], 1991; NRC, 1996; see Chapter 6).

The practice of teaching is complex. It involves repeating phases of planning, acting, observing, and reflecting. As outlined previously, teaching occurs in uncertain circumstances and requires constant decision making. It encompasses deep flexible knowledge and the ability to apply knowledge about students, content, the curriculum, instruction, assessment, and the school and local communities. Nevertheless, we believe that all teachers can practice in this way—in part by developing their practice for themselves as they build on their own classroom experience and expertise and in part by learning from the collected wisdom and experience of others.

There are a variety of activities carried out by teachers in such a practice. Effective teachers who understand the nature of learning pose challenging tasks more often than providing succinct explanations. They encourage their students to articulate their ideas and question each other about their reasons for holding their ideas rather than only correcting their mistakes. Effective teachers also set goals for instruction, create appropriate contexts for classroom activities, and pose problems that have relevance and meaning to the students. They organize activities in which students do much of the talking and doing, often in small groups without the teacher. They watch students' actions and listen carefully to students' arguments and explanations to understand what sense the students themselves are making. They monitor classroom activities and decide if, when, and how to intervene. When they intervene, they frequently do so by expanding the topic in ways that elicit more questions rather than prompting premature closure. They facilitate different levels of discourse needed in the classroom and are concerned not only with what students say about the topic but also with why they say it. They establish and maintain a classroom environment that provides opportunities for students to explore their own and others' ideas individually and collectively without fear of ridicule or sanction (NCTM, 1991; NRC, 1996).

These teachers create opportunities for all students to learn. They establish the learning environment as a place where students are respected and engaged participants, where student questions and ideas are valued, and where students are given the time, resources, and space necessary to explore and learn. They have a repertoire of strategies for responding appropriately to the variety of knowledge and experiences of their students, and they work to ensure equal access to equitable teaching for all students.

Finally, although we recognize that particular circumstances have an important influence on the quality of education in any given classroom, we strongly hold the following convictions:

- All teachers want to teach well and can do so, all teachers have classroom experience and expertise worthy of respect, and all teachers can attend to and respond appropriately to the variety of knowledge and experiences of their students.

- All teachers want all students to achieve.

- All communities want to support their schools, teachers, and students; although many people in communities think they are incapable of providing support, they can develop skills for doing so.

- The values and practices inherent in the community, the culture, and the educational system in which teachers work are at least as important as those of the teachers themselves in ensuring equal access to equitable teaching for all students.

- We must reach all students (all kinds of students in all locations) and all teachers through important, suitably differentiated and equitable learning activities.

The Nature of Science and Mathematics

As professional developers plan activities to increase teachers' ability to teach science and mathematics in ways consistent with national standards and state frameworks, it is important for them to understand and consider the current beliefs about the nature of these disciplines. Particularly in the education field, mathematics and science have long been viewed as bodies of established knowledge comprising facts that are true and that have been known for a long time. Science of this kind has been called a rhetoric of conclusions and final-form science (Duschl, 1990), and it represents a static conception of the discipline. People have a similar conception of mathematics: Some say "all the mathematics there is, is already out there" (Schifter & Fosnot, 1993, p. 12).

An alternative view of the nature of science and mathematics (the one reflected in national standards) asks not only "What do we know?" but also "How do we know it?" "What does it mean to 'do' mathematics and science?" and "Where does our knowledge come from?" This is a dynamic conception of these disciplines—a conception of "science in the making." It recognizes that science and mathematics are human pursuits—as much invention as discovery—with a long history in which schools of thought compete, fashions change, and some questions may never be settled (Schifter & Fosnot, 1993). This understanding of science and mathematics recognizes that these disciplines provide processes by which mathematicians and scientists produce knowledge and make judgments regarding whether it is "good" knowledge. Our current view of these disciplines recognizes that the processes of observing, describing, conjecturing, testing, explaining, revising hypotheses, predicting, observing, explaining, and so on, applied repeatedly to investigations, characterize the work of science and mathematics. The current view also recognizes the arguments that scientists and mathematicians advance to support their conclusions (NRC, 1996).

There are many similarities between mathematics and science that are reflected in practices common to both science and mathematics classrooms. For example, mathematics is like science and technology because it is used to answer fundamental questions and find solutions to practical problems (American Association for the Advancement of Science, 1993). This does not mean, however, that the disciplines are identical. Although mathematics provides a language that is an incredibly powerful tool for scientists, it is a discipline in its own right. It has been called the science of patterns and relationships. In particular, it is not constrained by science's goal of understanding and explaining the natural world, and it has no necessary relationship with the natural world. Nevertheless, many problems that it investigates do emerge from every part of the natural world, whether physical, biological, or social.

The relationship of science with the natural world is critical and complex. Science attempts to build a picture of the real world in terms of concepts, principles, theories, or constructs that can be used to explain what has been observed and predict what has not. Although this picture is most succinctly expressed in the language of mathematics, science also uses other forms of communication. For example, without a rich fund of images derived from experience with phenomena, scientific concepts that students learn are abstract labels and, for most individuals, seem unconnected with anything important, are distant, and are of little use. When students have accumulated a rich array of images, however, they are able to "see" the concept in the events associated with the specific phenomena; the phenomena become the metaphor for the concept. When students think of electric current, for example, they associate a definition and equations with their experiences of making a bulb light up, hearing their battery-powered radio begin to get faint, or seeing lightning flash.

The vision of excellent science and mathematics teaching illustrated in Chapter 1 reflects this view of these disciplines. In the examples, students are engaged in a dialogue with each other, with their teacher, with the natural world, with the ideas of others (both experts and laypeople), and indeed with themselves. In this dialogue, they speak, listen, and respond as they construct new meanings and formulate arguments. Through this process, they grapple with fundamental concepts in the discipline, learning not only what they are but also why they take the form that they do. In the process of developing these higher-order ideas and capabilities, students are also learning important basic information, such as facts and formulas, and doing exercises and procedures. These facts and procedures are not, however, ends in themselves; they also serve as integral parts of a broader context that gives these pieces of information meaning.

Professional Development

Professional development is a critical ingredient of science and mathematics education reform. During the past two decades, U.S. educators and policymakers have implemented a variety of programs aimed at increasing teachers' knowledge and skills. From these efforts, we have learned much about what constitutes effective professional development as well as the attributes and principles of best practice. For example, Loucks-Horsley and associates (1987) identified the attributes that are essential for effective professional development. Effective professional development experiences foster collegiality and collaboration; promote experimentation and risk taking; draw their content from available knowledge bases; involve participants in decisions about as many aspects of the professional development experience as possible; provide time to participate, reflect on, and practice what is learned; provide leadership and sustained support; supply appropriate rewards and incentives; have designs that reflect knowledge bases on learning and change; integrate individual, school, and district goals; and integrate both organizationally and instructionally with other staff development and change efforts. Note that many of these attributes parallel those of effective learning experiences for students. The idea of building new understandings through active engagement in a variety of experiences over time, and doing so with others in supportive learning environments, is as necessary for adults as it is for young people.

Many authors have surveyed research on professional development for science (Coble & Koballa, 1996) and mathematics (Clarke, 1994) teachers. In 1996, Loucks-Horsley, Stiles, and Hewson described a common vision of effective professional development in science and mathematics. To do so, they examined national efforts to develop standards to guide reform and noted a large degree of agreement in the documents produced by a variety of different organizations. These organizations included some interested in improving the subject matter of mathematics and science (NCTM, 1989; NRC, 1996) and some directly interested in professional development itself (National Staff Development Council, 1994, 1995a, 1995b). The authors also surveyed the work of the National Center for Improving Science Education (1993) that added to the knowledge base when it identified indicators of effectiveness for teacher development programs in science, mathematics, and technology. The common vision identifies the following seven principles that are addressed in effective professional development experiences:

1. Effective professional development experiences are driven by a well-defined image of effective classroom learning and teaching—for example, commitment to all children learning mathematics and science; an emphasis on inquiry-based learning, investigations, problem solving, and applications of knowledge; an approach that emphasizes in-depth understanding of core concepts and challenges students to construct new understandings; and clear means to measure meaningful achievement.

2. Effective professional development experiences provide opportunities for teachers to build their knowledge and skills. For example, they help teachers develop in-depth knowledge of their disciplines as well as

pedagogical content knowledge (listening to students' ideas, posing questions, and recognizing common and naive misconceptions), and they help in choosing and integrating curriculum and learning experiences.

3. Effective professional development experiences use or model with teachers the strategies teachers will use with their students. For example, they start where teachers are and build from there; provide ample time for in-depth investigations, collaborative work, and reflection; and connect explicitly with teachers' other professional development experiences and activities.

4. Effective professional development experiences build a learning community—for example, continuous learning is a part of the school norms and culture, teachers are rewarded and encouraged to take risks and learn, and teachers learn and share together.

5. Effective professional development experiences support teachers to serve in leadership roles—for example, as supporters of other teachers, as agents of change, and as promoters of reform.

6. Effective professional development experiences provide links to other parts of the education system. For example, professional development is integrated with other district or school initiatives or district or state curriculum frameworks and assessments or both, and it has active supports within the community.

7. Effective professional development experiences are continuously assessing themselves and making improvements to ensure positive impact on teacher effectiveness, student learning, leadership, and the school community.

These principles demonstrate how beliefs about professional development have changed during the past 25 years. In the early 1970s, professional development was called inservice; its goal was to bring outside expertise to teachers to increase their knowledge, often with regard to a discrete new program or approach. The contemporary focus of professional development has widened to embrace not only the teacher but also the organization to which the teacher belongs (Loucks-Horsley, 1995). This new focus brings with it new challenges. Although the education community has developed a large knowledge base about what constitutes effective professional development, we are just beginning to understand what it takes for whole systems and organizations to learn and set up ongoing mechanisms for learning.

Increasingly, leading-edge professional developers are attempting to help school organizations design the systems and structures they need to support continuous learning (Sparks, 1994). Although we know much about what constitutes "best practice," there is less guidance about how to design professional development so that it promotes continuous learning in the organization, is equitable for teachers and students, builds the leadership and infrastructure needed, fits with the school context, and gives teachers the range of experiences they need to learn. The design framework presented in this book is aimed at filling this gap. Throughout the book, other areas of the professional development knowledge base are discussed, as are issues that still need to be addressed.

The Change Process

Professional developers can be guided by the extensive body of knowledge about how effective change occurs in education settings (Fullan, 1991, 1993). Change is both an individual and an organizational phenomenon affecting each and every educator as well as the schools, districts, universities, and other organizations to which they belong. Principles that derive from the knowledge base on change include the following:

- Change is a process that takes time and persistence.
- As individuals progress through a change process, their needs for support and assistance change.
- Change efforts are effective when the change to be made is clearly defined, support and assistance are available, and leaders and policies support the change.
- Most systems resist change.
- Organizations that are continuously improving have ongoing mechanisms for setting goals, taking actions, assessing the results of their actions, and making adjustments.
- Change is complex because it requires people to communicate with one another about complex topics in organizations that are, for the most part, large and structured.

All educational changes of value require individuals to act in new ways (demonstrated by new skills, behaviors, activities, etc.) and to think in new ways (beliefs, understandings, ideas, etc.). The question of the relationships between thoughts and actions is therefore important for professional development. The conventional wisdom has been that changing teacher beliefs should be the primary work of professional development because when one believes differently, new behaviors will follow. Research on teacher change, however, indicates that changes in attitudes often result when teachers use a new practice and see their students benefiting (Guskey, 1986). Instead of being linear, changes in ideas and attitudes, and actions and behaviors, occur in a mutually inter-active process. On the one hand, people's current thoughts influence what choices they make and what they attend to as they plan and carry out educational activities. On the other hand, people's reflections on these activities and their outcomes influence their thoughts about educational matters. Therefore, change in attitudes and behaviors is iterative; well-conceived professional learning experiences address both, knowing that change in one brings about and then reinforces change in the other.

Fundamental change occurs over time through active engagement with new ideas, understandings, and real-life experiences. This explains why many teachers find it difficult to change how they teach: They experienced their own learning of mathematics and science in ways that are very different from those reflected in the national science and mathematics standards. They learned by memorizing information and others' explanations through a transmission model. These experiences serve as powerful models for their own teaching. Change occurs only when beliefs are restructured through new understandings and experimentation with new behaviors. Effective professional development experiences are designed to help teachers build new understandings of teaching and learning and to try the teaching strategies that help students learn in new ways. They guide teachers to construct knowledge in the same ways as do effective learning experiences for students. It is surprising, however, how often the principle of constructivism is conveyed to teachers in the context of how they should help their students learn, without its being the basis for how the teachers are helped to learn themselves (e.g., there are still many lectures on constructivism). Experiencing learning in ways that hold to constructivist principles is the only way for teachers to understand why it is important for their students to learn in this way and for them to break their old models of teaching (Little, 1993; Loucks-Horsley et al., 1990).

It should be no surprise that when change occurs, it does not happen in one step but is progressive. We learn from studies of individuals who change their practice over time that individuals go through stages in how they feel about the change and how knowledgeable and sophisticated they are in using it. The questions that people ask evolve from early questions that are more self-oriented (What is it? and How will it affect me?) to questions that are more task-oriented (How do I do it? How can I use these materials effectively? How can I organize myself? and Why is it taking so much time?) to questions focused on impact (Is this change working for my students? and Is there something that will work even better?) (Hord, Rutherford, Huling-Austin, & Hall, 1987). (See Chapter 4 for a detailed discussion of this developmental process.)

Professional development initiatives that are designed with the change process in mind have distinct characteristics (Fullan, 1991; Loucks-Horsley & Stiegelbauer, 1991). First, they are informed by the ongoing monitoring of the concerns, questions, and needs of teachers and focus interventions and support on what is learned. Second, they pay attention to implementation for several years for teachers to progress from an early focus on management to a later focus on student learning. Associated with this is the way they create realistic expectations in the system. It can take several years (most research indicates 3 to 5) for teachers to become routine in their use of a new practice or program; therefore, expecting student achievement to change in a short period is unrealistic. Third, once changes in teachers' practice become routine, other demands on their time may distract them from focusing on student learning. Effective professional development designs anticipate this and build in opportunities for organizational priority setting (Loucks-Horsley, 1995).

Although a major focus of change efforts is on the individuals changing, professional development can succeed only with simultaneous attention to changing the system within which teachers and other educators work. In the earlier wave of mathematics and science reform, impact studies reported the disturbing finding that many teachers who had experienced exemplary professional development returned to their schools to find no support for the kinds of changes they wanted to make, and therefore no change ultimately occurred. Education and businesses alike have learned much from similar experiences during the past two decades, and new attention to the structures in the system that support or block innovation and change has emerged. Here, the unit of change is the system and not the individual. A major premise of systems thinking is that the behavior of individuals in systems is dictated by underlying structures in organizations such as incentive systems, culture, and rules. Individuals are not to blame for breakdowns in the system that are caused by the system itself (Patterson, 1993; Senge, 1990). Effective change thus requires the organization to strive for continuous learning and to quickly adopt new approaches and strategies in response to new needs in the system. Educators at all levels are beginning to pay attention to "systemic change" by aligning components of the system, strengthening the relationship of the components to one another, and focusing their efforts on high standards for student learning (Smith & O'Day, 1991). Professional development is viewed as a critical component of reform—one that must be linked to those same clear goals for students as well as assessment, preservice teacher education, school leadership, and resources and staffing (National Commission on Teaching and America's Future, 1996).

The knowledge base discussed in this chapter provides important guidance to the design of professional development experiences. In Chapter 4, we examine another input into the design process: an array of strategies for professional learning that can, in combination, help professional developers create single experiences and large-scale initiatives that bring this knowledge base to life.

4 Strategies for Professional Learning

∎∎∎

At the very center of professional development planning is the decision about which strategies or approaches to use. As outlined in Chapter 2, the selection of strategies is informed by the goals, the knowledge base, and the context. In this chapter, we describe 15 specific professional development strategies. (Table 4.1 provides an "at-a-glance" description of each strategy.)

By a strategy, we mean a kind of learning experience that has identifiable characteristics that make it recognizable when implemented. In this chapter, we describe each strategy according to its (a) underlying assumptions—that is, the beliefs about teaching, learning, and professional development that designers must hold to select and use the strategy; (b) key elements—that is, the components of the strategy that help answer the question, How will I know it when I see it?; and (c) implementation requirements—that is, the resources and support needed to use the strategy, such as time, facilities, materials, and additional staff. We then give various examples of ways in which the strategy has been implemented and, in a commentary, we discuss some of the issues and challenges faced when selecting and using the strategy. Also, for each strategy, we identify additional resources—articles and books for obtaining further information as well as information about specific programs or initiatives that use the strategy.

As noted in previous chapters, professional development does not occur as isolated strategies. Every program, initiative, and professional development plan uses a variety of strategies in combination with one

TABLE 4.1 Strategies for Professional Learning

Immersion in inquiry into science and mathematics

> Engaging in the kinds of learning that teachers are expected to practice with their students—that is, inquiry-based science investigations or meaningful mathematics problem solving

Immersion in the world of scientists and mathematicians

> Participating in an intensive experience in the day-to-day work of a scientist or mathematician, often in a laboratory, industry, or museum, with full engagement in research activities

Curriculum implementation

> Learning, using, and refining use of a particular set of instructional materials in the classroom

Curriculum replacement units

> Implementing a unit of instruction that addresses one topic or concept and incorporates effective teaching and learning strategies to accomplish learning goals

Curriculum development and adaptation

> Creating new instructional materials and strategies or tailoring existing ones to meet the learning needs of students

Workshops, institutes, courses, and seminars

> Using structured opportunities outside of the classroom to focus intensely on topics of interest, including science or mathematics content, and learn from others with more expertise

Action research

> Examining teachers' own teaching and their students' learning by engaging in a research project in their classroom

Case discussions

> Examining written narratives or videotapes of classroom teaching and learning and discussing what is happening, the problems, issues, and outcomes that ensue

Study groups

> Engaging in regular, structured, and collaborative interactions regarding topics identified by the group, with opportunities to examine new information, reflect on their practice, or assess and analyze outcome data

Examining student work and student thinking and scoring assessments

> Carefully examining students' work and products to understand their thinking and learning strategies and identify their learning needs and appropriate teaching strategies and materials

(Continued)

TABLE 4.1 (Continued)

Coaching and mentoring

>   Working one-on-one with an equally or more experienced teacher to improve teaching and learning through a variety of activities, including classroom observation and feedback, problem solving and troubleshooting, and coplanning

Partnerships with scientists and mathematicians in business, industry, and universities

>   Working collaboratively with practicing scientists and mathematicians with the focus on improving teacher content knowledge, instructional materials, access to facilities, and acquiring new information

Professional networks

>   Linking in person or through electronic means with other teachers or groups to explore and discuss topics of interest, set and pursue common goals, share information and strategies, and identify and address common problems

Developing professional developers

>   Building the skills and knowledge needed to create learning experiences for other educators, including design of appropriate professional development strategies; presenting, demonstrating, and supporting teacher learning and change; and understanding in-depth the content and pedagogy required for effective teaching and learning of students and other educators

Technology for professional learning

>   Using various kinds of technology to learn content and pedagogy, including computers, telecommunications, videoconferencing, and CD-ROM and videodisc technology

another to form a unique design. Each strategy is one piece of the puzzle, and how strategies fit together depends on the other elements of the design framework. The professional development designer's challenge is to assemble a combination of learning activities that best meets the specific goals and context.

One guide to selecting strategies is knowing the primary purpose of a strategy and matching it to the needs of participating teachers. As noted in the discussion of the knowledge base on change in Chapter 3, strategies support a process of learning that unfolds over time. Because people change in what they know and what they need, different strategies can be more appropriate for different phases in the change process. As professional developers and researchers have assembled and studied programs, they have created various schemas that often help to guide others in their selection of different strategies. We now present some of these schemas.

First, in selecting strategies wisely, it helps to know that some strategies fulfill some purposes better than others. For example, some strategies (such as workshops) are more appropriate for building knowledge, whereas others (such as case discussions) help teachers think deeply about learning and teaching. The following are some different purposes for strategies:

- Strategies that focus on developing awareness are usually used during the beginning phases of a change, which call for introducing teachers to new approaches or content. The strategies are designed to raise awareness through the introduction of new information and to elicit thoughtful questioning on the part of the teachers concerning the new information.

- Strategies that focus on building knowledge provide opportunities for teachers to increase their understanding of science and mathematics content and teaching practices.

- Strategies that help teachers translate new knowledge into practice engage teachers in drawing on their knowledge base to plan instruction and improve their teaching.

- Strategies that focus on practicing teaching help teachers learn through the process of using a new approach, practice, or process with their students. As they practice new moves in their classrooms, they increase their understanding and their skills.

- Strategies that provide opportunities to reflect deeply on teaching and learning engage teachers in examining their experiences in the classroom, assessing the impact of the changes they have made on their students, and thinking about ways to improve. These strategies also encourage teachers to reflect on others' practice, relating it to their own and generating ideas for improvement.

Table 4.2 is adapted from a framework devised by researchers in the QUASAR project (Brown & Smith, 1997) to describe various ways of supporting teacher learning. The framework, in turn, reflects Shulman's (1987) model of pedagogical reasoning and action. According to Shulman, any act of teaching is cyclic. A teacher must comprehend the material to be taught, which then must be transformed into a form that can be taught. Then, instruction takes place and is accompanied by reflection on the effectiveness in fostering student learning.

TABLE 4.2 Purposes of Different Professional Learning Strategies

Strategy	Developing Awareness	Building Knowledge	Translating Into Practice	Practicing Teaching	Reflecting
Immersion in Inquiry	x	X			X
Immersion in Sci/Math World	x	X			
Curriculum Implementation		x	x	X	
Curriculum Replacement		x	x	X	
Curriculum Development/ Adaptation		x	X		
Workshops, Institutes	x	X	x		
Action Research		x			X
Case Discussion	x	x			X
Study Groups	x		x		X
Examining Student Work	x	x	x		X
Coaching and Mentoring		x	x	X	x
Partnerships	x	X			
Professional Networks	x	X	x		x
Developing Professional Developers		x	x	X	x
Technology	x	X	x		x

NOTE: A capital "X" indicates the primary purpose for each strategy, and a lowercase "x" indicates one or more secondary purposes.

Table 4.2 identifies the different types of teacher learning provided by engagement in each strategy. Note that individual strategies can serve more than one purpose. In this table, we have indicated what we think are the primary purposes for each strategy with a capital "X" and one or more secondary purposes with a lowercase "x." For example, engaging in the strategy of action research can be a source of new information (x), but this strategy is primarily a way to learn through studying teaching and student learning and reflecting on the results (X).

What is clear from this list of purposes is the developmental nature of learning. Several developmental models have been used by professional developers to select, combine, and sequence the strategies they use to support teacher learning. For example, the Concerns-Based Adoption Model, discussed briefly in Chapter 3, describes the emerging questions or concerns that educators have as they are introduced to and take on a new program, practice, or process (Hord, Rutherford, Huling-Austin, & Hall, 1987). These concerns develop from questions that are more self-oriented (e.g., "What is it?" "How will it affect me?" and "What will I have to do?") to those that are task-oriented (e.g., "How can I get more organized?" "Why is it taking so much time?" and "How can I best manage the materials and schedules?"), and, finally, when these concerns begin to be resolved, to more impact-oriented concerns (e.g., "How is this affecting students?" and "How can I improve what I'm doing so all students can learn?").

The concerns model suggests that teacher questions can guide the selection of strategies for professional development. For example, an immersion in inquiry into science or mathematics—that is, actually learning content in new ways—can help teachers see (and feel) what new teaching practices look like in action. They get a sense of new roles teachers must take, strategies for grouping and questioning, and the flow of instruction. Curriculum implementation helps teachers with their questions about the teaching task because it guides them to use of materials, time management, and classroom management techniques. Teachers' more impact-oriented questions can be addressed through opportunities for them to examine student work and score student assessments or conduct action research into their own questions about student learning.

Other schemas capture the developmental nature of teacher change in different ways. The National Gardening Association in Burlington, Vermont, depicts a teachers' progression toward inquiry-based science in several stages from no inquiry to textbook teaching, to use of hands-on activities in a cookbook fashion, to increasingly more student-guided investigations based on their questions and emerging scientific understandings. Each stage suggests different support materials and activities that help the teacher do a better job and move on to more student-centered inquiry.

Similarly, Bell and Gilbert (1996) propose a teacher development model from science education with three dimensions that need to be addressed and supported: personal, professional, and social. Each of these dimensions has three stages that can guide the kinds of strategies that teachers will find most helpful in their learning.

As noted previously, it is the combination of strategies that enriches the professional learning of teachers. For example, teachers might attend a workshop in which they use new curriculum materials, implement a unit from those materials in their classrooms with help from a mentor or coaching from a peer, review videos of their own or others' teaching in a case discussion group, and participate in a study group in which student work produced during use of the new curriculum is discussed. This set of strategies can nurture teacher learning through several stages of development and change in teaching practice.

Before discussing the 15 strategies in the following sections, we note some differences in the strategies selected by mathematics and science educators. We originally wanted to illustrate each strategy with both science and mathematics examples but soon learned that certain strategies were used more often by mathematics professional developers and others were used more often by science professional developers—and we can only speculate on the reasons. For example, science educators use curriculum implementation more often to support teacher learning; this may simply be because there have been more science curricula available, especially at the elementary level, that embody many of the principles of effective teaching and learning. Mathematics educators appear to focus more on examining student thinking through analysis of student products, classroom action research, and case discussions. In the discussions of strategies that follow, we have tried to present a range of examples and illustrations. The lack of examples of science for one strategy and mathematics for another is likely to reflect the preferences of the different content areas for how to support teacher learning; it is also possible, however, that we have missed a prime example. It is also interesting to note that currently there is more experimentation with strategies that have been successful in other content areas. For example, science educators have been working to develop science teaching and learning cases, and mathematics educators have been experimenting with the introduction of curriculum units to support teacher learning.

Immersion in Inquiry Into Science or Mathematics

Elaine, Teri, Kevin, and Shelly, mathematics teacher colleagues at Riverside school, were attending a seminar at a local university. As a prelude to a discussion on open-ended investigations, the teachers were presented with and asked to explore the following problem: How many 1 × 1-foot square floor tiles would you need to make a border on the floor around the edge of a rectangular room? The group began by trying to decide what the smallest room could be that would have a tile border as described. After some discussion of the meaning of "border," they agreed that a 3 × 3-foot room would be the smallest, and that it would have one tile in the interior. The group proceeded to build a model of the situation and concluded that the border would require eight tiles. At this point, Teri suggested that they look at a room that was 7 × 8 feet. (She had drawn a sketch of the tile border for a 7 × 8-foot room while the other three members of the group were determining the smallest case.) Kevin suggested that they subtract the area of a 6 × 5-foot rectangle from the area of the 7 × 8-foot rectangle because this difference would result in the number of tiles on the border of the 7 × 8-foot rectangle. He used Teri's diagram to explain this solution method to the members of the group. The teachers continued to explore different cases and to make conjectures regarding the number of square tiles in the borders of rooms with different dimensions. After much discussion and exploration, Kevin suggested an approach that seemed to "work" for rooms of any dimension. They then tested the suggested generalization and concluded that it did indeed work for any case.

Immersion in inquiry into science or mathematics is the structured opportunity to experience, firsthand, science or mathematics content and processes. First, by becoming a learner of the content, teachers broaden their own understanding and knowledge of the content that they are addressing with their students. Second, by learning through inquiry—putting the principles of inquiry-based science or mathematics teaching and learning into practice and experiencing the processes for themselves—teachers are better prepared to implement the practices in their classrooms. The goal is to help the teacher become a competent inquirer and an analytical student of his or her own process of learning through immersion in an investigation of science or mathematics content. Immersion experiences most often occur in settings in which the learning is guided by a knowledgeable and experienced "instructor" and the curriculum is designed specifically to highlight the inquiry approach to learning the mathematics or science content.

Underlying Assumptions

Using immersion in inquiry into science or mathematics as a strategy for professional development is based on several assumptions about teachers, learning, and professional development.

Teachers benefit from experiences as students that are based on the same principles as the ones they are expected to implement with students. The principles of human learning apply equally well to adults and children; they both learn through direct experience and by constructing their own meanings from those experiences using previous knowledge. If teachers are expected to implement inquiry-based science and mathematics teaching and learning in their classrooms, they first need to fully understand for themselves the processes that are involved in learning through these approaches.

Teachers must become mathematics or science learners by being challenged at their own level of competence. By engaging in activities that are appropriate for adult learners rather than doing student activities, teachers are able to investigate science or mathematics content for their own learning. This helps them develop an increased understanding of the content, which thus enhances teachers' ability to more effectively guide students in their learning of content.

Science and mathematics comprise inquiry and content. The content of science and mathematics is the understandings, meanings, and models that have been created and continue to be created by scientists and mathematicians. Science and mathematics as inquiry encompass the methodologies used to develop scientific and mathematics knowledge and understanding. Teachers must develop understanding and knowledge in both content and process.

Key Elements

The key elements of immersion in inquiry as a strategy for professional development are discussed in the following sections.

Immersion in an Intensive Learning Experience. Teachers are immersed in an intensive experience in which they focus on learning science or mathematics and are able to pursue content in-depth. As learners, they participate fully in the generation of investigable questions, plan and conduct investigations that allow them to make meaning out of the inquiry activities, collect and organize data, make predictions, measure and graph, and gain a broader view of the science or mathematics concepts they are investigating. They do all this to experience and learn the inquiry process for themselves.

Focus on How Students Should Learn. The goal of these experiences is to engage teachers in firsthand learning of what they are expected to practice in their classrooms—guiding students through inquiry-based science or mathematics activities.

Changed Conceptions About Science, Mathematics, and Teaching. One outcome from in-depth immersion in the inquiry process is a change in teachers' conceptions of the nature of science or mathematics learning and teaching. For example, as teachers begin to see science or mathematics teaching as less a matter of knowledge transfer and more an activity in which knowledge is generated through making sense of or understanding the content, they begin to see their own role as teacher changing from a direct conveyor of knowledge to a guide helping students develop their own meaning from experiences.

Implementation Requirements

For immersion in inquiry to be an effective means of professional development, certain requirements must be met.

Qualified Instructors. Because immersion experiences are characterized by guided activities, one key requirement is qualified instructors using appropriate materials. Guiding teachers through the inquiry process must be a specified goal of the immersion experience and one that is carried out by someone with experience.

Long-Term Experiences. Immersion experiences are not conducted in one-time-only workshops but usually extend over a long period of time. Often, such experiences are found only through programs in specific sites, such as the Workshop Center in New York, and are not accessible to teachers off-site. Some new programs and courses, however, are available through telecourses offered on the Internet, such as the Mathematics Learning Forums (see "Technology for Professional Learning" for a discussion of this course).

Examples

At the City College Workshop Center in New York, teachers attend a 2-week summer institute at which they immerse themselves in investigating a question in science. They learn how to conduct a science investigation using science inquiry as an approach. Scientists and center staff work with the teachers in developing and conducting the investigations. Teachers form hypotheses, design experiments, ask questions, record and analyze results, and present their findings. The philosophy behind these activities is that to help teachers teach inquiry science in their classrooms, they need to experience inquiry learning for themselves. Through this process, they also learn the science content. Teachers continue their learning throughout the academic year by attending sessions at the center that are focused on applying their new learnings in the classroom. The entire program is designed to bring about a paradigm shift in teachers toward a view that they have the capacity to inquire with meaning into phenomena and to successfully engage in science inquiry activities using phenomena and experiences that matter to them. The program also seeks to enable teachers to internalize an inquiry-based approach to the teaching and learning of science, implement it in their classrooms, and help their colleagues adopt it in their own practices (Dyasi, 1995).

SummerMath for Teachers is another example of an immersion program located at one site—at Mount Holyoke College. It is an intensive summer program for teachers that is designed to stimulate teachers' development of a constructivist view of learning. The program is based on the beliefs that teachers must become mathematics learners if they are going to teach for understanding, that this happens best when they are challenged at their own level of mathematics competence, and that they must be provided with experiences as students in classrooms that are based on the same pedagogical principles as the ones they are expected to implement with children (Schifter & Fosnot, 1993). Participating teachers have the opportunity to learn mathematics and discuss the experience of learning, the structure of the lesson, and the roles of the teacher and students. Schifter and Fosnot, however, point out that

> perhaps more important for [the teachers] than their investigation of any specific content area is the process of active self-reflection. By analyzing together their experience of the just-completed mathematics activity, teachers begin to construct an understanding of how knowledge develops and the circumstances that stimulate or inhibit it. (p. 26)

Commentary

Even with extensive course work in their preservice programs, many teachers come to the teaching of science or mathematics without having had opportunities to engage in inquiry themselves or to actually experience complex investigations that mirror how science or mathematics is performed. This immersion is beneficial, but it has its drawbacks as well. Teachers with limited time and programs with limited resources may not be able to afford the time required for in-depth investigation and may opt for shorter term experiences with, for example, the student learning materials.

Another interesting issue is where immersion in inquiry best fits into a learning sequence. At the Workshop Center, Dyasi uses it to initiate teachers into a new view of science. Others may choose it as a more in-depth enrichment once teachers learn to use and are comfortable with a set of materials for their students. They then gain a better understanding of how to help students explore important ideas, follow their own lines of investigation, generate alternative solutions to problems, or all three.

Additional Resources

CalTech Precollege Science Initiative (CAPSI), The Pasadena Modules Project: Modular Inquiries for Advanced Professional Development, Pasadena, CA. (Phone: 818-395-3222)

Russell, S. J. (1994). *Explorations in number, data, and space.* Palo Alto, CA: Seymour.

San Francisco Exploratorium's Teachers Institute Program, San Francisco. (Phone: 415-561-0313)

Schifter, D. (1993). Mathematics process as mathematics content: A course for teachers. *Journal of Mathematical Behavior, 12*(3), 271-283.

Schifter, D., Russell, S. J., & Bastable, V. (in press). Teaching to the big ideas. In M. Solomon (Ed.), *Reinventing the classroom.* New York: Teachers College Press.

ScienceAlive! A program sponsored by the Pacific Northwest Laboratory and the U.S. Department of Energy, funded by the National Science Foundation. Science Education Center, Richland, WA. (Phone: 509-375-2820)

Immersion in the World of Scientists and Mathematicians

As part of an 8-week immersion experience coordinated by the Department of Energy's Teacher Research Associates (TRAC) program at the Superconducting Super Collider Laboratory, Robert, a high school physics teacher, participated in a research study. He measured properties of scintillating tiles and fibers to understand the production and transportation of light in the tile and fiber assemblies for the Solenoidal Detector Collaboration (SDC) calorimeter. These data were used to understand how to optimize the light output of these assemblies and how to design a calibration system for the SDC calorimeter. His work included exciting tiles with an ultraviolet laser and measuring the light output with a photomultiplier tube under various conditions; measuring the transmission properties of samples of scintillators using a spectrophotometer; measuring the spectrum of the scintillation light in various samples using a fluorescence detector; and using a cosmic ray test station to study the response of a tower constructed from the tile and fiber assemblies. At the end of his research experience, Robert designed a transfer plan identifying ways he wanted to share his experiences with other physics teachers; he participated in workshops and attended presentations at which he shared his research on the "Correlation of Photoluminescence Spectra of Plastic Scintillator Tiles and Wavelength-Shifting Fibers With Light Output From Tile and Fiber Combinations."

The vast majority of science and mathematics teachers have never had an opportunity to actually "do" science or mathematics in a real-world setting. This situation perpetuates certain myths about the nature of science and mathematics because most teachers have no practical experience in the fields they are teaching. Immersion in the world of scientists and mathematicians is one way to resolve the dilemma and provides an opportunity for teachers to strengthen their knowledge base in content areas by becoming active participants in a mathematics or scientific community.

Frequently, the setting is a scientific laboratory, a mathematics research group, or a museum research department. Teachers join scientists or mathematicians in their work and fully participate in research activities. The purpose is for teachers to learn science and mathematics content; to learn elements of the research process, such as designing experiments, creating mathematical models, and collecting, analyzing, and synthesizing data; and to develop a broader and increased understanding of the scientific and mathematics inquiry approach to building knowledge and solving problems.

Underlying Assumptions

Using immersion in the world of scientists or mathematicians for professional development is based on certain assumptions about teachers, learning, and professional development.

Teachers who experience scientific or mathematics research firsthand increase their understanding and knowledge of science and mathematics content and processes. By becoming a scientist or mathematician in a research environment, teachers necessarily learn both content and the skills necessary for conducting research. They increase their knowledge of science and mathematics and, as part of a research team, develop skills in sharing and critiquing information with other professionals.

Teachers leave the research environment better equipped to teach science and mathematics in their classrooms. Quality research programs for teachers include components for transferring learned concepts and skills into the classroom; in many programs, a product of the experience is a detailed plan for extending experiences into the classroom. Many programs offer teachers support materials, electronic connections, and other networking facilities for continued contact and support once the teachers leave the environment and implement their plans. These experiences provide teachers with the background knowledge to "teach beyond the textbook" and to simulate in their classrooms the processes scientists and mathematicians use to solve problems.

Becoming part of the scientific and mathematics community is personally and professionally rewarding. Teachers need to have authentic experiences outside of the classroom. Most find that becoming an active member of a research team allows them to explore and develop their role as leader, equal partner, and contributing member of an interdisciplinary team and provides them with the opportunity to share their experiences beyond both the laboratory and the classroom (e.g., at national conferences).

Key Elements

Immersion experiences either in a scientific laboratory, with a mathematics research group, or in a museum research department have several components in common.

The experiences are designed as mentored research opportunities for teachers, as apprentice researchers, to learn the content, process, culture, and ethos of scientific or mathematics inquiry. Teachers often select their own area of research and are paired with a mentor scientist or mathematician, usually during an intensive summer program.

Teachers attend lectures and seminars and read materials on the science or mathematics topics related to the research. As part of their immersion into the scientific or mathematics community, teachers participate in activities outside of their research that enhance their experiences and contribute to their knowledge base.

Teachers actively participate as members of research teams, which sometimes include several scientists or mathematicians as well as university faculty. As part of their research experience, teachers contribute to the ongoing work of the research team by presenting oral reports on what they are learning, critically reviewing their own and others' work, and participating in team meetings.

A curriculum development component is facilitated by an expert. Teachers create action plans or instructional activities to transfer what they have learned to their classrooms. Although the main objective of immersion experiences is the professional development of teachers, one outcome is that as teachers obtain greater content and process knowledge, understanding of the research community, and experience in "being" a scientist or mathematician, they are better able to devise methods for sharing this with their students.

There are opportunities for follow-through with implementation and dissemination at local, regional, and national levels as well as opportunities for ongoing communication. Most immersion programs encourage all members of research teams to both individually and jointly present their findings and their experiences at meetings and in journal articles. Programs also encourage research team members to maintain communication with each other, view their scientist or mathematician mentors as resources, and, in some cases, invite their mentors to visit classrooms throughout the school year. Other programs offer "class reunions" at regional or national conferences, newsletters, and electronic networks for "graduates."

In addition to the key components mentioned previously, many programs incorporate journaling or writing about the immersion experience. Teachers find that writing about their experiences as they progress over time helps deepen the experience itself and helps them recognize that they have "become" a scientist or mathematician. The gaining of this perspective during the immersion program encourages teachers to return to the classroom with a different view of themselves.

Implementation Requirements

Immersion experiences for teachers in scientific or mathematics environments have several requirements that must be met.

Funding. Because this is a "one teacher at a time" professional development experience, it can be expensive—well over $10,000 per teacher.

Studies of the cost-effectiveness are ongoing, however, as are explorations of ways to reduce the cost or reach more teachers or both.

Access. Teachers need access to a research setting in which scientists and mathematicians are willing and able to serve as mentors. Accessibility is sometimes restricted by issues of safety, security, and competition.

Shared Expectations and Goals. All involved in the immersion experience need to have open, frequent communication and establish shared goals and expectations for the assignments and experiences of the teachers.

Resources and Support. Teachers need support from their school administrators to return to the classroom and use what they have learned. This may include additional resources and materials and permission to deviate from the standard curriculum.

Examples

Industry Initiatives for Science and Math Education (IISME) brings together teachers and professional scientists and mathematicians. IISME was created in 1985 by 15 companies in the San Francisco Bay Area and the Lawrence Hall of Science out of concern for the shortage of high school science and mathematics teachers and the declining number of students choosing to pursue technical fields. IISME bridges the gap between the classroom and the workplace by providing summer work opportunities for teachers in research laboratories. At each site, IISME teacher fellows work alongside industry mentors to learn how science and mathematics are practiced in the real world. The Lawrence Hall of Science provides year-round academic programs, follow-up support, and an electronic mail network so that IISME fellows can continue to interact with their colleagues after their summer internship. Outcomes of the IISME program range from specific classroom activities related to the teacher fellows' work assignments to teaching methods that stress cooperative working groups and interdisciplinary problem-solving patterned on real-world models. IISME "sister" programs now exist throughout California, in 15 other states, the District of Columbia, and Denmark.

Perhaps the single largest professional development program that enables teachers and scientists to work together is the TRAC program that is located at many of the nation's 28 National Energy Laboratories and that has support from the U.S. Department of Energy. One TRAC location is Brookhaven National Laboratory (BNL) in New York. This TRAC program is conducted in close cooperation with New York University (NYU). It began in response to a needs assessment of New York City teachers indicating that 90% of those surveyed felt uncomfortable with their science background, with many interested in personal interaction with a scientist in a laboratory setting. Currently, 10 teachers per year participate as interns at Brookhaven as part of a master's program for inservice teachers at NYU. As Leonhardt and Fraser-Abder (1996) state,

> Teacher interns arrive at BNL during the second week of July and quickly immerse themselves in their research. The interns perform laboratory and library research under the supervision of their scientist/advisers. Throughout the experience interns are treated as members of the scientific community. They have access to BNL resources and are encouraged to request assistance as needed and perform research as assigned. The interns live on-site for the duration of the internship. They participate in all programmatic and social activities, including weekly lunchtime discussions that focus on transferring the research experience to the classroom. The teachers form a cohesive group and share their laboratory successes, difficulties, and classroom strategies. Toward the end of their internships, teachers apply for small grants to support the transfer of their lab experience into their classrooms. At this time teachers also begin making preliminary plans to have either their scientist/adviser visit their classes during the fall semester or to have their classes visit BNL. (p. 33)

The University of California at Berkeley's University Research Expeditions Program (UREP) offers opportunities for teachers to work with UC Berkeley faculty in the sciences and social sciences on their current field research projects. UREP subsidizes teachers' field expeditions and provides campus workshops at which teachers develop curriculum based on the research performed on an expedition. The mission of the program is to provide teachers with the opportunity to engage in real science so that they can go back to their classrooms and perform similar activities; to teach the process of science rather than accumulating facts; and to open up channels of communication between scientists and educators. One teacher who conducted a wetlands research project in Belize summarized her experiences as follows (WestEd, 1996):

> I've seen teachers make incredible leaps in terms of their confidence. Even if we've had training in science, we've rarely had opportunities to participate in real scientific research. What we

do when we are isolated in classrooms is very different than what happens in universities, and UREP gives us a real understanding of how a scientist approaches a problem. (p. 9)

Project Growth in Education through a Mathematical Mentorship Alliance (GEMMA), in Dayton, Ohio, brings together teachers and administrators from school districts, mathematics and science educators from universities, and scientists and executives from several industries and businesses. Participants plan and take part in a variety of activities, with the purpose of improving the mathematics education of all students in the county's public schools. Project GEMMA provides opportunities for teachers to discover connections between mathematics and science, engineering, and other disciplines used in the workplace and disseminates to teachers materials about current real-world applications of mathematics. During the internship, a teacher is assigned to a mentor who guides the teacher through the completion of a project at the industry or business. The teacher is expected to make a contribution, not be just a spectator, as he or she also observes how people in industry operate, what skills they need, and how they use mathematics in their daily work.

During the internship, teachers attend seminars at which they discuss their experiences in the workplace, the applications of mathematics they are leaning and how they plan to share this with their students, and the teaching methods they are considering as a result of what they observe in industry. As a result of their experiences during the internship, they develop a booklet of applications problems that they pilot and revise during the school year. There are also follow-up "reunions" at which teachers reflect on what they experienced during the internship and what they are trying to transfer to the classroom. During the internships, teachers learn from one another how to transform successful industry content and methods into successful classroom content and methods (Farrell, 1994).

Commentary

Although an immersion experience can be extremely rewarding for teachers and result in changes in classroom practices, there are several "pitfalls." First, scientists and mathematicians sometimes prefer "helpers" who already have degrees in science or mathematics; those who fill the bill are commonly high school teachers. This somewhat limits the pool of teachers who can benefit from this kind of experience. There are, however, locations and assignments that welcome teachers with lower levels of experience.

Second is the question of the degree to which teachers are able to translate important aspects of their internship experience into the classroom. Staff at one program confronted this problem when past participants told them that, when they returned to their schools, they were frustrated by a lack of equipment and by colleagues and administrators who were unwilling to make changes in the school setting to accommodate an improved science program. Program sponsors addressed the problem by limiting admission to teachers whose administrators promised to provide support to maximize the teachers' effectiveness when they returned to the classroom. Other programs include partnership agreements with school districts or individual schools to implement changes that would use the teachers' research experience during the academic year. Many of these programs also provide structures for continued contact and support for teachers with their mentors, project staff, and fellow participants. Although imposing these types of contracts and partnership agreements on teachers and their administrators addresses the problems identified, it also limits the number and diversity of teachers who are able to participate in research opportunities to those with local support.

Third is the issue of whether teachers actually need to bring something back to the classroom other than a renewed interest in and commitment to their field and an increased understanding of content. Some believe that it is enough for teachers to develop this interest and knowledge, and that this will lead them to share their enthusiasm with students. Others believe that it is important to incorporate into the immersion experience strategic plans for implementing new learning in the classroom. In essence, this issue relates to how directly students need to be reached by their teachers' professional development and, in the case of teacher research participation, whether attention to classroom applications makes a significant difference.

A fourth issue concerns the relationship between scientists and mathematicians and teachers in the research environment. At best, it is collegial, and the scientist or mathematician has sufficient time to work with the teacher to involve him or her in the problem-solving process. There is the danger, however, that teachers will be given repetitive tasks with little explanation, or that they will be asked to read and attend lectures with advanced scientific or mathematics content and might then try to pass on the knowledge in a similar manner to their students. This problem can be addressed through careful orientation of mentors and guidance in selecting teacher research assignments. It arises less frequently with internship programs connected with museums, where teachers work closely with museum experts in developing exhibits, planetarium programs, or other activities for the general public. Because the main goal of museums is education, museum staff are frequently more effective coaches for how to translate learning to the classroom than are many scientists and mathematicians.

Finally, the cost of providing this strategy for teachers has led many to dismiss it as a viable opportunity for teacher professional development. Many believe that the money can be better spent in ways that reach more teachers. Some corporations and businesses are working with universities and research facilities to create sponsored internships for teachers. Many provide money for scholarships to purchase equipment and supplies for the classroom, pay for fellows' substitute teachers when they attend conferences and inservice workshops, and reproduce the materials they might develop during the internship (videos or software). Sponsored internships can help defray the costs associated with this strategy.

Additional Resources

Gottfried, S. S., Brown, C. W., Markovits, P. S., & Changar, J. B. (n.d.). *Scientific work experience programs for science teachers: A focus on research-related internships.* Unpublished manuscript.

Hays, I. D. (1994). *Scientists, educators, and national standards action at the local level: Forum proceedings, April 14-15.* Paper presented at the Sigma Xi, The Scientific Research Society Forum.

Industry Initiates for Science and Math Education (IISME), Lawrence Hall of Science, University of California, Berkeley, CA. (Phone: 415-326-4800)

The National Center for Improving Science Education. (1993). *Profiling teacher research participation programs: An approach to formative evaluation.* Andover, MA: Author.

Scientific Work Experience Programs for Teachers (SWEPT), Triangle Coalition for Science and Technology Education, College Park, MD. (Phone: 301-220-0870)

Teacher Research Associates (TRAC) program, U.S. Department of Energy, Washington, DC. (Phone: 202-586-0987)

University Research Expeditions Program (UREP), University of California at Berkeley. (Phone: 510-642-6586)

Curriculum Implementation

Sarah Johnson is a sixth-grade teacher in a district that has three middle schools, each with approximately 600 students, Grades 6 through 8. The school board has just voted to implement a new problem-centered mathematics curriculum. Sarah participated with other teachers in a preliminary meeting during the spring that provided an overview of this new cur-

riculum, but she really has little understanding of the total program or of what it will mean for her to actually use it.

The middle school coordinator has asked Sarah to join her, one seventh- and one eighth-grade teacher, and the principal from her school, along with similar teams from each of the other two middle schools in the district, to participate in a 1-week residential professional development institute that will introduce them to the curriculum. At the institute, she finds 18 other middle-grade teachers and their administrators from two other districts. This will be a good opportunity to learn with teachers who are from very different kinds of districts.

At the beginning of the institute, an overview of the structure and organization of the curriculum is provided. Very quickly, the leader moves to engaging participants in doing actual activities from the first module they will teach. Sarah jumps right in, as do the rest of her team members. They work through the various activities. Sarah is particularly attentive to some of the teaching strategies that the leader is using. In particular, she likes the way the leader expects different groups to take responsibility for initiating summary discussions about problems that have been investigated. She also notes that the leader makes a point of highlighting particular learning strategies as a way of pointing out the interaction of the teaching methods used and ways to promote student engagement and problem solving.

That night, participants are given homework problems to complete for the next day. Sarah and her team meet to work together on the problems; they are challenged as they solve problems and talk about the implications for use with their students. When they arrive at the workshop the next day, the leader designates various teams to take responsibility for presenting their solutions, providing a model for a strategy that Sarah plans to use as part of her classroom structure for the next year.

As the week progresses, the participants begin to understand the structure of the curriculum and how to use it with their students. The leader makes building a community of inquiry seem easy; Sarah wonders how she will develop such a community with her own students but is filled with enthusiasm. As the week draws to a close, the leader focuses on planning to use the curriculum; using the school calendar and the pacing guide provided with the curriculum, teachers from the same grade levels team up and lay out a schedule to implement the first module. Sarah feels confident about the detail provided in the teacher support materials, particularly because the curriculum has actually been field tested at a number of different sites for multiple years.

There are many things planned when Sarah returns to her district. She knows that the middle school coordinator is counting on her and the other teachers in her district to use the new curriculum in their classrooms this year and then to help introduce the curriculum to other teachers in their

schools the following year. The principals and the middle school coordi-
nator intend to be quite proactive in their efforts to support the teachers in
developing learning communities that are oriented toward problem solv-
ing and inquiry, and they will provide the teachers with opportunities for
peer coaching and support group meetings. Two more 1-day workshops
are scheduled throughout the year with the institute leader both to provide
time for discussion and to gain an understanding of other modules that
will be used at each grade level. Also, the institute leader will return to the
school district in the spring to conduct several 1-day sessions for the other
teachers in the schools.

For right now, Sarah is concerned with what will happen with her
students. For the first time in a long time, Sarah finds she is very excited
about teaching mathematics and that the curriculum seems to reflect her
beliefs about what constitutes good teaching and learning.

The implementation of new curricula in the classroom can serve as
a powerful learning experience for teachers. For curriculum implementation to support professional development, plans must be designed in
ways that enable teachers to learn about, try, reflect on, and share information about teaching and learning in the context of implementing the
curriculum with their colleagues. Through using curriculum in their
classrooms, reporting on what happens, and reflecting with others on the
strengths and weakness of different ideas and activities, teachers learn
about their own teaching and their students' learning (Ball, 1996).

Curriculum implementation involves using a set of materials that
includes both content and instructional guidelines. The "set" of materials may be from one publisher or developer, or it may have been selected
from a variety of quality materials available and organized by the school
or district for use at particular grade levels in the development of specific
concepts. For curriculum implementation to serve as an effective professional development activity, it is required that the curriculum selected
or organized for implementation meets quality standards for content and
for appropriate teaching strategies.

Curriculum implementation that is designed for professional development focuses teachers on learning about the new curriculum and how
to use it and on implementing it—not on researching, designing, testing,
or revising curriculum or all of these. The teachers' time, therefore, is
devoted to learning the science or mathematics content necessary to
teach the new curriculum, learning how to conduct the activities, learning how students can best learn the new material, and incorporating the
new curriculum into their long-term instruction.

The goal of this professional development strategy is not only for
teachers to implement a new curriculum but also for them to strengthen
their content and pedagogical knowledge and skills.

Underlying Assumptions

The use of curriculum implementation as a strategy for professional development is based on several assumptions about teaching, learning, and professional development.

Through an effective introduction to a high-quality set of curriculum materials, teachers can become clear about the goals for student learning so that they can make sound judgments about the use of materials and strategies in the classroom. For teachers, implementing a curriculum can clarify (a) the nature of the content itself and assumptions about what students bring to the content, (b) how the content can be taught (e.g., what is hard and what is easy for students as provided in the curriculum and as determined by the teacher's use of the curriculum), and (c) the nature of student knowledge—how students work and talk—and the nature of the discourse that teachers orchestrate to give them access to information about what and how students are learning.

Changing beliefs and attitudes about teaching and learning can result from practicing new behavior. Contrary to the view that beliefs must change before behaviors will change, there is mounting evidence that beliefs and behaviors interact in an ongoing way, and changes in one can bring about changes in the other. Guskey (1986) cites studies in which teachers were helped to change their approaches. The teachers were often unwilling at first, but once they observed their students learning, the teachers' belief in the new approaches and commitment to them changed significantly. Ferrini-Mundy (1997), through an examination of the influence and interpretation of the National Council of Teachers of Mathematics (NCTM) standards in several communities, found numerous instances in K through 12th-grade mathematics classrooms of teachers' commitment to new teaching behaviors once they observed new learning by the students. Ferrini-Mundy states, "We repeatedly saw skepticism giving way to confidence and belief through experimentation with various types of exploratory and open-ended activities, coupled with perceptive assessment of children's experiences of these situations" (p. 124).

The curriculum implementation strategy is based on the assumption that the concrete experience of actually teaching using new behaviors can help teachers change their beliefs and attitudes about the new ideas and move them toward real and lasting change. When teachers try new approaches and they observe their students learning in new and significant ways, the teachers develop or strengthen their commitment to change.

Teachers who experience new ways of teaching by actually teaching will develop and increase their understanding of the new way of teaching. Reflecting on and analyzing what they are experiencing in their classrooms increases their understanding. Teaching a curriculum that combines teaching strategies with specific standards-based outcomes and content is the optimal way to increase understanding and take on new ways of teaching. Structured discussion following these activities allows teachers to be reflective and analytical about their own classroom performance. They can articulate their experiences, get reinforcement for successes and help in understanding and addressing their problems, and receive and then work through challenges to their thinking. All this is best done when grounded in personal experiences.

Key Elements

There are several key elements of a curriculum implementation strategy for professional development.

Curriculum Materials. Curriculum is the way content is designed and delivered. It includes the structure, organization, balance, and presentation of the content in the classroom (National Research Council [NRC], 1996). Curriculum or instructional materials structure and organize the content and lend support for the teaching strategies and learning environments used by teachers to help their students learn. The curriculum implementation strategy relies on a high-quality set of curriculum materials, which are carefully developed by people with expertise in content and pedagogy, and sufficient resources and time to design, test, and refine the materials for use in diverse classrooms.

Learning the Curriculum. As teachers become familiar with the curriculum and go through the materials as learners, they practice the various teaching strategies they will use with their students. Teachers then try the new instructional materials and teaching practices in their classrooms and regularly discuss their results and progress with colleagues.

Planning and Support for Implementation. A plan contains the structure and timeline of the curriculum implementation (National Science Resources Center [NSRC], 1997). Teachers and professional developers work together to decide how and when the curriculum will be implemented and the milestones that will be met at different points in the implementation process. As the curriculum is introduced over a period of time, teachers are given different kinds of help and support that are tailored to their changing needs. Teachers share ideas and insights with one another as they implement the new curriculum. They also coach one another and conduct classroom visits to support implementation. (Usually, curriculum implementation involves using an entire curriculum for all grades in the school that covers all topics of the content area instead of only one topic or one grade level. The implementation process spread over time, however, may introduce units at one grade level at a time or introduce one unit at a time at each grade level.)

Implementation Requirements

For curriculum implementation to be used as a strategy for professional development, several requirements must be met.

A Quality Curriculum. A curriculum that meets the needs of the students in the school and district and is aligned with content and teaching standards must be selected for use. Materials needed for implementing the curriculum are available, and a system is in place that replenishes supplies and ensures that teachers have the materials they need when they need them.

Time. Teachers must have protected and structured time to learn about the new curriculum, try it in their classrooms, and reflect on their experiences and those of their students. School officials must acknowledge that implementing curriculum takes time, resources, and a commitment to reforming teaching and learning.

Teacher Development Opportunities. Teachers must have supported opportunities to become aware of the new curriculum, learn to manage materials in the classroom, teach the new curriculum, and assess both their own and their students' learning.

Policies. The school and district must anticipate and plan for institutionalization by ensuring that structures are in place for the continued use of the curriculum after the initial phases and that the curriculum is part of the overall school and district goals and policy. Plans must be in place for ongoing professional development for all teachers and support of new teachers or teachers who change grade levels.

Ongoing Commitment and Support. Teachers and school administrators must support the curriculum implementation over time (i.e., not just for 1 year) and avoid becoming distracted by other innovations and competing priorities. Administrators must ensure that the curriculum implementation meshes with other reform efforts currently in progress so that teachers are not overloaded and that the overall goals and vision for the school are coordinated.

Mechanisms for Assessment and Evaluation. Teachers must have routine meetings and interactions with other teachers to critique, reflect on, and process what and how they are teaching. Data are collected to assess the extent of implementation and the interim results from the new curriculum. Although these data may include information about student learning outcomes, data related to actual implementation strategies and use of the curriculum are essential, especially in the early stages. Teachers and professional developers use evaluation data to adjust what they are doing.

Examples

Since 1989, the Quantitative Understanding: Amplifying Student Achievement and Reasoning (QUASAR) project has fostered and studied the development and implementation of enhanced mathematics instructional programs for students attending middle schools in economically disadvantaged neighborhoods throughout the country. At each school site, the mathematics teachers and school administrators collaborate with "resource partners" to develop, implement, and modify an innovative mathematics instructional program for all students at the school (Stein, Silver, & Smith, in press).

One QUASAR school, Portsmouth Middle School, designed a program to implement Visual Mathematics (VM), an innovative curriculum that embodies many of the recommendations of the NCTM's *Curriculum and Evaluation Standards for School Mathematics* (1989). To prepare for implementing the VM curriculum, all the mathematics teachers attended two workshops conducted by the resource partners. The workshops included 60 hours of instruction designed to help teachers become familiar with the mathematical content and pedagogy of the curriculum and with issues related to current mathematics reform. Following the workshops, teachers also participated in monthly, full-day staff meetings at which they had opportunities to discuss problems and successes associated with implementing the curriculum in their classrooms. Throughout the year, as they implemented the curriculum the mathematics teachers continued to receive support both from the resource partners and, as they gained confidence in managing the initial steps in implementing the curriculum, from each other.

During the school year, consulting teachers visited classrooms, and teachers met regularly on their own to work with one another. Selected teachers were released from a portion of their teaching duties to serve as mentors for their peers—providing materials, conducting classroom observations, and holding discussions. Teachers also met biweekly after school and for 2 or 3 weeks each summer to undertake various project-related activities. Informal day-to-day sharing between teachers became routine, and teachers were provided with individual time for reflecting on videotapes of their own teaching practices and for writing in journals. Finally, teachers attended a variety of conferences and 1- and 2-day retreats at the end of the school year.

In another example, Montgomery County, Maryland, began its reform effort in 1988 when the superintendent of schools convened a task force to assess the county's K through 12th-grade science program. Under the guidance of the coordinator of elementary science, teachers began reviewing and field testing new curriculum materials that fit within the state framework. By 1990, teachers had selected one unit per grade level to implement in each elementary classroom. The county established an intensive professional development program, and the school system made the commitment to purchase the materials needed to implement the new program. The district held a 2-week summer institute in inquiry-centered pedagogy for 40 lead teachers who would field test the units in their classrooms. Throughout the year, the 40 teachers attended monthly meetings that addressed such topics as the nature of science, learning theory, a constructivist approach to learning, cognitive development, and cooperative learning, and they worked closely with scientists and science educators from the community. The following school year, an additional 28 lead teachers joined the implementation team.

As these teachers implemented the new curriculum, they also considered whether the curriculum reflected the new pedagogy and included examples of authentic assessments. They met monthly to discuss the experiences in their classrooms. From this process, the lead teachers selected curriculum materials from a range of national curriculum programs. Once the curriculum units had been selected and assembled, the district initiated a plan to provide all elementary teachers in the county with support and professional development opportunities as the teachers implemented the new units over a period of years. This began with a weeklong summer institute at which teachers received an overview of the new curriculum and then worked with their peers and experienced lead teachers in small groups that were formed by grade level. Throughout the school year, the teachers implemented three units in 12-week cycles. Before receiving any of the units, all participating teachers were released for a half day of workshops that were focused on materials management for the new units. Once they started teaching the units, teachers attended after-school support meetings to share their experiences and solve problems. Also during the first 2 years, the county established a science materials center. Staff at the center replenished kits, delivered them to teachers, and picked them up from teachers once the teachers had finished teaching them.

Administrators throughout the district also support the implementation efforts: They release teachers to attend meetings and institutes, they give teachers science content credit for attending the summer institutes, and they attend a summer institute focused on the new pedagogy and the science units. Recently, the district formed a partnership with the American Physical Society, and 45 scientists began working with the teachers. The combination of administrative support, professional development for all teachers, exposure to the materials for the units before actually teaching the units, a comprehensive materials distribution center, and quality curriculum has contributed to the county's efforts to implement the new science curriculum successfully.

Commentary

Although virtually all schools implement new curricula at some time, often they do not organize the implementation in ways that promote effective professional development. Designing initiatives so that teachers reflect on and learn from their experience is an efficient and effective professional development approach.

There are several benefits to using curriculum implementation as a vehicle for professional development. First, such an initiative combines two major aspects of the system—curriculum and teaching—so that changes will necessarily align and reinforce the two aspects. (Note that it is not uncommon for curriculum to be changed and teachers to have opportunities for professional development with no connection between the two.) A second and related benefit is the efficiency of teachers learning directly what they need to teach. This is the role that curriculum plays in this strategy. (In Chapter 7, two of the five professional development programs illustrate this strategy.) This contrasts with the situation in which teachers learn content and teaching strategies, but they have no ready-made vehicle to put these together in their classrooms. Finally, this strategy is also beneficial because it provides a focus for teacher reflection. Teachers can share issues, concerns, children's work, and so on in the context of discussing the new curriculum. Such discussions create the conditions for a more effective implementation of the new curriculum because support is provided for teachers to identify and solve problems and evaluate results.

In addition to its benefits, there are also pitfalls in the curriculum implementation strategy. First, there is a tension between the "mandates" to implement a new curriculum with fidelity and teacher creativity and independence. It is important for teachers to know how much adaptation they can do and still be viewed as implementing the curriculum effectively. Some changes in the new curriculum (e.g., finding and developing appropriate connections to other subject areas) can enhance the materials' effectiveness. Others can be harmful (e.g., when science teachers decide that live things are too difficult to manage or that demonstrations work better than having each student doing his or her own investigations). The nature of acceptable adaptations requires early and ongoing negotiation.

Schools can ensure continual use of the curriculum by proactively supporting all teachers and providing orientation for new teachers or teachers who change grades. The needs of teachers change over time. Initially, teachers may be focused on the "how-to's" and "whats" for using the new curriculum. Given the nature of problem-centered curricula, this focus could span the first few years of implementation as teachers develop frames of reference with respect to the nature of both the tasks and the students' thinking. Once teachers are comfortable at this stage, more complex issues related to promoting inquiry and understanding the impact of the curriculum surface. At this point, broader considerations of the nature of the mathematics or science content being addressed and how to better understand students' thinking may surface, necessitating a different orientation to professional development. Eventually, teachers may find themselves at points at which they want to "fine-tune" or make modifications or both in the use of the curriculum to better meet the needs of their students.

A final caveat: With this approach, there is a real danger that professional development support will stop once (or before) the curriculum is fully in place. This disregards the need for continuously increasing teacher knowledge and skills. The mechanisms for teacher reflection, sharing, assessment, and adjustment should become part of the overall school routine.

Curriculum Replacement Units

Jessica was enthusiastic about the school district's decision to adopt the Science and Technology for Children (STC) science units for Grades K through 6. During the past school year, she had attended a workshop at a regional National Science Teachers Association (NSTA) conference that highlighted one of the units for second grade that focused on balancing and weighing. During the summer before school started, she attended the district-sponsored weeklong institute for all second-grade teachers and was delighted to learn that the unit she had explored at NSTA would be the one implemented in all second-grade classrooms in the district; each grade was implementing one unit each year for the next 4 years. During the first few days of the institute, teachers from another district who had already taught the unit for a few years introduced Jessica and colleagues to the overall philosophy and design of the STC curriculum and worked with small groups of teachers as they "walked through" each lesson. At first, Jessica was overwhelmed with the kit of materials and panicked at the thought of having to manage the balance beams, buckets, marbles, plastic cups, and a myriad of objects, from plastic spoons to acrylic cylinders, in a room with 30 second graders. Once she and her group explored the contents of the kit and learned about the management tips in the teacher's guide, however, she felt more comfortable.

In the second half of the institute, Jessica and the other teachers worked through the lessons in the unit, completing the activities, exploring the materials, reading the background sections, hearing about "little glitches" and classroom discoveries from the teachers who had taught the unit, and asking questions about how those teachers had incorporated the integration ideas for other curriculum areas.

When school started, Jessica was nervous about trying to teach a messy, hands-on unit with her students but found that having the other second-grade teachers implementing the unit at the same time provided an opportunity for sharing experiences and solving problems. By the end of the 8 weeks, Jessica felt elated by her own success in handling the materials and presenting the activities to her students and by the learning her students had expressed in their journal writing and embedded assessment activities. In particular, she discovered much about what each student had learned as each child described the mobile he or she had designed and built, identifying fulcrum points and how he or she had resolved a "tippy" mobile that was too heavy on one side. Her students were ready for more "fun science," and Jessica was looking forward to teaching a unit next fall that would focus on solids and liquids.

Curriculum replacement units offer a window through which teachers can get a glimpse of what new teaching strategies look like in action. They also offer a way for teachers to engage in new and different teaching practices without completely "overhauling" their entire yearlong program. There are two ways in which replacement units are used for professional development. First, it is not the intended outcome for the units to be "adopted" or used over the long term. Rather, the units are used to stimulate teacher reflection and discussion. Through the experience of teaching the units, teachers change how they think about teaching and embrace new approaches that stimulate students to problem solve, reason, investigate, and construct their own meaning for the content. The second use of replacement units shares these goals, but it also has an additional goal. The intention here is to replace the entire curriculum over time, one or two units at a time, as in the previous vignette. This strategy helps teachers gradually learn a new way of teaching and some new content, leading ultimately to an entirely new curriculum through replacing some units each year.

Many reform initiatives have selected high-quality replacement units that are frequently developed by expert curriculum developers. The professional development programs introduce teachers to the units that can be used as replacements in their existing curriculum. The units are well-constructed sets of activities that address specific topics or concepts, with the most effective ones having been designed to elicit thoughtful, investigative problem solving from children. They are not designed as activities to supplement or enhance the existing curriculum; rather, they are coherent chunks of curriculum that are used to provide an alternative experience with traditional topics or to introduce new topics that are not currently part of the curriculum. They embody and thus illustrate what standards documents state should be taught and how teachers should teach.

Underlying Assumptions

Using replacement units as a strategy for professional development is based on several assumptions about learning, teaching, and professional development.

Trying a small dose of something is an effective way to "take the plunge." The demands on teachers are so great that the idea of completely revamping their teaching can stop them from considering anything new. This strategy assumes that, when teachers are not overwhelmed by a request or challenge, such as implementing an entire curriculum, they can be convinced by a small-scale experience to venture into larger-scale changes.

Practicing new behaviors in the classroom often results in changing beliefs and attitudes about teaching and learning. Contrary to the view that beliefs must change before behaviors will change, there is mounting evidence that beliefs and behaviors interact in an ongoing way, and changes in one can bring changes in the other. As noted previously in studies in which teachers were first helped to change their approaches, once they observed their students learning, the teachers' belief in the new approaches and commitment to them changed significantly. Similarly, the replacement unit strategy is based on the assumption that the concrete experience of actually using new behaviors as they teach can help teachers change their beliefs and attitudes about these new ideas and help them move toward more and lasting change. When teachers try new approaches and observe their students learning in new and significant ways, they develop or strengthen their commitment to change.

Reflecting on and analyzing what teachers are experiencing in their classrooms as a result of adopting new behaviors increases their understandings. Teaching a unit that combines teaching strategies with specific standards-based outcomes and content is the optimal way to increase understanding and take on new ways of teaching. Structured discussion following these activities allows teachers to be reflective and analytical about their own classroom performance. They can articulate their experiences, get reinforcement for successes and help in understanding and addressing their problems, and receive and then work through challenges to their thinking. All this is best done when grounded in personal experience.

Key Elements

There are several key elements of a curriculum replacement unit strategy for professional development.

Teachers must have access to high-quality replacement units. Replacement units focus on appropriate concepts and skills, present content that is based on standards and frameworks, and provide assessment that is aligned with both what is learned and how it is learned. As Burns (1994) notes, quality replacement units in mathematics

> integrate important mathematical topics and help students make sense of mathematics; appeal to students because the activities stimulate their thinking and imaginations and make mathematics interesting; appeal to teachers because they have been tested in classrooms and reflect input from teachers with experience teaching them; offer clear teaching plans, yet are broad enough to accommodate teachers veering from the plans to follow leads from students or add their own ideas; provide direction for assessing student understanding; allow for a span of abilities and interests; encourage students to communicate about mathematics, both orally and in writing; and provide opportunities for students to work individually and cooperatively. (p. 2)

Replacement units must be developed. The best replacement units are carefully and thoughtfully designed with sufficient investment in money, time, and expertise devoted to the development task. Given teachers' limited expertise, time, and other resources they have to devote to the task, curriculum units developed by expert curriculum developers are usually better learning tools than units that teachers develop themselves.

Teachers must learn how to implement replacement units. Teachers are grounded in the theoretical and practical aspects of the new teaching approach. They have opportunities to read and reflect on the units, try the activities as learners, attend workshops at which they can explore the rationale and learn from teachers experienced in the units, and practice new techniques.

Teachers must have opportunities to use the units and then reflect on their experiences. Teachers try out the units in their own classrooms, providing them with the opportunity to increase their understanding of and ownership for the new content or teaching strategies or both. Merely practicing new behaviors is not sufficient, however; teachers need opportunities for debriefing their experiences, discussing the implications for change in their teaching, and evaluating the impact that these practices have on students. Opportunities for reflection and dialogue increase understanding and can motivate teachers to broaden their application of the new approach to other parts of their curriculum.

Implementation Requirements

There are several requirements that must be met for replacement units to be successfully used as a catalyst for changing the way teachers think and teach.

Access to the Replacement Units and Materials. Replacement units can come from several places—for example, from new curriculum materials being developed by publishers or curriculum development organizations. Criteria for their selection include the following: The units must teach important mathematics or science concepts in ways recommended by the national standards, the units must stand alone and require only equipment and materials readily available or accessible to the teacher, and the units must be grade-level appropriate and accessible to a wide range of students. Ideally, replacement units are selected for the opportunities they provide for teachers to "see" their students doing significant mathematics or science in new and meaningful ways, and they provide opportunities for teachers to engage in discussions about what they see.

Preparation for Using the Replacement Units. Before teaching the units, teachers must learn from qualified people who are familiar with teaching the units. Not only do teachers need to understand the purposes of the units but also they need to know how to manage materials, how to allot time for presenting the materials, and how to manage classroom behaviors, such as providing guidance to their students in how to work together effectively. This typically includes significant time for experiencing the unit as learners and actually doing key parts of the unit themselves.

Agreement to Depart From the Standard Curriculum. If teachers are expected to try new teaching practices in their classrooms—usually with content that deviates from the required textbook curriculum—they need assurances that they are supported by administration and parents. Teachers cannot be expected to add a new curriculum to their overloaded existing curriculum. Something has to be "abandoned" for teachers to successfully implement replacement units and to have time to explore new ways of teaching.

Time, Resources, and Support for Teachers to Reflect on Their Classroom Experiences. Once teachers have begun teaching the units, it is essential that they have time to discuss and analyze what they are experiencing and learning. This reflective process requires that resources and support be available. For example, teachers at the same grade level need time to meet and discuss their concerns with each other and have access to support personnel for coaching and help in addressing concerns. This implies that the process is ongoing and long term; it is not just a one-time-only event.

Examples

The California Mathematics Renaissance Network has used replacement units to improve the teaching and learning of mathematics in middle schools throughout the state. During the 1994 and 1995 school year, more than 1,500 teachers from more than 400 middle schools engaged in the program's year-round professional development, which focused on discussing mathematics reform, experiencing hands-on mathematics, learning how to teach new state-of-the-art curriculum replacement units, and exploring the conditions that create opportunities for learning. Inherent in the professional development strategy of using replacement units is the following belief of the Mathematics Renaissance leadership (Acquarelli & Mumme, 1996):

Teachers must experience reform in their own classrooms and have opportunities to grapple with the difficulties that arise. Focusing the talk on [replacement units] has been particularly helpful to the process. Teachers have attended unit workshops and then taught the units while cluster leaders observed them. They've brought questions, concerns, and successes to their cluster meetings and shared their students' work with their colleagues. Their experience with alternative curricula has prompted examination, inquiry, and collaboration. This approach has allowed teachers to be exposed to big mathematical ideas in coherent, practical-sized chunks—pieces small enough to seem manageable to even the most reticent. (p. 482)

The Great Explorations in Mathematics and Science (GEMS) program, from the Lawrence Hall of Science, is a series of teacher's guides to hands-on, minds-on science. GEMS units are often used as replacement units because they provide step-by-step instructions for novice teachers and guidance in using a constructivist approach. Activities generally begin with questions so that the teacher can find out what his or her students already know about a topic. Then, they progress right into fun, involving activities, followed by students' discussion of their results and guidance for the teacher in helping the students to construct useful concepts in light of their recent activities.

The GEMS guides have been used as the focus for a number of teacher institutes in which teacher leaders are expected to bring new ideas back to their home districts. The following is a letter from one of the participants—a mentor teacher for science in her elementary school—that was written a few months after returning home (Sneider, 1996):

When I returned from the institute I worked with Ms. Carter, the fifth-grade teacher. Ms. Carter was a traditional teacher, she had worked predominately out of textbooks but was very open to new ideas. We were able to sit down once a week and plan our weekly class activities. I started out by sharing the GEMS guides, and after doing a weeklong *Oobleck* unit with four classes in our wing, she was hooked. After working with her closely through three GEMS guides, I found she began to instigate further hands-on science activities. Ms. Carter is now very enthusiastic and is going to be part of the NTEP program this summer with Los Alamos Labs. I really believe that participating in the institute allowed me to expand my personal and professional horizons and expand that excitement not only to Ms. Carter, but to many other teachers who I have since contacted. (p. 21)

Commentary

One of the benefits of the replacement unit strategy is that it helps teachers move at their own pace toward changing the ways they think about teaching and learning. Teachers are not expected to completely change their teaching practices throughout the school day or with the entire curriculum. Instead, replacement units provide an opportunity for teachers to "try on" a new teaching style within one specific aspect of the content. This helps teachers who prefer to develop their skills slowly become comfortable with new practices. An added benefit is that, because new ways of teaching are actually practiced in the classroom, teachers' typical early concerns about "What is it?" "What does it look like?" and "What will it feel like to do it?" are all addressed by the firsthand experience.

One of the key elements of this strategy, providing time and opportunities for "debriefing" experiences in the classroom, is also one of its greatest advantages. Teachers are not expected to attend a workshop and go back into their classrooms and simply implement the new teaching practices. Instead, they receive ample exposure to, training in, and discussion regarding both the management and the theoretical underpinnings of the replacement units; they then have ongoing opportunities to discuss what they are learning. It is this chance to openly share the problems they encounter and receive support and guidance in how to address them that enhances teachers' own professional growth and development. Too often, professional development strategies fail simply because teachers do not have this essential opportunity to reflect on their practices.

Replacement units are a cost-effective approach to providing professional development. Often, schools and districts cannot afford to completely overhaul the existing curriculum and purchase new materials and curriculum units. Investing in replacement units offers a less costly alternative. For example, in several school districts reforming their elementary science program, teachers are introducing into their curriculum one new science unit per year or semester. In all cases, the district has developed a content matrix to guide selection—that is, the district has determined what concepts or topics or both will be taught at each grade level—and in some cases it has actually selected all the units. Introducing them slowly, however, makes it more financially feasible to change the entire curriculum.

No professional development strategy is without its disadvantages. One disadvantage of replacement units is that teachers place too much emphasis on the units and not enough on the learning experiences—both theirs and their students'—that come from using them. They often view them as pieces of the curriculum that can be taught every year and begin to teach the units without examining how to make the new content an integral part of their curriculum and the new practices more a part of their teaching repertoire. This was a struggle that Mathematics Renaissance faced: Acquarelli and Mumme (1996, p. 480) stated, "How do you develop a deep understanding of the issues in mathematics education when teachers have a strong desire for things to take back, for recipes to add to their files?" To address this, Renaissance teachers selected student work from specific sections of a unit and used this work to examine how students from different settings approached challenging tasks. They "revisited" replacement units a second year, thus allowing them to delve deeper into student understanding and focus less on the mechanics of the unit.

Another disadvantage of replacement units arises out of teachers' enthusiasm for the units. Because teachers like the units, they often look for other pieces to add to their units or to other parts of their curriculum. They end up creating a incoherent, nonarticulated group of activities that do not build conceptual understanding. Sometimes, the replacement units become simply supplemental activities to the existing curriculum and do not have the intended outcome of helping teachers learn new ways of teaching. In fact, teachers who want or feel pressed to implement a new way of teaching may use the units to do so and at other times teach the "old way," arguing that students need both. In some cases, teachers attempt to combine a series of replacement units to create a whole curriculum. This well-intentioned effort often results in a curriculum that lacks a scope and sequence, a conceptual flow, and any coherence.

Teachers who do begin to change their teaching practices through using replacement units and move toward integrating them into the rest of their curriculum often experience a major stumbling block: finding quality instructional materials that incorporate the new teaching practices. In the absence of new materials, individual teachers seek to modify and adapt the existing curriculum. This creates a new professional development challenge: how to help teachers ensure that appropriate skills and concepts are still presented to the students and how to evaluate commercially produced materials to select those that are appropriate for their students and also incorporate the new content and teaching practice. Several resources are available to assist teachers and others to evaluate instructional materials aligned with standards (National

Research Council, in preparation; National Science Resources Center, 1997; Roseman, Kesidou, & Stern, 1996).

Additional Resources

GEMS, Great Explorations in Mathematics and Science, Lawrence Hall of Science, Berkeley, CA.

Math by All Means (a series of replacement units published by Math Solutions), Cuisenaire Company of America. (Phone: 1-800-237-3142)

Science and Technology for Children, Grades K through 6 science curriculum developed by the National Science Resources Center, Washington, DC. (Phone: 202-287-2063). Published by Carolina Biological Supply Company, Burlington, NC. (Phone: 1-800-334-5551)

Curriculum Development and Adaptation

At the request of the district superintendent, a group of volunteer K through sixth-grade teachers gathered with the district science curriculum specialist to form a curriculum committee to coordinate and revise the science curriculum in the district. Their first step was to review the current literature on trends, research, practices, and attitudes in science education. They also carefully studied the district, state, and national standards in science education. The teachers analyzed and discussed what they had read and synthesized their findings. They also conducted a needs assessment of their peers, community members, parents, and administrators. They discussed the relevance of current trends and standards, the needs of those affected, and how well changes in the curriculum could be applied in their district. After developing a plan for revision of the entire curriculum, they proposed a content matrix and curriculum materials matrix that identified specific hands-on, science units to address the content at each grade level. The teachers then obtained various units for pilot testing by teachers throughout the district. At the end of the year, they reviewed the results of the pilot test and identified a final selection of units for each grade level. The district adopted both the content and the materials matrices as well as the teachers' proposal for a long-term plan for implementing the units and providing professional development for all teachers in the district. At the end of the third year, a new group of volunteer teachers convened with the goal of revising some of the hands-on units based on feedback supplied by teachers at the end of teaching each unit. This group of teachers developed a plan for revising the units during the summer, inviting local scientists to sit at the table with them and provide content expertise and guidance in infusing more inquiry into the units. The district supported this plan and the teachers were paid stipends to participate in the refinement process.

In many cases, the goal of curriculum development or adaptation has been simply to create a new curriculum that will then be implemented in the classroom, either schoolwide or districtwide, within a science or mathematics department, or for individual courses. Increasingly, curriculum development and adaptation are being viewed as legitimate and effective strategies for the professional development of science and mathematics teachers.

Here, the term *curriculum* refers to content-specific materials used in classrooms and the articulated content matrix used to guide instruction, both of which are illustrated in the previous vignette. Given this broad definition of curriculum, the curriculum development process refers to both the creation of specific units of study to be implemented in the classroom and the creation of a districtwide or schoolwide content matrix that identifies the concepts and themes to be addressed at each grade level and the specific materials to be used to address those concepts and themes. Curriculum adaptation refers to the process of taking existing curriculum materials or content matrices and modifying them to more fully meet the needs of those involved—the students, teachers, school, and district.

Underlying Assumptions

The use of curriculum development and adaptation as a strategy for professional development is based on several assumptions about teachers, learning, and professional development.

Those closest to the level of implementation are best suited to develop curriculum. Through the process, teachers increase their content and pedagogical knowledge and reflect on their teaching. Teachers come to the table with a wealth of knowledge that prepares them to develop or adapt science or mathematics curricula. They know how students learn and which concepts are age appropriate; they often know how to teach the content that is the topic of the curriculum being developed or adapted. Their primary goal is to develop an appropriate curriculum that is applicable in the classroom. As they do so, however, teachers increase their knowledge of science or mathematics content through research or discussions with scientists or mathematicians; they also increase their awareness of diverse pedagogical approaches through reflecting on their own teaching in light of the new or revised curriculum.

The development of curriculum provides teachers with numerous opportunities to learn from others who have expertise outside of the classroom. As teachers work together on a science or mathematics curriculum, they engage in research, consult with others, collaborate with experts in relevant fields, and develop networks with peers and experts. In many cases, scientists and mathematicians are active participants with teachers in the process of developing or adapting curriculum, thus adding to teachers' opportunities to learn.

Teachers can increase their understanding of both content and pedagogy by thinking carefully about the broad goals of the curriculum and the specific concepts, skills, and attitudes that students need to acquire. Development or adaptation of parts of a curriculum cannot be accomplished unless teachers strongly consider how the specific section "fits" into the broader goals of the entire curriculum. For example, to develop or adapt curricula, teachers need to ask the question, "Do the specific units or materials build conceptual understanding of the content over time through a logical sequence of activities?" They need to understand state and local frameworks, national standards, the appropriateness of content and concepts that are presented at each grade level, and the sequence of other topics or units in the content area offered at each grade level. Whether developing individual units for instruction or creating a content matrix to be implemented schoolwide or districtwide, it is important that teachers have these understandings. By addressing the larger picture, teachers gain new knowledge and develop insights into how the content meets curriculum goals and enhances the learning of students.

Key Elements

There are two key elements of curriculum development or adaptation as a strategy for professional development.

Teachers undertake a process of developing or adapting curriculum that leads to a new product and learning. Although the outcome of curriculum development is a new or modified curriculum, it is the process that provides the opportunity for professional development. In the process of developing the curriculum, teachers learn new science or mathematics content; collaborate with peers and experts; design assessment that matches the content; examine their own classroom practices; work with others to solve problems; improve their own knowledge, skills, and attitudes to enhance classroom teaching; and engage in in-depth interaction with subject matter and pedagogy. All these activities enhance the professional growth of individual teachers and lead to more effective classroom practices that benefit the students.

Curriculum development or adaptation is a collaborative activity. Although individual teachers may be qualified to develop or modify curriculum for their own classrooms, the process of collaborating with a team enriches the professional development opportunities. Through discussions with other teachers, scientists, mathematicians, and administrators, individual teachers build their own knowledge of the content, curriculum organization and design, and content-specific pedagogy. Often, as teachers examine the curriculum, their attitudes about what constitutes effective science or mathematics teaching and learning change, and they return to their classrooms with new views. Also, by collaborating with others, teachers become less isolated in their individual classrooms and develop a broader perspective of science or mathematics education.

Implementation Requirements

For curriculum development or adaptation to be successful as a strategy for professional development, several requirements must be in place.

Voluntary Participation. Curriculum development or adaptation is most successful as professional development for teachers when it is voluntary. Developing and adapting curricula are complex and intensive tasks in which teachers must choose to participate.

Clear Expectations. Most curriculum development or adaptation efforts begin with specific expectations and guidelines, ideally designed by all involved. Teachers and administrators set clear goals, define products, and develop an effective timeline, instituting procedures for continued communications during the development or adaptation. Teachers must also have a clear understanding of the district standards or curriculum framework, and its goals and guiding principles for science or mathematics education, to align the curriculum with these.

An Established Procedure. Development or adaptation of any curriculum begins with evaluating current practices, assessing what is needed by teachers and students, determining what implementation procedures must be in place for the effort to be successful, and identifying a process for testing and evaluating the final curriculum. Often, once the curriculum is developed or adapted, teachers pilot test the curriculum in their classrooms and make revisions based on their evaluations.

Content Knowledge. Curriculum development or adaptation benefit from the guidance and in-depth knowledge of content of scientists or mathematicians.

District or School Administrative Support. Curriculum reform efforts are usually undertaken at the request of or at least with the sanction of administrators. Administrators encourage the process, provide time and incentives for teachers to participate, ensure access to resources and experts, and support ongoing, long-term improvement of the curriculum that is ultimately developed. Teachers are given the authority to implement the curriculum they develop or adapt. When teachers are merely asked to propose a curriculum that someone else has the authority to condone or reject, it can undermine their efforts, sending the message that they are not professionals with the expertise needed to make the final decisions.

Examples

As in many other school districts throughout the country, Spokane, Washington, district administrators provided the impetus for reforming the science program in the district. In 1989, the science coordinator and a team of teachers, administrators, and a local scientist developed a comprehensive K through sixth-grade science action plan while attending the National Science Resources Center's Elementary Science Leadership Institute in Washington, D.C. The first phase of the plan called for an in-depth curriculum review and development process. The science committee spent time identifying topics to be covered in the curriculum, obtaining input from teachers, and developing a comprehensive curriculum matrix made up of life, physical, and earth sciences strands. Once the strands were established, the district invited representatives from publishing companies to visit and present their curriculum materials. Teachers in the district piloted several units from various publishers, and the science committee ultimately designed a curriculum matrix with units from several publishers and some developed by teachers in the district.

As they implement their new district curriculum, they continue to improve it. Recently, a subcommittee of teachers has begun to identify the essential learning goals for each unit and to correlate them with the goals defined in state and national standards. The teachers continue to engage in professional development to increase their knowledge and understanding of how the overall curriculum and individual units meet the needs of their students and the goals of their teaching.

Not all curriculum development or adaptation efforts occur at the school or district level. One example of a program that has national application is Global Systems Science (GSS). (For more details, see the GSS case description under "Resources.") GSS is an interdisciplinary course for high school students that emphasizes how scientists from a wide variety of fields work together to understand significant problems of global impact. The GSS course materials include a wide variety of activities developed by teachers, including laboratory experiments, discussion activities, and simulations. Most of these activities have been developed at the Lawrence Hall of Science in Berkeley, California, during 3-week summer institutes for experienced high school teachers from around the country.

The goal of the GSS professional development component is not only to implement a new course of integrated studies but also to enable teachers to actively carry out new education reforms in science. Before they arrive at the summer institute, teachers spend 4 to 6 weeks pilot testing a model GSS unit in their own classrooms. During this phase, the goal is for teachers to become familiar with and develop opinions about the new approach. Then, at the summer institute, teachers share their insights about the content and process of teaching the new materials. They develop new activities and assessment tasks based on their discussions and experiences with the curriculum in their own classrooms; this leads to the revision of the curriculum. The teachers also continue to expand their knowledge base by meeting with scientists, visiting research laboratories, and reading books and articles on selected topics. Throughout the process, teachers collaborate with their peers and with scientists, reflect on their own teaching strategies, and discuss their perspectives on student learning as they revise and adapt the existing curriculum. They then implement the new activities from the GSS course in their classrooms.

Commentary

Many of the benefits of using curriculum development and adaptation for professional development of science and mathematics teachers have previously been identified throughout this section. As with any professional development strategy, there are challenges and issues to consider.

Time. Teachers usually do not have the time to devote to the intensive process of developing curriculum—researching, writing, piloting, revising, testing, and revising again. Frequently, teachers are available only during the summer months to devote time to intensive efforts such as developing curriculum. Although adapting an existing curriculum is a more reasonable task for a summer, even this process is better conducted over a longer period of time. Without time to reflect on the work, the professional development benefits of developing and adapting curricula are limited, and the effort becomes one of simply creating a product.

Teacher Expertise. Many people argue that teachers are not the most qualified to develop curriculum because although teachers often know which teaching and learning strategies are effective in a classroom, how children best learn content, and what content is age appropriate at certain grade levels, they do not have the "big picture" perspective on the overall curriculum—for example, across grade levels and within specific content topics. Nor do they have specialized expertise of instructional design and curriculum planning or the in-depth content knowledge needed to craft a full sequence of learning experiences that build across grade levels. It is certainly possible, however, for teams of teachers from across grade levels, with experience in various areas of science or mathematics, to collectively possess sufficient knowledge that, when given the time and access to resources such as scientists or mathematicians, they can be effective in designing a curriculum that addresses the needs of all students and the goals of the school or the district. The issue is not whether this is possible but whether starting curriculum development from scratch is the best use of limited resources. This is certainly where adaptation has advantages over development. In either case, there is clear benefit to the professional learning that occurs during the process.

Additional Resources

Ball, D. L., & Cohen, D. K. (1996). Reform by the book: What is—or might be—the role of curriculum materials in teacher learning and instructional reform? *Educational Researcher, 25*(9), 6-8, 14.

Branham, L. A. (1990). Tying professional development to math curriculum development. *Journal of Staff Development, 11*(3), 2-6.

Global Systems Science (GSS), Lawrence Hall of Science, Berkeley, CA. (Phone: 510-642-9635)

Killion, J. P. (1993). Staff development and curriculum development: Two sides of the same coin. *Journal of Staff Development, 14*(1), 38-41.

National Science Resources Center, Elementary Science Leadership Institutes, Washington, DC. (Phone: 202-287-2063)

National Science Resources Center, National Academy of Sciences, Smithsonian Institution. (1997). *Science for all children: A guide to improving elementary science education in your school district.* Washington, DC: National Academy Press.

Russell, S. J. (1997). The role of curriculum in teacher development. In S. N. Friel & G. W. Bright (Eds.), *Reflecting on our work: NSF teacher enhance-*

ment in K-6 mathematics (pp. 247-254). Lanham, MD: University of America Press.

Workshops, Institutes, Courses, and Seminars

In the summer of 1992, Tony Sanchez and the other mathematics teachers at his school participated in a 2-week summer institute held at the school. The institute was intended to help them develop their knowledge base related to algebra. The instructor, in this case a teacher educator who would be available to teachers during the following school year, regularly used the algebra pieces, which were available in each algebra classroom, to engage teachers in exploration of traditional algebraic concepts and procedures from new perspectives. The teachers often worked in small groups and then shared their solution strategies with the whole group. Following an activity, the instructor and teachers would discuss both what the teachers had done and what the instructor had done to support their learning. They would talk about how the algebra pieces had been used, the kinds of questions that arose, and the decisions the instructor had made.

Workshops, courses, institutes, and seminars are structured opportunities for educators to learn from facilitators or leaders with specialized expertise as well as from peers. These professional development sessions usually occur outside of the classroom and often bring together educators from different locations for common experiences and learning. They provide opportunities for participants to focus intensely on topics of interest for weeks (e.g., institutes) or for an extended period of time (e.g., courses). Workshops and seminars, however, tend to be offered for shorter periods of time and address more discrete learning goals, such as learning to use a particular set of lessons or try a new assessment strategy. Workshops are characterized by hands-on activities for participants to help them try ideas and materials. Seminars tend to be more oriented to sharing knowledge and experiences through discussions and reactions to others' practice or research results. Depending on the learning goals for a particular group, a professional developer might choose to combine one or more of these strategies, such as an intensive institute followed by a seminar series.

Underlying Assumptions

The use of the professional development strategy of workshops, institutes, courses, and seminars is based on certain assumptions about learning, teaching, and professional development.

External knowledge is valuable. Educators must constantly expand their knowledge of both their teaching fields and how to teach them. The structures of workshops, institutes, seminars, and courses provide teachers with opportunities to connect with outside sources of knowledge in a focused, direct, and intense way.

Learning outside of the work environment allows in-depth study and practice needed for success. Workshops, courses, seminars, and institutes provide teachers with time away from their classrooms and the opportunity to reflect, think deeply, argue alternative explanations, interact with other educators, and practice new ideas and techniques in safe settings. Adults benefit from time spent as focused learners being guided through new material and helped to make meaning of it for their own growth and experience.

One size can fit all. Because workshops, courses, seminars, and institutes are attended by groups of people, they assume that a well-crafted learning activity can indeed meet the needs of many. Although individuals each bring something different to a learning experience, and inevitably take away something different, this structure assumes that many can benefit from the same experience.

Key Elements

Effective workshops, institutes, seminars, and courses have several elements in common.

Clearly Stated Goals. Leaders of effective workshops, institutes, seminars, and courses communicate with participants about the goals of the learning experience prior to and during the sessions. They receive input from learners before setting goals so that the learning experience addresses the learners' needs.

A Leader or Facilitator. The leader or facilitator also guides and supports the participants' learning, often by being a primary source of expertise or bringing in other information through readings, consultants, the participants' experiences and knowledge, and structured experiences.

Defined Time Frames, Frequencies, and Group Structures. Defined time frames are of a certain duration (e.g., 8 a.m. to 3 p.m.) and a certain frequency (e.g., once a week for 3 hours.) Also, they are intended for groups of people. The learning environment is designed so that it is collegial for participants to learn from one another and from the leader of the session.

Often disparaged as the "traditional form of professional development," workshops, courses, institutes, and seminars, like other professional development strategies, can range in quality, depending on the extent to which they reflect the principles of effective professional development discussed in Chapter 3. At their best, they provide adult learners with important and relevant new knowledge and opportunities to try new ideas, practice new behaviors, and interact with others as they learn. The following paragraphs describe what these strategies look like "at their best."

Workshops, courses, seminars, and institutes can use the "training" model, which has a strong research base for helping teachers learn new behaviors that contribute to improved student learning (Joyce & Showers, 1988). This model includes the following steps: explanation of theory, demonstration or modeling of a skill, practice of the skill under simulated conditions, feedback about performance, and coaching in the workplace. An example of the application of this model would be training in cooperative learning strategies for use in science and mathematics teaching.

These structures also lend themselves to a teaching or learning model for developing conceptual understandings, such as those on which many science curricula are based. For example, a model developed by the National Center for Improving Science Education suggests the following four stages: invite, explore, explain, and apply (Loucks-Horsley et al., 1990). These stages can help structure a multiday institute, a workshop or seminar series, or a course. Table 4.3 indicates how professional developers can structure appropriate activities at each stage.

For example, during a 5-day professional development institute on inquiry in environmental education, participants might engage in a 2-day inquiry into participant-generated questions about a beach area (invite); 2 days of analysis and limited tryout of activities from different environmental education curriculum materials (explore); discussion of that analysis with regard to questions of congruence with the *National Science Education Standards* (NRC, 1996), clarification of the scientific concepts and processes embedded in the activities, and an opportunity to share insights (explain); planning for tryout in participant classrooms (apply); and follow-up in-classroom coaching and support group meetings to review, revise, and retry (apply and recycle).

By nature, courses are ongoing, which provides time for teachers to practice new ideas and behaviors and return to the course setting to reflect together on problems and successes. Effective course instructors provide time for these important reflections and help participants generate clear ideas about how they will apply what they learn. Likewise, the best workshops, seminars, and institutes are designed to include a

TABLE 4.3 What the Professional Developer or Designer Does

Stage	Consistent With the Model	Inconsistent With the Model
Invitation	• Creates interest • Generates curiosity • Stimulates dialogue • Raises questions • Elicits responses that uncover what the teacher/learners know or think about the concepts/topics	• Explains concepts • Provides definitions and answers • States conclusions • Provides closure • Lectures
Exploration, discovery, and creativity	• Encourages the teachers/learners to work together without direct instruction from the professional developer • Provides or stimulates multiple opportunities or experiences to explore an idea, strategy, or concept • Observes and listens to the teachers/learners as they interact • Asks probing questions to redirect teachers'/learners' investigations and dialogues when necessary • Provides time for teachers/learners to puzzle through problems and challenges • Acts as a consultant to teachers/learners	• Provides answers • Tells or explains how to work through the problem • Provides closure • Tells the teachers/learners that they are wrong • Gives information or facts that solve the problem • Leads teachers/learners step by step to solution
Proposing explanations and solutions	• Encourages teachers/learners to explain concepts and definitions in their own words • Asks for justification (evidence) and clarification from teachers/learners	• Accepts explanations that have no justification • Neglects to solicit teachers'/learners' explanations

(Continued)

TABLE 4.3 (Continued)

Stage	Consistent With the Model	Inconsistent With the Model
	• Formally provides definitions, explanations, and new labels (e.g., through lectures) • Uses teachers'/learners' previous experience as the basis for explaining concepts	• Introduces unrelated concepts or skills
Taking action	• Expects teachers/learners to explain concepts and definitions in their own words • Encourages teachers/ learners to apply or extend concepts and skills in new situations • Encourages and coaches teachers/learners to apply concepts and skills to their own situations • Reminds teachers/learners of alternative explanations • Refers teachers/learners to existing data and evidence and asks, "What do you think . . ." (strategies from the previous stage also apply here) • Looks for evidence that the teachers/learners have changed their thinking or behavior • Asks open-minded questions, such as "Why do you think . . . ?" "What evidence do you have?" "What do you think about x?" and "How would you explain x?"	• Provides definitive answers • Tells teachers/learners that they are wrong • Lectures • Leads teachers/learners step by step to a solution • Explains how to work through the problem or challenge

variety of modes through which learners can process information. These include journal writing, analysis of case studies, role playing, small group discussions, modeling lessons, engaging in problem solving, building things, exploring questions, and so on. Learners have ample time for follow-up opportunities to discuss the application of their learning, solve problems, and generate new ideas for teaching.

Implementation Requirements

Workshops, institutes, courses, and seminars have several requirements for implementation.

Expert Knowledge. A person or persons must be available to provide or facilitate access to the expert knowledge that learners will be exposed to during the sessions.

Time Away From the Workplace, With Arrangements for Substitutes or Stipends. Most workshops and seminars meet during regular school hours and require that a teacher have a substitute for the classroom. Teachers usually participate in courses and institutes during nonteaching time (such as during the summer or evenings and weekends). For these sessions, teachers may be paid a stipend for their time.

Curriculum or Syllabus. Learners should know what content they will learn through the professional development experience. Courses that are offered with graduate credit also require prior review and approval of content. A curriculum guide or syllabus addresses these needs.

Access to Resources and Materials. Depending on the content of the course, workshop, institute, or seminar, classroom materials, student work, texts, or articles are needed.

Incentives. There are a variety of incentives that can be offered for participation. For example, teachers can be given stipends when time is taken beyond regular school hours. Teachers can also be rewarded for their participation in these learning activities through recognition and graduate or professional development credit.

Examples

An example of an effective workshop structure is that used by the Math Talk project at Children's Television Workshop. This project conducted workshops and follow-up sessions with teachers to help them use supplementary mathematics curriculum materials to address the national standards. Teachers were offered the opportunity to participate in the workshops through the Eisenhower Regional Consortia in the Northeast. The goals for the sessions were stated up front, and teachers agreed to implement the Math Talk curriculum materials. The sessions were led by knowledgeable mathematics educators who combined demonstrations of the materials and explanations of the mathematics content within the materials to prepare teachers to teach with Math Talk. Teachers shared their misconceptions about certain content (e.g., rules of probability or measuring area and perimeter), and the mathematics experts helped to increase the teachers' understanding of the mathematics behind the classroom activities. Workshop leaders also helped teachers with their plans for introducing the materials in the classroom. During follow-up sessions, the teachers reported on their use of the materials, asked questions, and helped one another with plans for introducing more units. Again, the workshop leaders led discussions and demonstrations to increase the teachers' knowledge of mathematics content. Teachers also practiced using hands-on activities that they would reproduce in their classrooms. The cost of teacher substitutes was paid to the districts, and the teachers were given stipends for some Saturday sessions. They also received professional development credit toward recertification.

Participatory Oriented Planetariums for Schools was a National Science Foundation-supported summer institute program in which teacher-leaders came to the Lawrence Hall of Science in Berkeley, California, to learn how to use constructivist teaching methods in the context of a small planetarium. The intensive 3-week residential institutes involved exposure to new ideas and programs, visits to important facilities for research and teaching in astronomy and space science, creative efforts to adapt and devise new planetarium and classroom activities, and opportunities to interact with a wide variety of talented individuals who shared similar interests and goals.

The Math Learning Center at Portland State University offers a series of courses related to the *Visual Mathematics* curriculum, which has been developed during the past decade with funding from the National Science Foundation. The courses are designed to help teachers become familiar with visual thinking (a hallmark of the curriculum) and its role in the teaching of mathematics. They include readings related to philosophy of the curriculum and current mathematics reform and considerable exploration of mathematical content based on a constructivist approach to learning. The courses put teachers in the role of learner and give them opportunities to explore mathematics concepts and connections, discuss solutions and strategies with their colleagues in a manner similar to that which they would use with their own students, and develop powerful representations or mathematical abstractions. The courses are offered nationwide by workshop leaders (often classroom teachers) who have considerable personal experience using the curricular materials.

The Mathematics Learning Forums Project conducts on-line seminars hosted by graduate faculty members of Bank Street College in New York City. These 8-week seminars offer K through eighth-grade teachers instruction on how to teach mathematics. The teachers connect to the seminar via the Internet at their convenience and interact with the faculty and other seminar participants. After each session, teachers try new activities in their classes, and then they debrief their experience and get help improving their practice through subsequent electronic conversations.

Commentary

From research on teacher change, it is clear that a one-time workshop or seminar is unlikely to result in significant, long-term change in the practice of a teacher (Fullan, 1991; Joyce & Showers, 1988; Little, 1993). Rather, change requires multiple opportunities to learn, to practice, to interact using, and to reinforce new behaviors. Thus, although a single workshop may be a good kick-off for learning and can result in new knowledge or awareness on the part of participants, additional opportunities are needed for long-lasting change.

Because as stand-alone strategies workshops, institutes, courses, and seminars fall short of providing a well-rounded professional development experience, ideally one-time workshops, and even long-term courses, are combined with other strategies to enhance the learning experiences of the participants. For example, simply attending a workshop on mathematical pedagogy is insufficient to equip teachers to alter their practices. Teachers also need opportunities to translate their learning into practice (e.g., through modifying their curriculum), implement the new knowledge (e.g., with coaching), and reflect on their practices (e.g., through case discussions). When the principles of effective professional development are incorporated into the design of workshops, institutes, courses, and seminars and are then combined with other strategies, such as those suggested previously, the benefits for teachers are strengthened.

For optimal professional development, workshops, institutes, courses, and seminars must reflect the following features of effective adult learning (Regional Educational Laboratories, 1995):

- Opportunities for learners to shape the content of the workshops, institutes, courses, or seminars

- Time for reflection, predictions, and explorations
- Multiple modes of presentations and information processing
- Support and feedback from people with expertise
- Connections between new concepts and information and current knowledge and experience
- A safe environment to try new ideas and approaches

Additional Resources

Great Explorations in Math and Science (GEMS), Lawrence Hall of Science, University of California at Berkeley. (Phone: 510-642-9635)

Mathematics Learning Forums, Bank Street College of Education Mathematics Leadership Program and The Center for Children and Technology of the Education Development Center, Inc., New York. (Phone: 212-807-4207)

Math Talk Project, Children's Television Workshop, New York. (Phone: 212-875-6478)

The Math Learning Center, Portland State University, Portland, OR. (Phone: 503-725-4850)

Participatory Oriented Planetariums for Schools (POPS), Lawrence Hall of Science, University of California at Berkeley. (Phone: 510-642-9635)

Action Research

After attending a workshop on equity issues in the classroom, Pat and Linda, two 10th-grade geometry teachers, were inspired to examine whether they treated boys and girls differently during their classes. In particular, they decided to focus on how many times they called on boys versus girls to answer questions and whether they responded differently to answers offered by boys versus girls. After reading some additional research on gender issues and consulting their school's psychologist, Pat and Linda developed their research design, which included audiotaping several of their classes and keeping running logs of how many boys versus girls were called on during those lessons. Analyzing the audiotapes proved to be a significant challenge for the teachers, but after discussions with an educational researcher from a local college they developed a coding scheme that allowed them to characterize four different types of teacher responses to student comments.

As they had suspected at the start of the project, they discovered a fair amount of gender bias in their approaches to teaching geometry. Through discussing the audiotapes and observing each other's teaching, they were able to work at increasing their awareness of gender equity and develop strategies to address it in their classrooms. As a result of sharing their research findings with other mathematics teachers in their department, three other teachers joined Pat and Linda to form an ongoing action research group, which focuses on issues and concerns relevant to mathematics teaching and learning.

Action research has a long and varied history. First introduced by Kurt Lewin in the 1940s, action research has evolved in the education community into an ongoing process of systematic study in which teachers examine their own teaching and students' learning through descriptive reporting, purposeful conversation, collegial sharing, and critical reflection for the purpose of improving classroom practice (Miller & Pine, 1990).

Through action research, teachers reflect on their practices by studying what they are doing. When teachers conduct action research, the emphasis is on practice-based professional inquiry. Its main tenet is that practical reasoning and problem solving are adequate for generating scientific knowledge, and the natural language of practitioners is just as suitable for creating scientific understanding as empirically derived statements framed in technical language (Duckworth, 1986). This form of knowing comes from experience and direct interaction with students.

Holly (1991, p. 133) notes that "action research as a major form of professional development is now seen as central to the restructuring of schools." The strength of action research as a professional development strategy is that teachers either define the research questions or contribute to their definition in a meaningful way. Therefore, they have ownership over the process and are committed to promoting changes in practice that are indicated by the findings.

The form of the action research can vary, with teachers working together in collaborative teams of inquiry or with other researchers who are often from universities or research centers. Individual teachers may also pursue their own research studies, with opportunities to discuss their progress and findings with fellow teachers or researchers. In another variation, teachers examine relevant research, which is then used as a basis for collecting and analyzing data from their own classrooms (Loucks-Horsley et al., 1987).

The characteristics of any particular action research project will depend on the goals emphasized, the degree of collaboration between teachers and outside researchers, the process used in carrying out the research, the relationship of the project to the school, and the project outcomes. For example, in some action research projects, the goal is to improve teaching through teacher-led research and reflection on teaching and other classroom strategies. If outside researchers are involved, their role is to help build teachers' skills in research methodology and guide teachers in the reflective process.

In some instances of action research, the goal is to not only contribute to teachers' professional growth but also add to the education knowledge base. In these projects, teachers engage in the action and reflection process on a practical issue of classroom teaching, and their findings also contribute to answering larger questions that may be under investigation by the school district, a university, or other research organization.

Whichever goal is being pursued, action research lets teachers examine their teaching practices in a systematic, ongoing way with the purpose of changing those practices. It is not simply about identifying a problem to be solved but rather is more a process based on a vision of creating "learner-centered classrooms and building knowledge through inquiry" (Watkins, 1992, p. 4). Although this can apply to any area of education, it is especially relevant to mathematics and science, whose national standards encourage this vision explicitly.

Underlying Assumptions

The use of action research as a strategy for professional development is based on several assumptions about teachers, learning, and professional development.

Teachers are intelligent, inquiring individuals with important expertise and experiences that are central to the improvement of education practice. Action research begins with what a teacher knows and relies on that knowledge to explore and formulate new understandings. It assumes that significance and meaning are inherent in the actual situations of teaching and learning and that knowledge about teaching and learning should be determined in part by what teachers and learners actually do (Miller & Pine, 1990). This approach further assumes that the teacher is interested in learning about the phenomena of teaching and learning. Such a desire to explore is a prerequisite to engaging in action research. The knowledge and skills of actually performing research are not a prerequisite and can be developed.

By contributing to or formulating their own questions, and by collecting the data to answer these questions, teachers grow professionally. Educational research has typically been done "on" or "to" teachers and not "with" or "by" them. Researchers have assumed that research relevant to teachers would be picked up by them and used. The action research strategy assumes that a more intense teacher involvement with research will increase the likelihood that they will learn from their practice and use research results, thus contributing to their growth as teachers. It assumes that meaning can be constructed through action and reflection. It gives teachers the power to make decisions and puts the teacher in the position of accepting responsibility for his or her own professional growth (Miller & Pine, 1990; Sparks & Simmons, 1989; Wood, 1988).

Teachers are motivated to use more effective practices when they are continuously investigating the results of their actions in the classroom. Teacher research helps to link classroom practices with results. If teachers discover that certain strategies are more effective than others for presenting science or mathematics content, they are more likely to make greater use of them and abandon use of less effective ones. Classroom processes, interactions, and strategies are extremely complex and often differ widely from place to place. Professionals who use ongoing inquiry can better understand what is happening, and why, in their classrooms.

Key Elements

There are several key elements of action research as a strategy for professional development.

Teachers use an action research cycle. Action research involves a cycle of planning, acting, observing, and reflecting. Teachers identify a subject of research and develop a plan of action, often in collaboration with others. The questions pursued through action research are usually focused on the behaviors and processes of teaching and learning. Data are collected by observation, anecdotal records, checklists, videotaping, logging, collections of children's work, interviewing, and surveying, among other techniques. Data are analyzed, reflected on, and used to inform further planning and subsequent action.

Teachers are linked with sources of knowledge and stimulation from outside their schools. Action research projects are often informed by others' research and resources. Effective projects draw on available knowledge and build on it rather than re-create it. Furthermore, individuals and resources that offer expertise on research methodology help teachers to ensure the quality of their methods (Holly, 1991).

Teachers work collaboratively. Action researchers typically work together on all aspects of the project—setting common goals, mutually planning the research design, collecting and analyzing data, and reporting the results. The collaborative nature of the interactions allows for mutual understanding and democratic decision making and requires all participants to communicate openly and freely. For all participants, this requires an openness to discussing problems and limitations, to the ideas of others, and to learning new skills and behaviors needed for the research process (Oja & Smulyan, 1989).

Learning from research is documented and shared. Sharing learnings from action research can make a significant contribution to professional development. Opportunities to write about a project, to present findings to various audiences, to participate in discussions of the implications of findings for teaching and schools, and to develop materials that other teachers can use are just some of the ways that teachers can increase their skills and knowledge beyond what they learn from their own action research (Loucks-Horsley et al., 1987).

Implementation Requirements

For action research to be an effective means of helping teachers learn through reflection, certain requirements must be in place.

Access to Research Resources. If teachers have never conducted action research, they need access to an experienced researcher as a member of the research team or as a consultant. This person assists teachers with data collection and analysis, ensuring that the results of the research are valid. He or she may provide training in research methodologies, data-gathering techniques, and other processes that aid teachers in making sense of their experiences.

Time. Teachers need legitimate time to conduct action research. If their research is self-initiated, school administrators need to know that the teachers will be using planning time or other blocks of time outside of the classroom to conduct their research. Often, the time for data collection comes from managing the classroom differently and using equipment such as videocassette recorders. Teachers may need help rethinking how they spend their classroom time or getting equipment to document classroom processes or both. Teachers also need an environment with limited interruptions for discussion, investigation, collaboration with the research team, and reflection. In addition, there must be the recognition that action research occurs over a significant period of time and that teachers must be engaged in the process for the entire length of the research project.

Administrative Support and an Atmosphere Conducive to Experimentation. Administrators who support action research as a professional development activity make material and financial support available to teachers and recognize and reward collegial interaction. They ensure that teachers feel that they can try various strategies within their classrooms and support teachers in making decisions that influence their teaching. They provide a forum for teachers to share what they have learned with their colleagues.

Opportunities to Share the Results of Their Research. Once the findings of the research project have been obtained and analyzed, teachers need opportunities to share their results through in-house publications, professional conferences, workshops, journals, or other means. Assisting teachers to identify and use the best vehicles for sharing is an appropriate role for the professional developer.

Examples

The Continuous Assessment in Science Project (CASP) at The NETWORK, Inc. offers a model of professional development in science that is based on inquiry and action research. While elementary school teachers use hands-on, inquiry-based science teaching in the classroom, they also collect data about how and what students are learning. The teachers determine areas of focus for their research, gather data, and write cases describing their observations and findings. They use strategies such as observation, questioning, listening, and documentation through videotape and audiotape recording and still photography to gather and analyze data.

Through this program, teachers learn to observe the behavior of students at work and to use their observations to adjust learning activities to better meet learners' developmental needs. By aligning everyday assessment with good instructional strategies, teachers help children reach the goals of science learning the project espouses—that is, understanding science concepts through engaging in the processes and habits of mind of science (The NETWORK, Inc., 1996).

In Australia, mathematics educators at a local university organized action research teams of high school teachers and researchers at the university. One team focused on investigating the benefits to teachers from their examination of students' writing in high school mathematics classes. From the outset, the collaborative nature of the action research was emphasized: Miller and Hunt (1994) wrote,

> From the perspective of the university researchers, the study would not be successful if the teachers participated for the benefit of the university researchers. The intention was that the teachers participate because they want to investigate an alternative approach to learning how well their students understand the mathematics being studied in school. (p. 297)

Teachers on the team periodically asked their students to respond, in writing, to a "prompt," which is a statement or question designed to elicit students' understanding of a concept or skill. Teachers kept their own journals documenting thoughts and reflections on their impressions of the students' responses to the prompts and what they were learning. Teachers and university mathematics educators met periodically to discuss the teachers' experiences.

One of the teachers, Neil Hunt, discovered that his students' responses to the prompts consistently showed an incorrect use of the term *coefficient*. His reaction was to "use more prompts that focused the students' writing on the correct use of mathematics vocabulary" (Miller & Hunt, 1994, p. 300). He shared his observations at a team meeting and found that other teachers were observing the same misuse of mathematics vocabulary. Within a few days of the team meeting, one of the university team members observed Neil's classroom. During the discussion following the observation, the university researcher noted that Neil consistently misused, or avoided, mathematical vocabulary (Miller & Hunt, 1994):

> "Were you aware that not once in the whole lesson did you use the word *coefficient?*" At first I didn't believe her. Suddenly I realized that she was right. I had repeatedly asked the students to tell me what happened when we increased or decreased "the number in front of *x*." Why had I not used the word *coefficient?* She also indicated that I had said *the answer* rather than *the quotient* and that several times I had referred to *the number underneath* rather than *the denominator.* (p. 301)

Neil Hunt's research into his students' understanding of concepts led him to recognize that his teaching was contributing to his students' confusion and resulted in a more conscious effort to change his teaching. At the end of the semester, Neil found that after he consistently used mathematics vocabulary with his students, the students were more comfortable using the vocabulary both in class and in their written responses to prompts.

Action research is a component of the Colorado College Integrated Science Teacher Enhancement Project. Teachers who participate in this 3-year master of arts in teaching program attend 6-week, science-rich summer institutes, develop and build teaching units that they implement during the school year, attend academic year seminars, and formulate and conduct an action research project. One elementary school teacher participant, for example, decided to experiment with teaching science at the beginning of the day rather than at the end, and she documented what happened. She learned that science permeated the day, often became a focus for language learning and mathematics, and encouraged students to inquire more in their learning across the curriculum. A journal article and permanent change in her teaching day resulted (Strycker, 1995).

Commentary

Science and mathematics teachers interested in continuous assessment and improvement can benefit greatly from action research projects. Benefits are generated by both the process and the products of the action research. For example, in the process of conducting an action research project, teachers gain knowledge and skill in research methods and applications (Lieberman, 1986; Miller & Pine, 1990; Oja & Smulyan, 1989). They can become more flexible in their thinking, more receptive to new ideas, and better able to solve problems as they arise. They can change their definitions of professional skills and roles, feel more valued and confident, increase their awareness of classroom issues, become more reflective, change educational beliefs and align their theories and practice, and broaden their views of teaching and learning. Teachers gain new knowledge that helps them solve immediate problems, broaden their knowledge base, and learn skills that can be applied to future interests and concerns (Oja & Smulyan, 1989).

Action research can also support overall change efforts in schools because findings can help prepare the school staff for needed improvements. The school culture can also shift positively. The action research team unites teachers and encourages collegial interaction. The collaborative nature of action research has the potential to encourage greater professional talk and action related to teaching, learning, and school problems. In addition, a collaborative team provides possibilities for teachers to assume new roles and exhibit leadership, with feelings of powerlessness transformed into a greater sense of empowerment (Lieberman, 1986).

Another benefit of action research is its contribution to narrowing the gap between research and practice. This occurs when researchers work closely with teachers to define and conduct research. New educational theory and knowledge are generated (Loucks-Horsley et al., 1987). As a result of learning more about research and research methods, teachers make more informed decisions about when and how to apply the research findings of others.

With its many benefits, action research can be a powerful professional development activity. As teachers and schools engage in action research, however, some of the implementation requirements discussed previously are not addressed. Some of the issues that arise are discussed in the following sections.

Time. Action research requires a great deal of time and focus. Research involves many steps, and it takes time to observe how different strategies work with different students and in different circumstances. Teachers should be recognized for the time spent in action research projects and have it count toward district or state professional development or recertification credit. Teachers and administrators can examine the school schedule to find common time, during the day if possible, for teachers to work together on a research project. Administrators can help teachers find time by cutting back on faculty meetings and using print or electronic messages to communicate routine information and announcements. Unnecessary paperwork can also be eliminated to free up teachers to conduct their research and share their findings.

Legitimacy of the Action Research. Often, professional development that is not in the form of institutes or workshops receives no legitimate recognition in schools. This calls for both administrators and participating teachers to communicate more and publicly acknowledge the value of the research. Teachers can help convey the importance of action research by providing regular updates to all staff on their progress. All staff can become aware of the purpose of the action research project and how its findings can be used.

Readiness of Action Research Participants. This approach to professional development may not be for all teachers at the same time. Teachers differ widely in their priorities and interests, and these change over time. As noted at the beginning of the chapter, some teachers may be more "ready" to benefit from this strategy than others. Teachers who are struggling to get new practices working may not be ready to collect data and then step back and reflect on the data. Teachers who are less concerned with trying to master new practices in the classroom and more concerned about the effectiveness of their teaching and its impact on student learning may be in the best position to benefit from action research projects.

Additional Resources

Calhoun, E. F. (1993). Action research: Three approaches. *Educational Leadership, 51*(2), 62-65.

Calhoun, E. F. (1994). *How to use action research in the self-renewing school.* Alexandria, VA: Association for Supervision and Curriculum Development.

Colorado College Integrated Science Teacher Enhancement Project (CC: ISTEP) (Paul Kuerbis, Director), Colorado Springs, CO.

Danielson, C. (1996). *Enhancing professional practice: A framework for teaching.* Alexandria, VA: Association for Supervision and Curriculum Development.

Sagor, R. (1992). *How to conduct collaborative action research.* Alexandria, VA: Association for Supervision and Curriculum Development.

Case Discussions

Sharon Friedman is a fourth-grade teacher, case writer, case discussion facilitator, and researcher involved with the Mathematics Case Methods Project. In her reflections on her involvement in case discussions, she writes the following (Barnett & Friedman, in press):

> *When I first participated in a math case discussion, I thought that I would be examining instructional practice. I thought that I would share what I do in the classroom and hear about alternatives, which would lead to better informed decisions for my mathematics program. I was right, except for my understanding of what it means to "examine" instructional practice. I quickly learned that the "examination" entailed more than merely acquainting myself with various instructional methods. Through the discussions we looked deeply into the way instructional practice influenced and responded to student thinking. Any teaching practice, it seemed, had a consequence in terms of its effect on student thinking. Some curricula even led to confusion. We delved into the thoughts and misconceptions that students carry with them to our math classes, derived from past instruction, experience, and intuition. Good instructional practice, I was to discover, is an interaction between what the teacher says and the experiences he or she provides, and what the students do with it. Good practice is not, as teachers are often led to believe, a preset formula that does what it is supposed to do because the curriculum writers say so. I learned the*

*importance of focusing the impact of my words and actions on chil-
dren, on framing instruction that could anticipate student thinking as
much as possible, and on responding effectively to the results. In planning, I learned to consider an interaction rather than simply a teaching method that does not take student thinking into account.*

Case discussions offer groups of teachers the opportunity to reflect
on teaching and learning by examining narrative stories or videotapes
that depict classroom teaching or learning situations. Cases are narra-
tives (whether in print form or on videotape) that offer a picture of a
teaching or learning event and are specifically designed to provoke discussion and reflection. They are not simply stories about teaching or
learning but are, as Shulman (1992) notes, focused on events such as a
teaching dilemma, students engaged in mathematics or science investigations, images of student thought processes, or teaching strategies in
action.

Case discussions are used in a variety of ways with different goals
and purposes. For example, educators and researchers promote the use
of case discussions to examine student thinking and learning as a means
of professional development. In these instances, cases are used as a window into children's thinking within a specific context. Teachers listen to
students' ideas about mathematics and science and examine students'
responses. By analyzing children's thinking and how their ideas are developing and by identifying what they understand and where their confusions lie, teachers become aware of how children construct their
mathematical and scientific ideas. Being able to see mathematics and
science through the child's eyes helps teachers know and anticipate how
students may misunderstand certain concepts and enables them to
choose instructional experiences that can capitalize on the child's thinking. Teachers develop a greater recognition that student misunderstand-
ings can be a valuable teaching tool. These activities promote professional development when they cause teachers to reexamine their
perceptions of students' capabilities and their own assumptions about
what "understanding mathematics and science" really means (Schifter,
Russell, & Bastable, in press).

The process of reflecting on students' thinking and learning through
case discussions often results in teachers "trying out" the ideas or activities contained in the cases in their own classrooms (Barnett, 1991;
Davenport & Sassi, 1995; Schifter, 1994). The powerful images of students in the case discussions prompt teachers to wonder about the thinking of their own students, how they might pose similar problems in their
classes, and what might happen as a consequence. Teachers discover that
they are better able to provide their students with experiences that help

them articulate their confusion and with activities that help them resolve those confusions.

In addition, when teachers confront mathematics and science issues through the lens of students' perspectives, they often increase their own mathematics and science knowledge (Schifter & Bastable, 1995). As teachers reflect on students' thinking and approaches to solving problems, and assess the reasoning of students' responses, they begin to think through the mathematics or science again for themselves, often seeing new aspects of familiar content and expanding their own understanding (Russell et al., 1995). Case discussions can also be a powerful tool for helping teachers examine their own teaching practices. In these instances, cases typically convey a contextual problem, dilemma, or issue in teaching as well as the thoughts, feelings, and internal struggles of the case teacher (Schifter, 1996b).

Cases can present "whole stories" that include an ending that describes how the case teacher addressed the dilemma (Schifter, 1996b). Others stop short of describing how the case teacher handled the problem and instead end with a series of open-ended questions to be addressed by the case discussants. Some are "packed full" of information to convey the complexity of teaching (Merseth, 1991), whereas others focus on discrete instances of teaching. Finally, some cases are grouped into clusters based on cases that have one or two similar dominant themes or that illustrate different aspects of the same principle. Examining clusters of cases requires teachers to retrieve, understand, and grapple with the domain or theme in different contexts and under different conditions (Barnett & Friedman, in press).

Whatever the focus of a case, all case discussions share common goals: to increase and enrich teachers' fundamental beliefs and understanding about teaching and learning; to provide opportunities for teachers to become involved in critical discussions of actual teaching situations; and to encourage teachers to become problem solvers who pose questions, explore multiple perspectives, and examine alternative solutions (Barnett & Sather, 1992; Shulman & Kepner, 1994).

Not only is participating in case discussions a powerful professional development strategy but also the process of writing and developing cases enhances teachers' growth and development. The act of writing cases and then discussing them with colleagues helps teachers analyze their own instructional practice.

Usually, teacher-writers follow a structured case development process that progresses from identifying a topic or issue of concern to collaborative work with an editor or facilitator who helps turn the narrative into a case that has benefits for a larger audience. Most teachers who have written cases report that the writing process has a strong impact on their professional life, how they think about their teaching and students, their strategies and modes of instruction, and the ways in which they interact with colleagues regarding their experiences (Shulman & Kepner, 1994).

Underlying Assumptions

The use of case discussions as a strategy for professional development is based on several assumptions about learning, teaching, and professional development.

Teachers can guide their own growth and development, and they construct knowledge through collegial interactions. In this way, case discussions are consistent with a constructivist perspective of learning. By examining and reflecting on cases with their colleagues, teachers can further develop their understanding of teaching and learning.

Case discussions provide a more focused picture of a specific aspect of teaching or learning than one could observe in real time in the classroom. Often, observers in a classroom focus on management behaviors and miss opportunities to focus carefully on specific teaching or learning episodes. By using cases, all participants are examining the same experience of the case teacher and students and have the immediate opportunity to reflect on those experiences during the case discussion.

The opportunity to carefully observe and analyze actual teaching and learning situations leads to changes in teachers' beliefs, attitudes, convictions, and, ultimately, practice. Advocates of case discussions (e.g., Barnett & Sather, 1992; Nelson, 1995) believe that teachers will not implement real reform unless their basic beliefs about teaching and learning are confronted and changed. Case discussions raise teachers' awareness of important issues in teaching and learning, cause them to rethink their attitudes and beliefs, and, perhaps, change their classroom practice.

Case discussions are an effective way to illustrate theory in practice. Case discussions create a context for teachers to integrate their research-based knowledge into their view of children's learning and their own teaching and to apply this to their instructional practice. Vivid descriptions of the classroom process provide grounding for theoretical principles where contexts for interpreting these abstractions are lacking (Schifter, 1994) and help teachers tie abstract learning to the complexities of real-world application (Filby, 1995).

Case discussions provide images of reform-oriented mathematics and science teaching and learning. New teaching in mathematics and science requires teachers to change their beliefs about the nature of knowledge and learning and how knowledge is derived, increase their knowledge of content, and reinvent their classroom practice (Nelson, 1995). Translating the ideals of these new ways of teaching and learning into actual classroom practice, however, is often the most complex and challenging task teachers face. Some cases offer an image of what reform-oriented classrooms look like and how teachers implement the principles of reform. Far from being examples of the "unattainable," teachers have found that they can identify with many of the struggles faced by teachers and students in the cases and have found them motivating and inspiring (Schifter, 1996b).

Key Elements

There are several key elements of case discussions as a strategy for professional development.

Nature of Teacher Interactions. Much of the learning takes place through discussion. Through verbalization and interaction, teachers formulate ideas, learn from each other, become aware of alternative strategies and perspectives, internalize theory, critique their own and others' ideas, become aware of their own assumptions and beliefs, increase their pedagogical content knowledge, and engage in "collaborative reflection" on real problems faced by teachers (Barnett & Sather, 1992; Far West Laboratory, 1990; Filby, 1995).

When reflecting on cases that promote discussion about teacher actions, discussants may focus on what the case teacher should do next or evaluate the action that was taken. This process engages teachers in an analysis of why and how to use certain teaching strategies, challenges some of their assumptions and beliefs about the appropriate use of strategies, and broadens their repertoire of strategies for planning and implementing instruction (Shulman & Kepner, 1994). The ultimate goal of reflecting on cases focused on teacher action is to develop in teachers an attitude of inquiry toward and strategies for inquiring about classroom practice.

Facilitation of Cases. Case discussions require a knowledgeable and experienced facilitator who prompts reflection by case discussants. The facilitator helps participants identify and understand the problem or situation in the case, evaluate the approach taken or examine the source of students' confusion, discuss alternative actions, and reflect on the theoretical underpinnings of the action taken and discuss the consequences for learning.

Facilitation notes are often developed and published in a facilitator's guide that accompanies a case book or video. These notes help the facilitator shape the discussions so that the richness of a case is fully explored.

Focus on Group Dynamics. Case discussion groups establish supporting norms for interaction and commit to the long-term nature of the process. Together, they establish ground rules and group norms that create an atmosphere of learning and trust. Participants demonstrate their commitment to improving their teaching practice and willingness to help others explore their teaching practices (Filby, 1995). (Note that groups do not always establish effective ways of working together, and this can seriously influence the amount that participants learn.)

Relevant and Recognizable Cases. Although some cases depict teaching or learning situations that reflect the "ideal image" of what teaching and learning can look like, teachers need, at least initially, to be able to identify aspects of their own teaching within a case. Ideally, teachers encounter situations similar to the cases in their own teaching and can draw on their experiences during the discussion. Once teachers feel a sense of connection with a case, they can delve deeper into how the case is either similar or dissimilar to their own teaching approaches and beliefs. For example, some cases will parallel a teacher's own approaches or philosophy and can provide opportunities to examine and evaluate the consequences of specific decisions based on those ideas. Other cases will present notions that conflict with the beliefs of the teachers and can provoke critical analysis of the perspectives presented; "wrestling with the resulting disequilibrium" is what leads to changes in teachers' thinking about teaching and learning (Barnett & Sather, 1992).

Documented Learning. Case discussions are most effective when individual participants document what they are learning in the discussions and what they do in their classrooms as a result.

Implementation Requirements

For case discussions to succeed as a strategy for professional development, there are several implementation requirements.

Attitudes and Skills of Participants and Facilitators. Effective case discussions require certain attitudes on the part of both participants and facilitators. Participants must have a shared commitment to improving their teaching practice, a willingness to share and critically discuss aspects of practice, and curiosity about important assumptions that underlie teaching and learning (Davenport & Sassi, 1995). Facilitators must also share these attitudes.

In addition, facilitators must have an in-depth understanding of the science and mathematics being taught, learned, or both, in the cases. Also, they must have the skills and experience to manage discussions that are at once intellectually stimulating, challenging, supportive, at times confrontational, and, ultimately, useful. Handbooks and training opportunities are available for facilitators to develop these skills (see "Additional Resources").

Participants rely on discussion to tease out learning and insights. Therefore, they and the facilitator need fairly sophisticated communication skills to challenge assumptions, understand different mental models and perspectives, and dig deeply into underlying structures and assumptions that support teaching and learning. If participants do not have experience engaging in this type of dialogue, they need coaching by the facilitator before beginning their case discussions.

Time. Thoughtful discussions require time to unfold and become meaningful. They can happen in large chunks of time, such as during professional development days, or in smaller chunks but more frequently, such as during a common planning time or faculty meeting. Often, case discussions are held during graduate or inservice courses to follow up workshops at which new strategies or approaches are learned.

Access to Quality Cases. Case discussions must be clear, thorough, and well developed. The best strategy may be to work with published cases that have been used successfully with other groups before having participants write their own cases. Many cases are available in print and electronically (see "Additional Resources").

Examples

Cases and their discussion are the focus of the Mathematics Case Methods Project at WestEd in San Francisco. The project aims to build the capacity of teachers to make informed strategic decisions that draw on and anticipate student thinking through the development and analysis of mathematics cases. The cases are accounts of classroom experiences written by teachers and describe an instructional sequence in which the teacher is surprised or perplexed by students' responses or by the results of an assessment task (Barnett & Friedman, in press). Included in the cases are descriptions or samples of student work or dialogues. After reading a case, teachers discuss questions and issues raised by the case in a session that is guided by a facilitator. The facilitator is a teacher with case discussion experience who has chosen to take on a leadership role and has been formally prepared to facilitate the sessions. In each case discussion, a different case is read and discussed. Barnett and Friedman identify many outcomes from teachers' participation in case discussions: the case discussions provide a powerful stimulus for changes in teachers' beliefs about how children learn and how mathematics should be taught, they lead to improvement in teachers' mathematical content knowledge, they increase the complexity of teachers' pedagogical content knowledge, and they lead to changes in teachers' classroom teaching practices.

The Cambridge-based education research and development organization, Technical Education Resource Centers (TERC), has developed the *Sense Making in Science* video series (1996). This series offers visual cases of 12 teachers as they work together exploring what it means to learn and teach science. The series is a resource for teacher self-study or professional development sessions conducted by a facilitator. The videotapes depict teachers investigating scientific ideas, trying new teaching practices, and learning how to explore their students' thinking. Each video includes a summary of the video, recommended reading, and questions for discussion to help observers reflect on and analyze the teaching and learning occurring in the scenes.

Developing Mathematical Ideas is a professional development curriculum that uses sets of classroom episodes developed by teachers participating in Teaching to the Big Ideas, a professional development and research project. These episodes form the bases for case discussions designed to help teachers focus on the mathematical thinking of students and to raise issues related to classroom practice, pedagogy, and mathematics content.

In addition to case discussions, Developing Mathematical Ideas gives teachers opportunities to share and discuss actual student work, to participate in facilitated mathematics lessons, to develop their own cases, to review current mathematics research and carry out research in their own classrooms, and to view and discuss videotapes of mathematics classrooms and interviews.

Commentary

Case discussions create a stimulating environment in which teachers use their expertise and professional judgment to consider underlying assumptions, analyze situations, and draw conclusions about teaching and learning. As a professional development strategy, they have many benefits. Teachers' ideas and insights are valued and challenged, leading them to reflect on and change their beliefs about how children learn and how and what they teach. Mathematics cases have also been shown to increase teachers' content knowledge, and there is reason to believe the same may hold true for science cases. Case discussions recognize the expertise teachers have while providing them with opportunities to have in-depth conversations about teaching and learning.

Several critical issues surround the use of case discussions as a professional development strategy. For example, one question currently being asked is whether case discussions must be conducted face-to-face or whether they can be done electronically. Bank Street College conducts very successful electronic case discussions as part of its telecomputing courses. Outside evaluations have shown this approach to be highly valued by and beneficial to participants. (Bank Street's program is discussed in detail in "Technology for Professional Learning.") There is good reason to argue, however, that because they often challenge teachers' deeply held beliefs about teaching and learning, case discussions are best conducted in person. The interpersonal, face-to-face dimension can be critical to establishing rapport and trust and to communicating disagreements in respectful and constructive ways. Preserving these benefits from the interpersonal dimension via electronic means presents a considerable challenge.

Another similar issue that has been raised is whether teachers can benefit from reading cases on their own and addressing key issues in solitary reflection. Because a serious time commitment may be required to be part of a case discussion group, it is sometimes tempting for teachers to cut the recommended corners and read about, rather than participate in, cases. Although teachers can certainly learn many things from reading cases, the real benefits of this strategy derive from the group process itself. It is difficult, if not impossible, to throw oneself into the kind of disequilibrium Barnett and Friedman (in press) have shown to be the essential first step to changing beliefs and practices. In addition, the diverse contributions of the group are what determine the unique nature of each case discussion and even cause discussions of the same case to have a distinctive character.

The question of whether unfacilitated discussions are as effective as those that are facilitated is at the heart of another critical issue. A small group of teachers who are committed to using this approach or who are reluctant to designate a facilitator may still benefit from case discussions, but they would need very effective communication skills and would need to have at least some organized method of recording and tracking the group's progress.

The role of the facilitator in many case approaches is more than that of a guide. Particularly in those instances in which the approach includes published case facilitation guides or notes, the facilitator can be responsible for encouraging the group to address certain issues raised in the guides. Without a facilitator, some of these issues might be left unexamined.

Another danger inherent in nonfacilitated case discussions is that they may become more like study groups and lose the essence that characterizes cases as a professional development strategy.

Finally, people who use case discussions, and especially those who write their own cases, must be concerned about the confidentiality and ethics involved in this strategy. Case discussions must be treated like cases in other professions, such as health, law, and social services. Participants must ensure that materials such as videotape, print descriptions, and pictures are used with consent and that all materials viewed are kept confidential by the group (Kleinfeld, n.d.). This also sets up the right climate for those interested in writing, and then sharing, their own cases.

Additional Resources

Barnett, C., & Friedman, S. (in press). Mathematics case discussions: Nothing is sacred. In E. Fennema & B. Scott-Nelson (Eds.), *Mathematics teachers in transition*. Hillsdale, NJ: Lawrence Erlbaum.

Barnett, C., Goldstein, D., & Jackson, B. (Eds.). (1994). *Mathematics teaching cases: Fractions, decimals, ratios, and percents: Hard to teach and hard to learn? Facilitator's discussion guide*. Portsmouth, NH: Heineman.

Barnett, C., & Ramirez, A. (1996). Fostering critical analysis and reflection through mathematics case discussions. In J. Colbert, P. Desberg, & K. Trimble (Eds.), *The case for education: Contemporary approaches for using case methods*. Needham Heights, MA: Allyn & Bacon.

Casebooks from WestEd, San Francisco: Shulman, J., & Mesa-Bains, A. (1993). *Diversity in the classroom: A casebook for teachers and teacher educators;* Barnett, C., & Tyson, P. (1994). *Enhancing mathematics teaching through case discussions;* Barnett, C., Goldstein, D., & Jackson, B. (1994). *Mathematics teaching cases: Fractions, decimals, ratios and percents—Hard to teach and hard to learn?;* WestEd Eisenhower Regional Consortium for Science and Mathematics Education & Distance Learning Resource Network. (1996). *Tales from the electronic frontier.*

Cases Institute (D. Schifter, Director), Education Development Center, Newton, MA. (Phone: 617-969-7100)

Center for Case Studies in Education (R. Silverman and W. Welty, Codirectors), Pace University, Pleasantville, NY. (Phone: 914-773-3879)

Hansen, A. (1997). Writing cases for teaching: Observations of a practitioner. *Phi Delta Kappan, 78*(5), 398-403.

Mathematics Case Methods Project (C. Barnett & S. Friedman, Codirectors), WestEd, San Francisco. (Phone: 415-565-3000)

Roderick MacDougall Center for Case Development and Teaching. (1994, August). *Catalogue of K-12 case materials.* Cambridge, MA: Harvard Graduate School of Education.

Rowley, J. B., & Hart, P. M. (1996). How video case studies can promote reflective dialogue. *Educational Leadership, 53*(6), 28-29.

Schifter, D. (1995). Teachers' changing conceptions of the nature of mathematics: Enactment in the classroom. In B. S. Nelson (Ed.), *Inquiry and the development of teaching: Issues in the transformation of mathematics teaching* (pp. 17-25). Newton, MA: Center for the Development of Teaching Paper Series, Education Development Center.

Study Groups

After several years in a project focused on mathematics education reform, the teachers at McKinley Middle School were still fine-tuning their practice. Their instructional tasks were good, their curriculum was sound, and their organizational and management skills were honed. Somehow, however, they felt that things still were not going as well as they could. They decided that they needed to focus on the instructional tasks they were using in their classrooms. In particular, they thought that the tasks did not always seem to play out in the ways they intended. They had attended a session at a recent NCTM conference in which a framework was presented that described ways in which the cognitive demand of tasks sometimes declined as students implemented them. The teachers wanted to explore this framework further to determine if it might offer some insight into how and why their lessons sometimes did not seem to deliver their potential. They decided to meet biweekly after school to share videotapes of their teaching and use the framework to reflect on whether or not the cognitive-demanding tasks that they usually set up in their lessons were indeed being carried out by students in a way that maintained their high-level demands. Each week, a teacher would volunteer to show a 20- to 30-minute clip of instruction that would then be discussed using the framework as a guide. A McKinley teacher commented later that year, "This sustained, deep attention to practice was absolutely what was needed to take us over the top." Another commented that the regular group sessions were the motivating force that pushed everyone to be more critical and reflective.

Study groups offer teachers the opportunity to come together to address issues of teaching and learning. The topics addressed in these groups vary from current issues in mathematics and science education to whole-school reform. Groups may be composed of small numbers of teachers interested in pursuing a topic together or entire school faculty addressing whole-school reform issues. Regardless of the topic or issue being addressed, study groups provide a forum in which teachers can be inquirers and ask questions that matter to them, over a period of time, and in a collaborative and supportive environment.

Underlying Assumptions

The use of study groups for professional development is based on certain assumptions about teachers, learning, and professional development.

Teachers have the knowledge, skills, and desire to make decisions regarding their own professional growth. As adult learners, teachers know what teaching and learning issues concern them and are able to work with their peers to address these issues. By exercising control over their own professional growth, teachers can design and implement study groups that best meet their own needs and those of their students.

The context within which teachers work provides worthwhile content for their collaboration with each other. Addressing issues related to their own practices in their own classrooms allows teachers to develop new practices that are directly related to their local contexts. Unlike professional development experiences designed by others or ones that provide teachers with an innovation to implement, study groups provide a forum in which teachers can address issues that embody central values and principles relevant to their own environments (Little, 1993).

Collegiality, cooperation, and communication among teachers are valued by the school community. Given the belief that teachers are respected as self-directed, adult learners, the school community encourages teachers to work collaboratively with each other. Teachers' participation in study groups helps create a community of learners that promote continuous improvement and growth as a way of life in the school. Moving out of the isolation of working individually in a classroom to sharing ideas and new learnings with peers in a supportive group fosters a sense of collegiality and professionalism among teachers. Study groups also provide an opportunity for teachers to develop a common language to talk about and reflect on classroom instruction.

Key Elements

For study groups to succeed as a strategy for professional learning, several key elements must be in place.

Varied Topics and Issues. One of the primary elements of this strategy is that groups are organized around a specific topic or issue of importance to the participating teachers. These topics range from school-based concerns to curriculum and instructional issues. For example, grade-level teachers might form a study group to learn more about assessing their students' understanding of science concepts. Over a period of time, they might meet to discuss research they have read, share examples of assessments and critique the appropriateness of the assessments, or invite school or district personnel to join the group to discuss other assessment requirements and how these impact classroom practice. Other study groups might be composed of entire school faculties or departments that focus on implementing specific school improvement initiatives.

Varied Structures. Depending on the nature of topics discussed or issues addressed, the form study groups take varies. Makibbin and Sprague (1991) suggest four models for structuring study groups. First, the implementation model is designed to support teachers' implementation of strategies recently learned in workshops or other short-term sessions. The goal is to provide teachers with an ongoing system for discussing, reflecting on, and analyzing their implementation of strategies after the workshop has concluded. Second, the institutionalization model is used once teachers have already implemented new practices in the classroom and want to continue refining and improving these practices. Third, research-sharing groups are organized around discussions of recent research and how it relates to classroom practice. Fourth, investigation study groups are a way for teachers to identify a topic or practice about which they would like to learn more. In this model, teachers read about, discuss, and implement new strategies that are relevant in their own contexts. These models have been successfully implemented by teachers of mathematics and science as they investigate content, instructional practices, and student learning.

Implementation Requirements

There are several requirements for implementation of study group experiences for teachers.

Time. Like most other strategies for professional development, participating in a study group requires time not only to meet and address the issues but also to do so over a long period. Some suggest a minimum of at least once a week over a period of several months (LaBonte, Leighty, Mills, & True 1995; Murphy, 1992, 1995). Regardless of how frequently the group meets, however, it is critical that groups keep a regular schedule of consistent contact with the expectation that their work is ongoing.

Support From Administrators. The formation and success of study groups requires direct support from school administrators not only for the time for the group to meet but also for the endeavor itself. Administrators send a clear message of the importance of professional development for teachers if time is set aside during the school day for study groups to convene. Administrators can also offer support by providing access to resources, technology, or experts when teachers request assistance in meeting their goals.

Substantive Topics. Teachers forming study groups must identify their members (by grade level, across grade levels, schoolwide, or departmentwide) and identify a topic or issue that is "complex and substantive enough to hold the group together while individuals are developing the skills of working together as a cohesive group and developing trust and rapport" (Murphy 1995, p. 41). For teachers just embarking on collaboration with their peers, this new format for sharing knowledge and ideas will require that they become comfortable with the process and make adjustments as they progress. In addition, if the topic selected is too narrow or can be addressed in a very few sessions, the group may find itself moving from topic to topic without really reflecting on what they are learning.

Study Group Activities. Study groups must also identify a process for how to address the issues or topics. Most study groups use a variety of activities, including reading and discussing research; learning about new teaching and learning approaches through reading, attending workshops or other sessions, or inviting experts to work with the group; and implementing new practices in their classrooms and using the study group time to reflect on and analyze the experience both for themselves and for their students.

Self-Direction and Self-Governance. Teachers should join and form study groups voluntarily and determine their own focus for learning and the format for the sessions. Murphy (1995) suggests the following problem-solving cycle that can help teachers effectively structure their study groups:

- Collect and review the data relevant to the selected topic or issue.
- State what the "problem" is and what it should be.
- Categorize and prioritize the problems.

- Specify the intended results for teachers and students that will indicate that the problem is lessened or solved.

- Select strategies to implement that will reach the intended results.

- Specify procedures for organizing and sustaining groups.

- Implement the plan.

- Track changes through logs or journals.

- Evaluate the implementation, and institutionalize the changes.

Group Interaction Skills. As with other strategies organized around cooperative group work, group interaction skills are important. Successful groups have members who share a common goal and are committed to accomplishing the goal; work to create an environment of trust, openness, and foster communication; believe that diversity is an asset and that each member brings something unique to the group; value risk taking and creativity; are able to plan and implement strategies; share leadership and facilitation of group processes; are comfortable with consensus decision-making procedures; and are committed to building a team that reflects deeply on their learnings.

Examples

One example of a group of teachers that formed their own study group illustrates almost all the underlying assumptions, key elements, and implementation requirements discussed here. Ten elementary teachers in Cleveland organized a study group called Journeys after realizing that they were ready to explore issues in their science teaching; they wanted to begin the process of self-reflection (Badders et al., 1996). The members had compatible philosophies about teaching, expressed an interest in enriching their understanding about the craft of teaching, and were willing to seek opportunities for intellectual professional growth. The group reflected a wide range of teaching experience and varying backgrounds, knowledge, and skills in inquiry-based science teaching. Each teacher expressed a sincere commitment to the goals of the study group and clearly displayed a joy for teaching and a desire to explore his or her teaching in-depth.

The Journeys group convened regularly for 4 years. Initial sessions were more social than intellectual, helping them to develop an environment of mutual trust and understanding. They then forged ahead on their goals. During the 4 years, their goals varied: to connect theory and practice; to conduct classroom-based action research; to intensely study issues in inquiry-based science teaching, coaching and mentoring, constructivism, and assessment; to get involved in professional science teacher organizations at the local, state, and national levels; and to apply the vision and goals of the *National Science Education Standards* (NRC, 1996) to the classroom.

During the 4 years, the conversations among the teachers caused them to question their own assumptions about teaching and learning. The group critically reflected on their pedagogy, their content understanding, their knowledge of teaching, and issues of assessment concerning instruction and what their children were coming to know and understand about science concepts. Constructive feedback from group members helped them analyze their practices in the classroom.

In addition to what they learned in their study group, the Cleveland teachers expanded their roles outside of the classroom. They joined local, state, and national organizations and attended and presented at these organizations' conferences. The group was selected to be involved in a multistate portfolio project focused on assessment. Most members started study groups with other teachers. Journeys members continue in their professional growth and learning: Badders et al. (1996, p. 3) stated, "We believe that we have begun to discover the meaning of lifelong learning."

The Pasadena Unified School District in California provides another example of educators implementing study groups with teachers. Elementary teachers in Pasadena have been actively teaching kit-based, inquiry science for many years and are involved in numerous science education reform initiatives. In 1993, two individuals, in collaboration with the district, began to work with teachers who had been teaching kit-based, inquiry science for at least 2 years with regard to issues of pedagogy and assessment. The goal was to help teachers who had become accomplished at implementing the curriculum in their classrooms begin to delve into and reflect on their own teaching and their students' learning. Fifty teachers formed study groups in two areas: assessment and pedagogy.

Each pedagogy study group consisted of four teachers from one grade level, one scientist, and one master resource teacher from the district who served as the facilitator. The study groups met once a month for 3 hours after school during a period of one and a half years. Groups selected their own topics, which included investigating the appropriateness of using cooperative learning groups in first grade; carefully examining student science journals and lab books in third and fourth grades; analyzing both teacher expectations and student learning; and modifying an existing fifth-grade science unit to reflect more open-ended, inquiry learning for students.

Each assessment study group consisted of three teachers, one scientist, and one master resource teacher from the district. Each group was facilitated by an outside assessment expert and met once a month for 3 hours after school during a period of 3 years. Each study group investigated issues regarding how best to assess what their students were learning from the kit-based curriculum using both embedded and end-of-unit assessments. They developed assessments, tested them in classrooms with students, and evaluated their effectiveness.

Within all the groups, facilitators served the role of asking provocative questions, providing guidance, and challenging teachers to delve further into topics. Scientists in the groups played similar roles and also helped provide teachers with science content when needed. Periodically, the groups invited experts and guests to join them for discussions and to share resources. Both groups of teachers presented their findings to their peers twice a year at all-day Saturday conferences and received feedback and critique from other teachers. Both the teachers and the scientists received stipends for their work in the study groups.

Commentary

Study groups require the participation of teachers who are committed to reflecting on their work and taking initiative for their own learning. It is not a strategy that lends itself to raising awareness about a topic in a short period of time but rather one that encourages teachers to "go deep" and question and reflect on their own practices.

Because study groups necessarily involve teachers in reflection outside of the classroom, it is difficult to sustain study groups in traditional school cultures. Although they may be slow to get started in such environments, once study groups "take hold" in a school, teachers enthusiastically support their continuation. Often, administrators come to recognize their benefit and realize that study groups lend themselves well to investigations and inquiries into numerous topics and issues of concern to both teachers and the entire school community. For example, study groups concerned with finding time for professional development, using national and state standards to improve teaching and learning, or developing community support for science or mathematics reform can benefit teachers and students while building ownership and commitment by a broader school community.

Additional Resources

Brown, M. I. (1995). Study groups at Elder Middle School. *Journal of Staff Development, 16*(3), 53.

Budnick, S. (1995). Study groups at Mission Bay High School. *Journal of Staff Development, 16*(3), 52.

Carter, S., Crane, P., Moss, M., Pearce, K., Roudebush, J., & Witte, B. (1995). Study groups: The productive "whole." *Journal of Staff Development, 16*(3), 50-52.

Charles, L., & Clark, P. (1995). Whole-faculty study groups at Sweetwater Union High School. *Journal of Staff Development, 16*(3), 49-50.

Little, J. W. (1990). The persistence of privacy: Autonomy and initiative in teachers' professional relations. *Teachers College Record, 91*(4), 509-536.

Roy, P. (1994). *A primer on study groups.* Wilmington, DE: Patricia Roy.

Stein, M. K., & Smith, M. (in press). The mathematical tasks framework as a tool for reflection. *Mathematics Teaching in the Middle School.*

Turner, P. (1995). Study groups at Sarah Cobb Elementary. *Journal of Staff Development, 16*(3), 53.

Examining Student Work and Student Thinking and Scoring Assessments

Teachers from two middle schools were distressed because their students did not do well on the new state performance assessment. Wanting to help them do better, the teachers decided to look carefully at their students' work to uncover where the problems might lie. They selected 10 students in different classrooms and then gathered and studied the students' portfolios, scoring sheets, and other records. The teachers did the assessment tasks themselves and explored several questions: What were the tasks asking? How were the responses scored? What does one need to know and be able to do to do the task? and How did the students interpret and approach the task? As a result of their discussions, the teachers were better able to "see" the students' work and understand their thinking. They listed the kinds of understandings that the assessment seemed to tap and the kinds of problems they saw in students' work. This guided subsequent discussions of how they could help students improve their performance on the state assessment and their understanding of important mathematical ideas (Ball & Cohen, 1995).

Underlying Assumptions

Evans (1993, p. 72) states that "real student work gives teachers a starting point for conversations that get to the essence of what happens in classrooms. Samples of student work are concrete demonstrations of what is known and what is not known."

The use of the professional development strategy of examining student work and student thinking and scoring assessments is based on several assumptions about learning, teaching, and professional development.

Student learning is the ultimate outcome for professional development, and the closer the professional development opportunity brings teachers to student learning the better. This is different from professional development that focuses on teaching practices. Examining student work and student assessments focuses teachers' attention on the consequences of their teaching for the learners, which demonstrates to teachers discrepancies between what they believed they were teaching and what students appear to have learned (Driscoll & Bryant, in press).

More learning occurs when teachers confront real problems—ones that they face in their classrooms on a daily basis. Such is the case with student work and assessments, which teachers use to judge the quality of learning and, in some cases, teaching. As Ball and Cohen (1995) indicate, there is value in using a real task of practice as a context for learning.

Student products can reflect what they know and the nature of their thinking. Thus, when teachers examine student work, they gain insights into their students' learning and guidance for designing new learning experiences.

Key Elements

There are several key elements of using student work and student thinking and scoring assessments as a strategy for professional development.

What Teachers Have Plenty of: Student Work. The richest discussions are stimulated by work samples that are varied in their nature and quality, require more than short answers, and include students' explanations of their thinking (e.g., why they answered the way they did and what made them do what they did).

Focus of the Discussion. The focus of discussion may vary. In the opening vignette to this section, for example, teachers had a compelling reason to examine student assessments and did so using the actual test that had been given. At other times, teachers might bring to open-ended discussion groups examples of student work that puzzle them. In some situations, teachers may begin with a rubric supplied by others to apply to a set of student work (e.g., the contents of portfolios or the results of performance tasks) or may take the opportunity to develop their own rubric through examining student work. Also, the focus for a discussion may be a videotape of children's explanations of their understanding of a problem or situation.

Teacher Discussions. Although an individual teacher can certainly examine student work or reflect on student thinking in isolation, there is power in examining student work as a team. As elementary teacher Christine Evans (1993) points out, working together greatly enhances what is possible to consider and to learn. Among her teaching group, their ideas differed about the mathematics, the tasks, and particular students. Their discussions broadened what any one person could do. Together, they began to develop shared ideas and standards that could guide their collective efforts. Creating a supportive environment in which teachers can work with each other and examine their own values about teaching and learning enhances the process, as noted by Rebecca Corwin (1997, p. 187): "Doing mathematics together in a responsive group creates a safe professional community in which to explore issues and raise questions about both mathematics and pedagogy."

Implementation Requirements

For examining student work and student thinking and scoring assessments to succeed as a strategy for professional development, several requirements must be met.

Focused Time for Discussion and Reflection. Like many professional development opportunities, this strategy requires a focused period of time without distractions to study the material and reflect on what it suggests about students' thinking and learning needs.

The Guidance of an Experienced Content Expert. There is a need for the participation of someone who has recognized expertise in the mathematics or science that is being examined (there is more often a need for this at the elementary level than at other levels, at which teachers typically have greater content preparation). Often, delving deeply into understanding what students are thinking by analyzing their written work or responses on assessments requires substantial knowledge of the science or mathematics. Similarly, if students' responses on assessment instruments or the effectiveness of the instruments themselves are being examined, it is helpful to have the guidance of someone with experience in assessment.

Because student work is something teachers have in abundance, there are few additional requirements for supporting this learning strategy.

Examples

In one middle school, teachers worked with a mathematics educator from a nearby university to discuss the in-depth analysis of students' responses to specific performance tasks. In one task, students were asked to circle the number that has the greatest value: .08, .8, .080, or .008000. Students were to choose the number and explain their answer. Many students could select the correct answer, but they could not successfully explain how they arrived at it. For their part, teachers differed in how important they thought it was to have an explanation at all. The group examined several examples in which students had the right answer but did not understand why. One student gave an intricate, illustrated explanation; one simply noted, "it has the greatest value"; and another wrote, "the .8 is the greatest because it has no zeros before the number or after the number. The more zeros the lesser it is." With regard to this experience, Parke and Lane (1996/1997) noted the following:

> When the teachers compared the explanations, they began to see how much insight those explanations can provide into a students' level of understanding. This discussion was one of the first meaningful interactions these teachers had about their students' conceptual understandings and what they were learning in the classroom. (p. 27)

Another example of teachers examining student work and thinking is provided by Project IMPACT (Increasing the Mathematical Power of All Children and Teachers), a collaboration between the University of Maryland at College Park and Montgomery County Public Schools in Maryland. The project addresses a constructivist perspective of mathematics learning and focuses on how to promote student and teacher understanding through interaction. The intent is for teachers to organize their instruction to build on students' existing knowledge, relating mathematical procedures and curriculum objectives to problem solving (Campbell & Robles, 1997). During summer teacher enhancement programs, teachers examine an activity, rather than actual student work, to explore how the activity might facilitate a child's reexamination of a mathematical construct. Teachers also write questions that they could ask of students to determine what mathematical ideas the children were constructing as they completed the activity. To encourage teachers to transfer what they themselves have learned in an adult-level mathematics session to their students, they are challenged to define a task or an activity that would address the same mathematical topic at a level appropriate for their students. These activities encourage teachers to reflect on their students' thought processes as the children develop mathematical constructs, helping the teachers design more effective and challenging activities for learning.

The Cognitively Guided Instruction (CGI) project of the University of Wisconsin at Madison helps teachers examine student thinking, as well as their own thinking, as a means of professional development. CGI "helps teachers gain an understanding of children's thinking by having them construct relationships between an explicit research-based model of children's thinking and their own children's thinking" (Fennema, Carpenter, & Franke, 1997, p. 193). With an experienced facilitator, teachers view videotapes of children solving and discussing mathematical problems. Through extended discussions, teachers begin to recognize patterns in the way children approach certain problems and how children's solutions can be used to help predict their responses to other problems. Ultimately, as Fennema et al. (1997), the directors of the CGI project, note, "Knowledge of their own children's thinking enables teachers to make instructional decisions so that children's learning of mathematics improves" (p. 195).

For elementary teachers in California, scoring assessments has helped deepen their appreciation of the value of this activity as a professional development strategy. Assessment comes alive for them when they examine a range of student responses to the challenge to create a "Critter Museum." The teachers learn a complex scoring rubric and procedure to assist them in their scoring task. At the same time, they enhance their own understanding of important science concepts and how students exhibit what they know and are able to do (DiRanna, Osterfeld, Cerwin, Topps, & Tucker, 1995).

Commentary

There are many who see this strategy as the most powerful way to help teachers improve their practice. Clearly, it is totally "authentic" in that teachers work with products of student thinking and study closely the very thing they are responsible for improving. As professional development becomes more results oriented, there is no better way to focus on learning.

It is useful to think about how this strategy can be combined with others to optimize professional learning. For example, teachers implementing a new curriculum can bring examples of student work to follow-up sessions. Case discussions can (and often do) relate to student work, discussing in some depth what students did and what teachers can learn from that. In their action research and peer coaching, teachers can pay special attention to students who are talking to each other or working on problems or investigations; teachers can question the students about what they are doing and why. Video cases of teaching, including CD-ROMs, can be accompanied by student work so that teachers viewing and discussing them can get a clearer and larger picture of what students are learning.

The most important aspect of this strategy is that teachers have access to and then develop for themselves the ability to understand the content students are struggling with and ways that they, the teachers, can help. Pedagogical content knowledge—that special province of excellent teachers—is absolutely necessary for teachers to maximize their learning as they examine and discuss what students demonstrate they know and do not know.

Additional Resources

Cain, R. W., Kenney, P. A., & Schloemer, C. G. (1994). Teachers as assessors: A professional development challenge. In D. B. Aichele & A. F. Coxford (Eds.), *Professional development for teachers of mathematics, 1994 yearbook* (pp. 93-101). Reston, VA: National Council of Teachers of Mathematics.

Cognitively Guided Instruction Project (E. Fennema & T. P. Carpenter, Directors), University of Wisconsin at Madison.

Martin-Kniep, G. O., Sussman, E. S., & Meltzer, E. (1995). The North Shore Collaborative Inquiry Project: A reflective study of assessment and learning. *Journal of Staff Development, 16*(4), 46-51.

National Commission of Teaching and America's Future. (1996, September). *What matters most: Teaching for America's future.* New York: Author.

Coaching and Mentoring

Although initially hesitant about her ability to implement a new middle-school curriculum as part of the QUASAR project, Dorothy was comforted by the fact that she was not alone. In particular, she was fortunate to have daily interactions with Paul, a teacher-colleague who was more experienced in using the curriculum. During her first year in the QUASAR project, Dorothy taught mathematics with Paul in the same room. In fact, Dorothy did not have access to a free room during her prep period, so she would stay in Paul's classroom and observe his teaching. Although she complained at first about not getting work done during her prep time, eventually she came to enjoy it. Early in the first year, Dorothy wrote the following in her journal:

I know I will need a place of my own, but I will also learn a lot working in the room while Paul is teaching. Today I didn't get anything done during my prep because I was interested in Paul's lessons.

Dorothy's appreciation of her close, day-to-day contact with Paul continued, as she expressed to an interviewer as follows:

I know that they would have thrown me out of the math program in one week if it weren't for Paul, because Paul has everything organized. I share a room with Paul, so we collaborate. I see him a lot, like fourth period is my lunch and I always go in there and get ready for math during that time and he's usually there, and I can say, "God, I'm really feeling. . . ." And he says, "Dorothy, I felt exactly the same way last year at this time" and "You did this well and you did this well." He's in and out a lot when I teach. (Stein et al., in press)

Coaching and mentoring are professional development strategies that provide one-on-one learning opportunities for teachers focused on improving teaching practice. They take advantage of the knowledge and skills of experienced teachers, giving them, and those with less experience, opportunities to learn from each other. While typically more formalized and structured than in the previous vignette, they often have the same impact on teachers, providing them with confidence and abilities to improve their practices.

Numerous professional development practices have the label "coaching": technical coaching, collegial coaching, challenge coaching, team coaching, cognitive coaching, linguistic coaching, and peer coaching (see "Resources"). All incorporate a traditional supervisory model focused on classroom observations and use a preconference-observation-postconference cycle. Over the years, particular forms of coaching have emerged with different purposes and correspondingly different techniques, as suggested by the labels mentioned previously. In addition, for some the concept of coaching has broadened beyond the focus on classroom observation to include other activities, such as coplanning instruction, material development, and thinking together about the influence of their behavior on students (Showers & Joyce, 1996). In most instances, coaching is thought of as being done by peers—teachers who have equal competence.

By common definition, however, a mentor is an experienced adult who befriends and guides a less experienced adult. In education, mentors are experienced teachers working with beginning teachers or teachers who have experience and particular expertise in a program, teaching practice, or content area who work with others with less experience and expertise. Mentors can play roles of teacher, coach, role model, developer of talent, sponsor, protector, and opener of doors. The literature on mentoring beginning teachers is substantial; research indicates that effective mentoring programs can lower the attrition rate for beginning teachers, significantly decreasing the length and trauma of their induction period into the profession (Newton et al., 1994). Mentors in science and mathematics programs are typically teachers with more content knowledge or experience in using a particular program or practice who work with those less experienced. Sometimes, scientists and mathematicians can be mentors for teachers, helping them to develop an increased understanding of the content they are teaching and to insert in their instruction examples and discussions of real-world applications of the skills and knowledge they are helping their students to develop.

Underlying Assumptions

The use of coaching and mentoring for professional development is based on certain assumptions about teachers, learning, and professional development.

Reflection by an individual on his or her own practice can be enhanced by another's observations and perceptions. Experienced teachers are often on "automatic pilot" and thus are not conscious of many of the moves they make with their students and the teaching techniques they employ. Less experienced teachers are typically focused on managing the learning environment and, similarly, are not conscious of many of their interactions with students. By simply holding up a mirror, a coach or mentor can bring to consciousness some useful information for teachers with regard to their practice.

Teachers working to master new materials or teaching practices benefit from ongoing assistance. It is predictable that when teachers (or anyone, for that matter) try something significantly new to them, they encounter problems and obstacles, lack confidence and coordination, and benefit from help. Because their needs are often idiosyncratic—that is, what one teacher needs is likely to be different from what another needs—one-on-one help is needed. Coaches and mentors with more experience and expertise can help.

Teachers are competent professionals whose experience, expertise, and observations are valuable sources of knowledge, skill development, and inspiration for other teachers. This is a critical assumption to which professional developers must subscribe to consider using coaching and mentoring in their programs. Some people believe that what science and mathematics teachers need is assistance from outside of their colleagues and their schools that is delivered by trainers, program developers, scientists, and mathematicians. The critical and specialized knowledge that experienced teachers have—pedagogical content knowledge—is not acknowledged as worth sharing (Shulman, 1987). It is this very knowledge, however, that helps teachers understand what their students need, how they come to understand certain concepts and principles of the content, and what they need to increase that understanding. Sharing this kind of expertise is at the core of coaching and mentoring.

Key Elements

For coaching and mentoring to succeed as strategies for professional development, several key elements must be in place.

A Focus for Learning or Improvement. Coaching and mentoring are most successful when teachers agree that they will work on examining particular teaching techniques, student interactions, perplexing problems, or learning strategies. Sometimes, this is as focused as tallying the number and kinds of questions teachers ask of different students to understand any gender or cultural biases, which is of great importance in teaching science and mathematics. Other times, it is more general, such as techniques used to manage materials. Although being "on call" and supportive in general are important roles of mentors, when both coaches and mentors observe in classrooms they need a predetermined focus that they agree on with the teacher being observed.

Mechanisms for Sharing and Feedback. For classroom observations, preconferences typically are opportunities for the observer and teacher being observed to agree on the focus and set ground rules about the kind of feedback that will be helpful. Postconferences, then, are guided by these agreements. Different approaches to coaching and mentoring suggest different forms of sharing and feedback, some structured by classroom observation instruments and others as open as sharing detailed, but unstructured, observations of the flow of the lesson. Likewise, forms of feedback vary from simple description to particular forms of questioning.

Opportunities for Interaction. It almost goes without saying that for coaching and mentoring to work, teachers need opportunities to interact with each other. For example, just having time for classroom observations, without protected time to talk before and after, defeats the purpose of careful and shared examination and understanding of teaching practice. Although a novice teacher may pick up some "tips" from sitting in on a lesson, a follow-up discussion of what was done, why, and with what impact is critical to understanding teaching.

Implementation Requirements

For coaching and mentoring to succeed as strategies for professional development, several requirements must be met.

A Climate of Trust, Collegiality, and Continuous Growth. These are necessary because of the personal nature of coaching and mentoring. The ability to fail and learn from failures, acknowledge both strengths and weaknesses and build improvement strategies on both, welcome the role of a "critical friend" (Costa & Kallick, 1993), and accept that learning never ends must be the backdrop for coaching and mentoring relationships to be successful.

Long-Term Commitment to Interaction. Coaching and mentoring cannot have an impact unless they occur over time. Previously noted is the importance of building trust, which takes time. Teachers must also build an understanding about what each knows about teaching, learning, and content and what each can do with students in classrooms. As this understanding increases, teachers become of more help to each other. This can happen only if interaction occurs more than once, with some amount of regularity, so that suggestions and insights can be tried and reflections on their impact shared. It is only then that learning will be cumulative.

Skill Building in Coaching and Mentoring. Coaching and mentoring require special skills in communication (e.g., clarifying, paraphrasing, conflict management, and listening), observation, and giving feedback. Sophisticated training programs are available for this purpose (see the Association for Supervision and Curriculum Development and the National Staff Development Council under "Resources"). Furthermore, coaches and mentors benefit from understanding principles of adult learning and the change process. In addition, the more a coach or mentor understands about the content being taught and knows from experience how students learn it (and how to teach it), the better. Although good coaches and mentors can help teachers become more reflective in their practice, and better inquirers into problems and dilemmas of teaching, they can be of much greater assistance if they know the specific content being taught by the teachers with whom they are working.

Administrative Support. Coaching and mentoring require that teachers form special relationships and have time to build them. Administrators must recognize and articulate the importance of mentoring and coaching relationships and activities, allocate or reallocate time in ways that pairs have time to observe each other and work together, and nurture and support the building of a learning community in the school that has these teacher partnerships at its core (Garmston, 1987; Showers & Joyce, 1996).

Examples

In the Colorado College CC-ISTEP teacher enhancement program for teachers of science from primary through secondary schools, many teachers are from rural Colorado, coming from schools in which they are the only science teacher. They have never spent time in others' classrooms, nor have they had opportunities to coach others or to be coached. A model for teaching from a constructivist perspective (Loucks-Horsley et al., 1990) is used in the program and, consequently, forms the framework for classroom observations for participating teachers. Teachers' observations of each other's teaching focus on where the teacher and students are in the learning sequence and how interactions address students' stages of learning and with what impact.

Another project that incorporates coaching and mentoring is Teachers Empowering Teachers: Computers in Geometry Classrooms, at Saint Olaf College in Northfield, Minnesota. The project's main goal is to help geometry teachers develop the knowledge, skills, and confidence necessary to use computer-based tools in their classrooms (Wallace, Cederberg, & Allen, 1994). To reach this goal, the project is designed around an "expanding network" model: From college instructors, the network expands to master high school geometry teachers, then to less experienced teachers, and finally to colleagues in each teacher's school. "Experts" at each level work closely with teachers on the next level, serving first as a coach, then as a mentor, and finally as a colleague. As coaches and mentors, teachers serve as classroom assistants, facilitators of discussion groups, instructors during workshop sessions, observers during classroom teaching, and collaborative peers during lesson development. They also conduct simulated classroom sessions in which they model the teaching of geometry lessons that incorporate computers. Each level of the network provides unique opportunities for teachers to serve as mentors and coaches in these various roles.

Another university-based program, the Atlanta Math Project (AMP) at Georgia State University in Atlanta, uses coaching and mentoring as a key component in helping mathematics teachers implement the NCTM standards. As Grouws and Schultz (1996, p. 446) noted, the use of a "reflective teaching model includes monthly planning of at least one mathematics lesson with an AMP partner who then observes a live or videotaped lesson and follows up with a nonevaluative reflective debriefing." These coaching and observing partnerships occur during a yearlong period and are accompanied by sessions focused on mathematics pedagogy and the NCTM standards. Through assessment of the program, it has been found that the use of a peer partner to facilitate planning, teaching experiences, and debriefing sessions helps teachers construct pedagogical content knowledge and mathematics content knowledge as well as creates a support structure that facilitates risk taking in the classroom.

Commentary

Several issues arise when coaching or mentoring are introduced to teachers, whether in a department or schoolwide effort or as a part of a professional development program or initiative. First, norms of isolation and privacy work against many teachers' willingness to open their classrooms and their teaching to observation and scrutiny. Going slowly, developing trusting and sharing relationships before classroom observations, and having a very specific focus that is unthreatening at first but then introduces more challenging questions about teaching and learning are some ways that teachers living with those norms have accepted coaching as an opportunity.

Second, time for making and discussing classroom observations is a problem within a typical school schedule. Creative solutions to this have been found (Joyce & Showers, 1987); for example, hiring a roving substitute for the day who will take over as needed, relieving the observing teachers one after the other. Rearranging planning times, team teaching, and taking advantage of others, and not just teachers, to work with students have all been used successfully.

Finally, it is important that before coaching or mentoring is initiated, there is a study of the literature and the different kinds of approaches that are possible. As noted at the beginning of this section, not only does coaching have many labels but also each type has a different purpose, technique, and outcome. Likewise, the literature on mentoring is rich and approaches vary. Studying and then learning the techniques, through reading, focused professional development, or both, can maximize the impact of coaching and mentoring strategies. (See "Resources" for materials for review.)

Additional Resources

Association for Supervision and Curriculum Development (ASCD), Alexandria, VA (Phone: 703-549-9110). Contact this organization for information on professional development in peer coaching and mentoring.

Caccia, P. F. (1996). Linguistic coaching: Helping beginning teachers defeat discouragement. *Educational Leadership, 53*(6), 17-20.

Colorado College, CC-ISTEP Teacher Enhancement Program (P. Kuerbis, Project Director), Colorado Springs, CO. (Phone: 719-389-6147)

Costa, A., & Garmston, R. (1994). *Cognitive coaching: Approaching renaissance schools.* Norwood, MA: C. Gordon.

Ganser, T. (1996). Preparing mentors of beginning teachers: An overview for staff developers. *Journal of Staff Development, 17*(4), 8-11.

National Staff Development Council (NSDC), Oxford, OH (Phone: 513-523-6029). Contact this organization for information on professional development in peer coaching and mentoring.

Phillips, M. D., & Glickman, C. D. (1991). Peer coaching: Developmental approach to enhancing teacher thinking. *Journal of Staff Development, 12*(2), 20-25.

Shulman, J. H., & Colbert, J. A. (Eds.). (1987). *The mentor teacher casebook.* Eugene, OR/San Francisco: University of Oregon, ERIC Clearinghouse on Educational Management/Far West Laboratory for Educational Research and Development.

Partnerships With Scientists and Mathematicians in Business, Industry, and Universities

Julie, a fifth-grade teacher, is struggling to understand the concepts underlying why large, heavy boats float. She is working with a group of other teachers and scientists to improve the school's curriculum unit on floating and sinking. Julie has taught the unit to her students once and recognized many of the misconceptions her students held as they started the unit. She also watched her students' understanding grow as they progressed through the unit. She and the other teachers have found, however, that the science background information provided in the teachers guide is incomplete and often misleading. The teachers are working with scientists from the local university to (a) clearly understand the concepts and (b) revise the science content information that is provided to teachers in the guide. Julie thought she understood the concepts of buoyant force and displacement, but as she tried to articulate her understanding she found that her understanding was not as clear as she thought. Right now, she is listening intently as one of the scientists asks her to explain why the plastic spoon is floating in the tub of water on the table in front of her. She is confident that when she stumbles over her words, the scientist will encourage her to continue and will help guide her through a thought process based on what she is observing that will help her fully understand the concepts and not simply "give" her the answer. The next challenge will be to put her understanding of the concepts into words so that other teachers will also begin to grasp them!

The types of partnerships between teachers and scientists and mathematicians in business, industry, and universities are as diverse as the individuals involved in the partnerships. One form of partnership— teachers immersing themselves in the world of scientists and mathematicians—is a professional development strategy that we have discussed previously in this chapter. The partnerships discussed in this section focus on scientists and mathematicians coming into the world of the teacher: scientists and mathematicians serving as mentors, working side by side with teachers as resources for understanding and learning content, participating in the design and evaluation of curriculum materials, or sitting at the table during strategic planning and decision making. An important characteristic of the partnerships we discuss here is that both partners bring expertise to their endeavors, with the ultimate goal of improving teaching and learning of science and mathematics.

Underlying Assumptions

The use of the professional development strategy of participating in partnerships is based on several assumptions about teachers, learning, and professional development.

Quality science and mathematics education is a community responsibility. Partnerships for professional development are based on the assumption that the quality and effectiveness of science and mathematics teaching and learning is the responsibility of the entire community and not just the schools. Both education for students and professional development for teachers can be enhanced by the participation of those from the community.

Partners are equal. Partnerships, to be effective, must truly be a two-way exchange of resources and knowledge. Scientists, mathematicians, and teachers have equal but different roles to play. Their joint efforts are based on a mutual belief that each has expertise to share and can make important contributions to the effort (Loucks-Horsley et al., 1987).

Key Elements

Successful partnerships have several elements in common.

Collaboration Between Teachers and Scientists and Mathematicians. As Loucks-Horsley and associates discuss in *Continuing to Learn* (1987), partnerships for professional development can serve almost any purpose and include any number of activities. The authors describe the ways in which partnerships vary in scope and intensity and group them into three clusters: those based on support for each partner, those based on cooperation between partners, and those based on collaboration between partners. In the 10 years since Loucks-Horsley et al. wrote *Continuing to Learn,* an increasing number of partnerships have emerged that stress collaboration between teachers and scientists and mathematicians with the explicit purpose of teacher professional development.

Roles for Scientists and Mathematicians. Often, collaborative partnerships take the form of scientists and mathematicians working directly with teachers as part of a professional development program, institute, or initiative. In their roles as content experts, scientists and mathematicians strive to help teachers build confidence in teaching science and mathematics by modeling inquiry and providing them with new insights and experiences. Some of the roles they play include presenting at workshops, working with teachers to increase their content knowledge, being on-site resources, evaluating the scientific and mathematics accuracy of teaching materials, working with teachers to develop goals and classroom-based activities to achieve those goals, assisting in writing grant proposals, providing teachers access to equipment and materials, and inviting teachers into research labs for special seminars and demonstrations or to participate in experiments.

Consistent Values, Goals, and Objectives. Regardless of the specific activities, both partners need to ensure that their involvement is consistent with the values, goals, and objectives of the science or mathematics program; responds to a clearly understood educational need; supports and does not undermine either implicitly or explicitly an existing curriculum and instruction message; and has been considered and assessed by groups with different views.

Benefits to Teachers. What do the partners get from these relation-ships? For teachers, working closely with scientists and mathematicians provides exposure to role models and brings real-world application of subject matter into perspective. They have the opportunity to learn more about how the scientific and mathematics processes work—what scien-tists and mathematicians do and how and why they do it. Teachers are exposed to new perspectives and a different professional culture, and the partnership keeps them in touch with a broader knowledge base.

Benefits to Scientists and Mathematicians. For scientists and mathe-maticians, benefits include the opportunity to become familiar with the needs and realities of a school system and to become advocates for qual-ity science and mathematics education. They can examine their own teaching and become aware of how they model teaching strategies, espe-cially whether they promote active learning and quality process and con-tent teaching. Also, truly collaborative partnerships move scientists and mathematicians away from the traditional roles they have played in pub-lic education—as science fair judges, expert speakers, and hosts for field trips—and into more interactive and authentic roles of sharing the enter-prises in which they work with learners.

Implementation Requirements

For partnerships to succeed as a strategy for professional development, several requirements must be met.

Realistic Expectations. Scientists, mathematicians, and teachers must have realistic expectations about what kind of relationship they want to have, how long it will take to develop, and what is required to be successful. They must develop a history of shared experiences that, over time, build the trust and respect necessary for the high levels of involve-ment and commitment required by collaboration to improve science and mathematics teaching and learning.

Orientation and Knowledge Building. Given that the world of scien-tists and mathematicians is dramatically different from that of the teach-ers, an "introduction" to and understanding of both worlds is essential. Teachers are often intimidated by the experts, and the experts sometimes enter the education environment ready to bestow their knowledge and "fix" the problems. A successful partnership between scientists and mathematicians and teachers requires that each value the knowledge and expertise of the other, recognize the importance of the roles played by each person, and begin to learn about each other's work. For scientists and mathematicians, this includes learning about the development of children, the political and cultural environment of the school system, and the pedagogy involved in teaching science and mathematics. For teachers, this includes recognizing that scientists and mathematicians have knowledge to share with them, but that their own knowledge and skills are valuable; that they have a responsibility to help "educate" the scientists and mathematicians about their profession; and that they must help craft appropriate roles for scientists and mathematicians to play in supporting the teachers' own teaching and learning.

Involvement. Scientists, mathematicians, and teachers must all feel an equal stake in the success of the partnership, and they must be invested in quality professional development. Both partners must break out of their traditional roles and relationships (e.g., scientists and mathematicians as knowledge producers and teachers as translators of that knowledge) and develop new ones. During the process, each person's roles and expectations should be clarified. To remain interested and committed, partners must see significant results and some important benefits of being involved. When they do see results, they take credit as a team and celebrate the process and product of their joint efforts.

Commitment. A high level of commitment from all involved in the partnership is necessary to enable a partnership to be collaborative. Commitment involves significant allotments of time and energy. People often underestimate the amount of energy it takes to work with other people, especially in activities as complex as professional development. Thus, there must be administrative and organizational support for the partners. If the school and the teachers are to be more than the passive receivers of someone else's professional development program, school personnel must commit significant time and energy to planning, delivering, and following up on activities. Scientists and mathematicians also need flexibility in their schedules and their own professional responsibilities to devote the time and energy to the partnership.

Leadership. Partnerships do not form, nor do they thrive, without strong, visionary leadership. Because partnerships often feel above and beyond the call of duty to participants who already have a full work life, the motivating force of a leader (or leaders) is vital. In addition to motivation, good leadership keeps activities moving—coordinating people, timelines, and tasks so that everyone knows what is happening and the benefits are visible. In addition, within the partnership, leadership must be shared by the scientists or mathematicians and the teachers to ensure effective collaboration.

Examples

For many years, business and industry have formed partnerships with school districts and individual schools, often supporting schools in communities where they have corporate offices or plants. Those partnerships, however, have usually been characterized only by financial support for programs in the schools, the purchase of materials and resources, hosting of field trips, or presentations given in classrooms—endeavors focused more on students than on teachers. Increasingly, business and industry are examining ways of supporting the professional development of science and mathematics teachers. The NSRC in Washington, D.C., has worked for more than 10 years to connect school district teams with scientists, mathematicians, business, and industry in the pursuit of supporting teachers. Several companies, including Dow Chemical, Bristol-Myers Squibb Company, Hewlett-Packard Company, and Mile, Inc., have worked with the NSRC to provide financial support for teams of teachers, superintendents, curriculum specialists, and scientists to attend the annual National Science Education Leadership Institutes. These companies often provide financial support not only for purchasing science materials but also to establish materials distribution and refurbishment centers in the school districts once the teams have established a long-term plan for reform. In addition, many of these corporations provide funding for ongoing professional development for the teachers once they return from the institute and encourage their scientists and mathematicians to volunteer time to work with the teachers in a variety of capacities.

Project ASTRO was started by the Astronomical Society of the Pacific, which has brought together professional and amateur astronomers and teachers for more than a century. With support from the National Science Foundation, in 1993 the organization was able to play a much more active role in improving science in Grades 4 through 9. The first step was to recruit teachers and both amateur and professional astronomers who wanted to work together and to establish teams consisting of one or two teachers at a school site along with one or two amateur or professional scientists who were located as close to the school as possible.

The creators of Project ASTRO provided more than a structure for teachers and scientists to work together. They also tried to solve some of the long-standing problems. The staff were aware that most scientists who wanted to be helpful in education had little knowledge of how to do so. Frequently, scientists who volunteered time to help in the classroom tended to talk with students much as they would talk with their colleagues, emphasizing theories and technical details, and use overhead transparencies or slides that were difficult for students to understand.

Similarly, amateur astronomers would sometimes allow students to look through telescopes but rarely help students understand what they were looking at or to overcome common misconceptions in astronomy.

To avoid these pitfalls, future partners were introduced to each other at a 2-day workshop that provided training in hands-on activities and a brief background in the conceptual difficulties that students encounter when learning astronomy. In addition, each team was given a variety of resources for teaching astronomy at a level appropriate to the reasoning skills of the students. The scientists were encouraged to visit the school on at least four occasions during the ensuing school year, and they were provided with tips about how to interact with the students. An ongoing evaluation during the course of the project provided additional insights that were passed on to new participants.

The project had a positive impact on teachers, astronomers, and students. Ninety-one percent of the teachers felt that they were teaching more astronomy as a result of Project ASTRO, and 48% felt that they were teaching more science. Both teachers and astronomers felt that their knowledge of strategies for effectively teaching astronomy had increased significantly, and astronomers felt that they knew far more about how children learn and how to develop problem solving and reasoning ability in children. Many teachers also felt that their astronomy content knowledge had increased significantly as a result of Project ASTRO.

The Science for Early Educational Development project (SEED) was started as a collaborative pilot program between the California Institute of Technology and the local Pasadena Unified School District. To implement an experientially based science program, Project SEED has defined and enhanced a core program of hands-on science kits that have been successfully developed during the past 20 years by educators and scientists. An important aspect of the program is the involvement of working scientists on the teacher teams. During initial training, teams of teachers work through each hands-on science kit under the leadership of an experienced mentor teacher with the support of a science professional. In this way, the teachers become familiar with the science materials before attempting to use them in the classroom.

Rather than give lectures, scientists work side by side with the teachers as they explore the hands-on science units and focus their efforts on modeling the process involved in scientific reasoning and experimentation. When appropriate, the scientists also contribute to discussions on scientific content and the relevance of a particular science unit or topic to contemporary scientific questions. The focus of the scientists' involvement is on the actual materials the teachers use in their classrooms; this helps teachers feel comfortable and confident in their ability to teach hands-on science. Often, scientists also serve as resources to teachers because they are available to answer questions and discuss issues as they arise during the teaching of the units.

Prior to working directly with teachers, Project SEED staff meet with scientists to acquaint them with the program and to discuss their roles. The project staff have found that one of the most effective ways to orient the scientists is to have the scientists participate in the same process that the teachers, and later the students, experience. A lead teacher and an experienced scientist guide the new volunteer scientists through some of the activities in one of the hands-on kits, just as they will then do with the teachers.

The Kentucky K-4 Mathematics Specialist program has established a network of 435 K through fourth-grade mathematics specialists in 143 districts and 25 private schools throughout Kentucky. In addition to establishing a network, the program's primary goals were to implement the recommendations of the NCTM standards in elementary classrooms throughout the state and to provide opportunities for collaboration among university faculty, classroom teachers, and school administrators. Regional teams worked closely together to develop seminars to prepare K through fourth-grade teachers as mathematics specialists. The teams were composed of university mathematics educators, university mathematicians, classroom teachers, and school administrators. The program found these diverse teams to be highly effective. As Bush (1997) states, it was found that the

> regional team members gained a mutual respect for each other. Mathematicians learned to appreciate the complex task of teaching elementary school. Teachers learned to appreciate the mathematical and pedagogical expertise of the university faculty. The teachers also began to appreciate the depth of mathematics and theoretical perspectives held by the university faculty. The seminars were strengthened by the input and collaboration of persons with different backgrounds. The activities and information provided in seminars were mathematically sound, pedagogically sound, and classroom tested. (p. 174)

Commentary

Although bringing teachers together with scientists and mathematicians can be a powerful learning experience for all involved, there are often challenges to face and obstacles to overcome.

As noted previously, participants in the partnership face cultural and communication differences. Teachers, scientists, and mathematicians live in different worlds and have their own languages unique to their disciplines. It is imperative for successful partnering that all involved have opportunities to appreciate and recognize the value of each partner's discipline. At the onset of a partnership, teachers, scientists, and mathematicians need orientation to help them understand the realities of each other's worlds. Scientists and mathematicians must understand needs in science and mathematics education and know about student competencies and developmental learning. They must develop an understanding of how they can bring a piece of what they do in their own world to their interactions with the teachers and to give and receive feedback from teachers.

Sometimes, issues arise regarding the expectations that scientists and mathematicians have when entering into the partnership: that they are there to "fix" the situation, believing the educational problems can be solved if only the teachers will listen to them. If they have this perspective, they may want to take control and have difficulty treating teachers as equals with their own valid expertise. Also, some scientists and mathematicians see the school as an environment in which they can identify a handful of people interested in moving into their fields rather than a place where the knowledge of all can be increased. These views affect how they approach the professional development of teachers: If teachers' main purpose is to educate the selected few, scientists and mathematicians tend to be less cognizant of the need to enhance the teachers' overall knowledge base but, instead, focus more on specific content. Also, if these scientists and mathematicians teach through lecture, they will be less likely to value the inquiring nature of learning science and mathematics.

Scientists and mathematicians often face the obstacle of not receiving support, recognition, or encouragement from their organizations, institutions, or universities to pursue relationships and partnerships in settings outside of their normal working environments. They have conflicting demands to continue with research in the laboratory, publish journal articles and books, and make significant contributions to their fields. Although the values and priorities in many institutions are beginning to shift toward the value of scientists and mathematicians working with teachers, there is still a long way to go in moving this forward.

Finally, teachers sometimes fear intrusion by outsiders, especially those whom the teachers view as the ultimate experts. They can feel intimidated by the presence of scientists and mathematicians and not recognize that they bring their own expertise to the partnership. Feeling the respect of scientists and mathematicians for their work as teachers goes a long way toward solidifying and enhancing the relationship and ultimately benefiting students.

Additional Resources

Bowers, J. (1994). Scientists and science education reform: Myths, methods, and madness. In *Scientists, educators, and national standards: Action at the local level, forum proceedings, April 14-15*, Sigma Xi, The Scientific Research Society (pp. 123-130). Research Triangle Park, NC: The Scientific Research Society.

Friel, S. N., & Bright, G. W. (Eds.). (1997). *Reflecting on our Work: NSF teacher enhancement in K-6 mathematics.* Lanham, MD: University Press of America.

National Research Council, Commission on Life Sciences, Board on Biology, Committee on Biology Teacher Inservice Programs. (1996). *The role of scientists in the professional development of science teachers.* Washington, DC: National Academy Press.

National Science Resources Center, National Science Education Leadership Institute, Washington, DC. (Phone: 202-287-2063)

Project ASTRO, Astronomical Society of the Pacific, San Francisco.

Project SEED, Science for Early Education Development, Pasadena Unified School District, Pasadena, CA. (Phone: 818-791-8932)

Sussman, A. (Ed.). (1993). *Science education partnerships: Manual for scientists and K-12 teachers.* San Francisco: University of California.

Professional Networks

When Christine Moore applied to be a local coordinator for her state's science and mathematics reform initiative, she never dreamed how it would benefit her own teaching and increase her knowledge and skills. As a local coordinator, she became actively involved in two networks of teachers. The first was statewide and involved all the 30 teachers who were selected as local coordinators. The second was the network of teachers Christine created in her own local district. The statewide network meets once every other month to demonstrate use of new classroom materials, discuss developments from research and practice in the fields of science and mathematics teaching, and respond to one another's questions and issues. Between meetings, the state network members keep in touch through e-mail and phone calls. Several times each month, Christine replicates the state network meetings with teachers in her own district. In after-school meetings, teachers in her district demonstrate lessons, discuss student learning, and present issues and problems for discussion.

Christine has been amazed at the insight many of her district colleagues have offered, and she takes these ideas and information back to her state network for wider consumption. The district network teachers are working together on cross-grade projects and are generating enthusiasm

among other teachers. All the teachers participating in the network report
improvements in their teaching and more comfort asking other teachers
in their buildings for help and ideas.

A network is an organized professional community that has a common theme or purpose. Individuals join networks to share their own knowledge and experience with other network members and learn from other network participants. Networks appear through school-university collaborations; teacher-to-teacher or school-to-school linkages; partnerships with neighborhood organizations, teacher unions, and subject-matter associations; and local or national groups. In education, these communities are often organized to improve teaching of a particular subject matter, to address pedagogy for teaching certain content or students or both, or in support of particular school reforms.

Networks often articulate specific goals and purposes, recruit their members, and have scheduled activities, such as summer institutes, regular meetings, electronic discussions, newsletters, or chat rooms. In addition to drawing on the expertise of network members, many formal networks also involve individuals who are experts in areas of interest to the network participants. For example, a network of scientists and science educators who participated in writing the *National Science Education Standards* (NRC, 1996) might provide guidance to teachers as they implement the standards. A network that is focused on making high school curriculum and instruction relevant to students' futures might involve employers who can share information about the knowledge and skills needed in the workplace.

One of the most important elements of maintaining a network is to keep people engaged and connected. Effective networks have means to update members when they miss a meeting or other networking event. Mechanisms such as a buddy system or publishing minutes of discussions help to ensure continuity among participants.

Not all networks are structured formally; informal networks can also provide opportunities for exchanging information and getting professional support. For example, teachers in a city or region involved in implementing an innovation such as a new curriculum or trying to create more student-centered instruction might decide to meet regularly to discuss what they are learning, share resources, and identify and solve problems. Likewise, physics teachers from a district or region, who are often alone in their schools, may, through an informal network, share teaching materials and ideas and information about resources or learning opportunities. These informal networks can often benefit from being recognized by the teachers' schools or districts or both as legitimate professional development activities.

Underlying Assumptions

The use of professional networks as a strategy for professional development is based on several assumptions about teachers, learning, and professional development.

Adults are social by nature and benefit from interacting with other
individuals who have similar purposes and interests as they learn. Networks can nurture a professional community, developing norms of
collegiality, continuous improvement, and experimentation. Common
interests, experiences, and frequent interaction result in a common language regarding issues in science and mathematics that encourages
frequent communication about improvement. Teachers are no longer
isolated in their classrooms, struggling alone with issues of teaching and
learning. Active network members have access to a variety of opportunities for peer support in their efforts to experiment with new ideas and
practices in science and mathematics.

Teachers have knowledge and experience to share with one another,
and mechanisms that create opportunities for such sharing contribute to
improvements in practice. Networks build the capacity of their members
to identify and solve their own problems. Shared experiences increase
the knowledge pool within a network—ideas and knowledge build as
members try new approaches and have in-depth discussions about how
something did or did not work. As they grapple with their growing
understanding and reflect on and discuss their experimentation and implementation, teachers develop a sense of efficacy and confidence in
their individual and collective ability to identify and solve their own
problems and make improvements in their different contexts. Through
conferencing with each other, linking by computer networks, having
access to computer databases, visiting other schools, teaching others
about what they have learned, attending conferences, and participating
in partnerships, teachers gain new information that informs their decision making and enhances their ability to effectively address issues of
teaching and learning.

Meaningful improvement in educational programs occurs best when
members of an educational community share common beliefs and work
together toward common goals. Networks provide a forum for education
professionals to get to know one another over time and share and evaluate different perspectives and thoughts about educational practice. As
networks mature, members begin to identify and emphasize their com-

mon beliefs and make progress toward meeting the goals they have set for themselves.

Key Elements

Networks may emerge spontaneously or they may be more consciously created. Whatever their origin, networks share some key elements that lead to their effectiveness.

Interactions Among Members. Interactions within a network are ongoing and are focused on a particular subject or purpose. Networks are "discourse communities" that enable teachers to meet regularly (either in person or electronically, e.g., through e-mail) to solve problems, consider new ideas, evaluate alternatives, or reflect on specific issues in science and mathematics (Lieberman & McLaughlin, 1992). Sometimes they are self-directed, with the participants defining their own agendas; sometimes they are moderated by experienced facilitators who encourage the exchange of ideas within the community. In defining the focus, teachers build an agenda that is sensitive to their contexts and concerns and commit themselves to goals that are broader and more inclusive than their initial concerns. Learning networks must have a high level of trust among participants so that people feel free to disclose information about what they think, how they teach, and what they need and to take personal risks, such as being a critical friend to other members. Achieving the level of trust needed to support direct communication takes time but is useful as a ground rule from the very beginning of the network.

Membership. Membership in most networks is voluntary. Members are committed to a new idea or philosophy and develop loyalty to each other. Networks maintain an atmosphere of openness and sharing that helps fellow members see each other as problem solvers. In creating this atmosphere, members demonstrate trust, flexibility, and informality in their contacts with other network members.

Effective Communication. A network is not a network without ongoing communication. The more varied the interactions, the more likely the participants are to remain involved and committed to the efforts. Good communications allow all network members to benefit from one another's input and create records that are accessible by members who may have missed a particular meeting or interaction or want to review information. Ground rules encourage everyone to participate equally and to respect the ideas of others.

Broad Perspective. Networks help members develop perspectives that stretch beyond the walls of their classroom or school. Through interactions in the network, teachers gain new knowledge and access to research-based resources beyond their schools or districts. Effective networks promote sharing of information and ideas with other professionals in different environments and help teachers broaden their perspective of and exposure to issues. Creating an essentially new structure for teachers' involvement and learning outside of their workplaces results in new norms of collegiality, a broadened view of leadership, enhanced perspectives on students' needs, opportunities to be both learners and partners in the construction of knowledge, and an authentic professional voice for teachers.

Facilitation and Leadership. Effective networks require the clear assignment of responsibility for managing the network, orchestrating its activities, brokering resources from diverse segments of the community, and promoting and sustaining the involvement of teachers and others. In some formal networks, the designated leader(s) may be in organizations that have funding for network support. In informal networks, leadership is more emergent, it may rotate, but it is nonetheless critical to maintain momentum. Capable network leaders are visionary, effective in a variety of contexts (e.g., schools, universities, private sector, and community), comfortable with ambiguity and willing to be flexible, knowledgeable about the focus of the network and its communication mechanisms, organized, action oriented, and able to nurture leadership in participants.

Implementation Requirements

Successful networks share common implementation requirements whether they are organized around subject matter, teaching methods, school improvement, or restructuring efforts in mathematics and science. To successfully initiate and sustain a network, several requirements must be met.

Clear Focus of Activity. Networks need a purpose. As networks recruit participants, these new recruits need to know why they are joining and what they can expect to get from their investment of time. The focus of the network might be broadly defined at first, giving members the opportunity to fine-tune the purpose to address their common interests and objectives. New interests and more complex relationships may emerge through networking; there is, however, a need to retain the initial focus or declare that the purpose is shifting in response to a new condition. If the intent of the network becomes unclear, there is a greater chance that the network will become irrelevant for many participants.

Size and Logistical Requirements. The strength, endurance, and effectiveness of a network are often directly related to its lack of complexity and the low cost of active participation. Although some electronic networks may be able to handle large numbers of participants, networks that rely on in-person interactions and prompting from a trained facilitator must be a reasonable size to allow for adequate interaction among all participants. With adequate resources, strategies such as tiered or multiple leadership can allow for larger membership.

Communication Mechanisms. Whether network members have in-person meetings, attend local or regional association meetings, or meet electronically, their networks must have effective mechanisms for promoting communication. Mechanisms such as a collaborative calendar, newsletter, classroom visits among members, topic-specific discussion groups, or a resource book or other means for sharing new information and materials can expand the network and help members to make better use of the new knowledge and ideas they gain.

Monitoring Progress and Impact. Effective networks pay attention to how they meet the needs of members and how they can improve. They assign responsibility for monitoring the progress of the network. Because participants' needs change over time, it is important to keep tabs on whether the network is keeping pace. Asking members to comment regularly on their satisfaction with the network and suggest ideas for improvement can keep a network strong and vital.

Examples

The purpose of the Urban Mathematics Collaborative (UMC) is to support teachers of mathematics, and at some sites science, to address and resolve poor mathematics performance of inner-city students. Initiated by the Ford Foundation and involving some of the largest school districts in the nation, the network connects urban teachers with one another, other users of mathematics, and individuals involved in mathematics education reform. The UMC exposes teachers to new ideas, providing them with information about how students learn mathematics and what mathematics should be taught in the curriculum. The network focuses considerable resources on the development of teacher leaders. Teachers learn mathematics content and pedagogy and group facilitation skills, enabling them to lead presentations and support reforms in their schools.

The success of the collaboratives at sites throughout the country rests on many of the important assumptions and critical elements noted in this chapter: Teachers join the network voluntarily and with a commitment to improving their teaching; the network provides support for teachers' experimentation in their classrooms through collegial support and feedback; the collaboratives create a community of learners sharing a common vision of mathematics education reform; and they exist independently of the school district within which they function, with the goals and agenda of the interactions determined by the teachers themselves.

Another network at the national level, the Mathematics Learning Forums, helps teachers introduce new mathematics teaching practices in their classrooms. Teachers from throughout the country participate in this telecommunications network, a program of the Bank Street College of Education's Mathematics Leadership Program and the Center for Children and Technology of the Education Development Center, Inc. The network has a clearly defined purpose: to help teachers do mathematics with their students and talk about mathematics with their colleagues. Forums are convened by a facilitator who provides guidance about mathematics instruction and encourages teachers as they try new strategies. Teachers pay close attention to the learning of their students, their own learning, and that of their forum colleagues. Each forum is limited to 12 participants, and participants enroll for 8 weeks. In addition to on-line discussions, teachers view videotapes and work with students on new strategies for mathematics.

During the past 9 years, elementary school teachers in California have had the opportunity to become part of a statewide network, California Science Implementation Network (CSIN). CSIN actually began in 1988, prior to the National Science Foundation funding of the Statewide Systemic Initiative, as a fledgling teacher-leader network with one statewide director, 25 teacher trainers (science staff developers), and 50 schools. During its 9-year history, CSIN (with NSF funding) has grown to 12 regional directors and more than 200 staff developers. In the process, CSIN has assisted more than 1,700 elementary schools to plan and implement quality science programs, and it has influenced how schools operate—from finances to teacher collaboration and student learning.

The network has a strong leadership structure that provides assistance to its members (schools and teachers) and a clear purpose—to provide in-depth professional development for entire school staffs on the content and pedagogy of science instructional materials; to build site and district leadership capacity by creating an infrastructure for systemic change; to continue to develop staffs who are knowledgeable about science reform and who teach with confidence and content strength toward that effort; and to create an ongoing, living network that maintains an advocacy for elementary science as a basic and core subject while assisting elementary schools in holistic systemic reform of the elementary school program.

Four levels of interacting networks enable the "inside-out systemic reform strategies" to react to and advocate for programs and policies to meet the needs of the schools. At each school, the implementation team, science staff developer, and scientist cadre, with the assistance from the regional director, plan for and implement 50 hours of on-site professional development for the entire staff. On the local level, clusters of three to five schools meet monthly with their staff developer to share common concerns, successes, content knowledge, and strategies for implementation in the classroom. Three times a year, regional meetings bring together clusters, their science staff developers, and the regional directors to articulate common efforts and discuss issues related to content, pedagogy, and implementation. The meetings are for K through 12th-grade teachers and enable participants to network with other reform efforts. Statewide, the science staff developers, cadres, and regional directors meet twice yearly to determine implementation goals and strategies for improving science education. These meetings are devoted to enhancing the leadership skills, content knowledge, and teaching experiences of all CSIN professional development providers.

The Association of Science Materials Centers (ASMC) networks people in school districts from across the country. ASMC members meet annually to share information about the design of science teaching materials, resources for materials, and strategies for reducing the cost of inquiry-based science teaching. Members also provide information on how to establish and sustain a central science materials support center.

Commentary

Networks can be successful strategies for providing professional development for individual teachers and are especially effective in reducing isolation among teachers. Frequently, networks provide a forum for interaction with peers from other parts of the community and throughout the country or internationally. In the process, individual teachers become part of a collegial, cohesive professional community that examines and reflects on issues related to teaching and learning. In addition to engaging teachers in collective work on issues that emerge out of their own efforts, networks provide support, encouragement, motivation, and intellectual and emotional stimulation. For those involved in the process of change, networks provide a venue for teachers to recognize that they are part of a profession that is also in the process of change.

This can help legitimize local reform efforts and increase the communication between and among levels of the system.

Sustaining effective networks, however, can be difficult. Lieberman and McLaughlin (1992) discuss the following issues that network organizers and participants must address:

Application: Although networks provide a forum for teachers to explore and discuss issues relevant to teaching and learning, the intention is that the new practices and perspectives they acquire will influence their work with students. One challenge that networks face is that the network may draw teachers' loyalty and interest away from the school to the network itself. Consciously addressing this issue in discussions and activities within the network can help increase the likelihood that teachers will apply and implement their new learnings in their classrooms.

Gaining support within the school: Often, teachers in networks feel ostracized within their own schools by other teachers, the principal, or the administration. Addressing this issue is imperative; some formal networks require that all teachers in a department within a school participate in the network. This, however, "violates" the network credo of remaining voluntary and imposes a requirement that is not always conducive to the trusting environment inherent in effective networks.

Stability: Network participants and organizers must secure long-term funding and support. This includes not only financial support but also the establishment of structures to help ensure the long-term sustainability for the network, such as legitimate time for teacher participation and, when necessary, access to computers and other equipment needed to participate in the network.

Overextension: Managing a network is a fundamental problem for both networks and their sponsors. The more popular the network, the greater the demand on its limited resources. It is easy to underestimate what it will take to maintain and then to "scale up" a network. It requires new leaders to facilitate the network and nurture the new members. This challenge may require restricting membership to a size appropriate to both resources and capacity to serve members well.

Ownership: Some networks that are initiated by foundations, by schools and university partnerships, or by national or local reform efforts have their own agendas. This can result in a problem about who controls the agenda. Because the power of networks lies in their flexibility, their agendas are in a constant state of refinement rather than irrevocably fixed in time or place. Sometimes, however, the partners with the money or status or both become uncomfortable as teachers are emboldened to take more control.

Expanding objectives: Most networks are formed around specific goals, but as new responsibilities and roles emerge teachers often find themselves in roles they are unaccustomed to playing: political strategist, negotiator, policymaker, or conflict mediator. Networks must address the issue of emerging roles and how to provide teachers with opportunities for taking advantage of and learning from these new roles.

Evaluation: Networks need constant evaluation to gather information on results and how well they meet the needs of members. The success of networks relies on teachers' perceptions that their own goals are being served. Modifications in network practice should address deficiencies and maintain quality. This will help the network stay true to its purpose and avoid being influenced solely by issues of funding or political pressures.

Additional Resources

Association of Science Materials Centers, c/o Science and Social Sciences Resource Specialist, Mesa Public Schools, Mesa, AZ. (Phone: 602-898-7815)

Cusick, P. A. (1982). *A study of networks among professional staffs in secondary schools.* East Lansing: Michigan State University, Institute for Research on Teaching.

Dempsey, E. (1995). IMPACT II: A teacher-to-teacher networking program. *Educational Leadership, 42*(4), 41-45.

Honey, M., Bennett, D., Hupert, N., Kanze, B., Meade, T., Panush, E. M., Powell, K., Spielvogel, R., Dubitsky, B., Cohen, M., Melnick, H., & Peterson, L. (1994). The Mathematics Learning Forums online: Using telecommunications as a tool for reflective practice. *Machine-Mediated-Learning, 4*(2/3), 163-176.

Katz, M. M., McSwiney, E., & Stroud, K. (1987). *Facilitating collegial exchange among science teachers by writing: The use of computer-based conferencing.* Cambridge, MA: Harvard University, Harvard Graduate School of Education, Educational Technology Center.

Loucks-Horsley, S., Harding, C. K., Arbuckle, M. A., Murray, L. B., Dubea, C., & Williams, M. K. (1987). Networks. In *Continuing to learn: A guidebook for teacher development* (pp. 110-115). Andover, MA/Oxford, OH: The Regional Laboratory for Educational Improvement of the Northeast and Islands/National Staff Development Council.

Riel, M., & Levin, J. A. (1990). Building electronic communities: Success and failure in computer networking. *Instructional Science, 19,* 145-169.

Ruopp, R., Gal, S., Drayton, B., & Pfister, M. (1993). *LabNet: Toward a community of practice.* Hillsdale, NJ: Lawrence Erlbaum.

Webb, N., Tate, B., & Heck, D. (1995, February). *The Urban Mathematics Collaborative Project: A study of teacher, community, and reform.* Unpublished manuscript.

Developing Professional Developers

Sandra Hart had taught fourth grade for 5 years when her school became a pilot site for the district's new science program. She and her colleagues received the new set of instructional materials and participated in 3 days of workshops for each of the next 2 years. When the district recruited teachers to help prepare and support other teachers to use the program, she readily volunteered because she loved using it with her students and wanted to share the many strategies she had developed to make it work well in her classroom.

Sandra and nine other teachers became the staff developers for the program. They attended a 2-week leadership academy during the summer, at which they increased their understanding and honed their skills in the program; learned to conduct workshops; practiced skills in coaching, consultation, and collaboration; and learned about the change process. Released half-time to be staff developers for two schools each, the 10 teachers met weekly and, with the support and assistance of the district's curriculum coordinator, designed and implemented a plan for districtwide program change.

The strategy of identifying and developing professional developers has been widely used in mathematics and science improvement. When professional development was narrowly construed as training, this strategy was more commonly called "train the trainer." Now, however, as professional development has broadened to include a variety of strategies to support professional learning, so too have the roles and attendant skills of those who would help professionals learn. Train the trainer has become "professionally develop the professional developer!"

This strategy has two distinct benefits to the individuals involved. First, individuals who serve as professional developers increase their own knowledge and skills in mathematics and science, learning, and teaching. The following adage applies: There is no better way to learn something than to have to teach it. Second, the new professional developers acquire skills and knowledge well beyond what they need to teach students—those required to support change. These additional abilities help schools, departments, and districts become learning organizations with the capacities and dispositions to collaborate, experiment, and continuously improve. This can result in more learning for all students and all members of the school community.

The strategy of developing professional developers designates teachers, administrators, or other school personnel, or all three, as leaders or trainers for a particular program or change initiative. These individuals

are responsible for preparing others to use the new program or participate in the change. The preparation and support of these new professional developers is critical to their success and requires careful planning for effective recruitment, training, incentives, and support.

Effective professional developers need a broad range of knowledge
and skills. Depending on the roles they play—for example, trainer, mentor, coach, or consultant—they must develop expertise in organizational
change, adult learning and development, coaching, effective teaching
and learning, evaluation, and many of the professional development
strategies described in this chapter.

As an organization or project considers its long-term professional development plan, the strategy described in this section is very important.
There are many benefits to using local professionals to assume the many
professional development roles. It provides accessible local "talent" who
can implement new programs and professional development. It builds
local capacity for ongoing development and can serve as a reward for
teachers and other professionals who have the requisite skills, attitudes,
and interest. Investing in professional developers also provides the
school, district, or project with individuals who can connect those in the
organization to innovations occurring outside through national and regional networking.

The processes for preparing professional developers have been
evolving during the past two decades. Ten years ago, there were few formal programs for professional developers. Most grew into their roles by
implementing new instructional practices and sharing the good ones
with colleagues and sometimes attending "train-the-trainer" workshops.
The lack of a career path for these "homegrown" staff developers often
led them to leave their classrooms or schools to become consultants and
trainers in private and public organizations. Increasingly, as school
districts or other professional development initiatives seek to build local
capacity for continuous learning and development, they are using the
strategy of developing their own professional developers.

Underlying Assumptions

The use of the development of professional developers as a strategy is
based on several assumptions about teachers, learning, and professional
development.

*Well-prepared local professional developers are highly committed to
the success of the professional development program.* Individuals who are
prepared to use a particular program or approach, use it successfully
themselves, and then support the learning of their peers have a high

degree of commitment to making the change work. Their enthusiasm and commitment builds competence and ownership in others as they learn and implement new approaches.

Aspiring professional developers can learn and then successfully use the skills needed to support others to change. This assumes that, like teachers, good professional developers do not have to be born but rather can develop the requisite abilities. It also assumes that they can use these skills with their peers in their local settings and have the intended impact.

Local professional developers have a better understanding of their context than do outsiders and are able to adapt new programs to work best in their local settings. Outside consultants rarely know a school's local conditions well enough to anticipate the adaptations that may be needed in a program. Local professional developers can relate to the needs of the teachers and students in their schools and are able to identify and implement needed changes in the programs.

Key Elements

There are several key elements of developing professional developers as a strategy.

Professional developers have a critical set of knowledge, skills, and attitudes. These include a thorough knowledge of the best practices in teaching, learning, and school organization; self-awareness and the ability to be self-critical; willingness to learn from mistakes and successes; knowledge of schools, both the learning and teaching processes, and the political structures and culture; knowledge of how adults learn; and an understanding of the process of implementing and evaluating changes. Professional developers must also be skillful organizers and coordinators; often called on to raise funds for new programs, they must be skilled in grant writing and fund development. Effective professional developers are flexible, adaptable, and creative. They value the knowledge adults bring to their learning experiences and are willing to take risks and experiment with new approaches and ideas.

Professional developers work with teachers and other educators in a variety of ways. The work of the professional developer is varied depending on the goals of the change initiative and the strategy being used. When new curriculum is being implemented, professional developers conduct workshops and in-class demonstrations, coach teachers, facilitate after-school problem-solving or trouble-shooting sessions, brief and consult with administrators, and possibly organize material support systems. When content knowledge is being enriched, professional developers may teach content courses, lead study groups focused on content updates, and select and introduce replacement units that are rich in new content not previously taught by teachers.

Implementation Requirements

There are several requirements for implementing this strategy well.

Identify potential professional developers. One source is individuals who have had some other leadership experience, including those who have served as coaches or mentors, "certified trainers," instructors or clinical faculty for university courses, or team leaders or department chairs with teacher support responsibilities in their schools. These experiences are likely to have broadened the individuals' perspectives beyond their classrooms and to have given them opportunities to develop effective ways of working with adults. Professional developers can be teachers, especially good teachers whom others emulate and respect. Either way, successful professional developers have certain attributes in common. For example, they are open to change, are credible with teachers, are effective communicators, and have experiences and knowledge that are relevant to the staff with whom they will work. They are self-confident and organized, and they work well with their peers. They have the time available to engage in their own development and, ultimately, to work with others in a professional development role.

Master the program, knowledge base, or change that will support the learning of others. They know it, can demonstrate it, have made it a routine in their teaching, and have evidence that it works with their students. This usually takes at least two rounds of practice or application, which may mean 2 years, before they are able to teach and support others.

Develop competencies for effective professional developers. There is no one prescription for developing the requisite skills and knowledge of professional developers. Many colleges and universities now offer courses that address inservice education, coaching, collaboration, and change management in schools. Some institutions (e.g., the University of Maryland) offer doctoral-level training in staff development. More commonly, school-based professional developers develop the necessary skills through workshops on effective training, team development, and change management (many of which are offered by the Association for

Supervision and Curriculum Development and the National Staff Development Council) and by continuing their development in their particular area of expertise (e.g., science education, assessment practice, and action research). They are involved in self-study and networks and are mentored by more experienced staff developers. They read journal articles, attend training or conferences, and join on-line networks.

Allocate time to do the work. Designing and conducting learning experiences for others is not a job that can be done after school and on weekends if it is to be done correctly. When local professional developers are used well, they have time released from student responsibilities to do their work.

Communicate clear expectations for professional developers. One way the school administration supports local professional developers is to communicate clear expectations for performance, time requirements, and available resources. In addition, issues that can create problems or signal a lack of support are anticipated, such as how the new professional developers will be introduced to their peers and what, if any, benefits or rewards the professional developer will receive for taking on the new role.

Link with other professional developers. Collegiality and collaboration among professional developers leads to many positive outcomes. Professional developers need access to many resources—the latest findings from research and information about effective programs—and an awareness of the quality of training programs and curriculum. Professional developers cannot work in isolation; they must continually expand their knowledge and stay current in the field. Through national and regional networking, they gain access to these important resources and continue their own development.

Conduct ongoing evaluation of programs and performance. Evaluation of the professional development program is critical to ensuring the program's quality. The professional developer and school staff should gather formal and informal feedback on all professional development activity through a variety of mechanisms (e.g., surveys, observations, and interviews). Data should be analyzed to determine what, if any, changes are needed in the programs. Similarly, the performance of professional developers can be monitored on an ongoing basis, with opportunities to discuss strengths and weaknesses and areas that can be improved.

Examples

One role for a professional developer is as a facilitator in case discussions. Carne Barnett, whose work on mathematics case discussions has contributed much to understanding this professional development strategy, describes what she has learned in the process of becoming an effective facilitator of case discussions as follows (Barnett & Friedman, in press):

> As a facilitator, I also had to learn to depend on case discussion participants to modify their own opinions and ideas as their pedagogical content knowledge grew. However, it was not a laissez-faire approach. I learned ways to evoke deeper analysis of student thinking, to elicit alternative points of view by playing devil's advocate, and to press for justifications and consequences of various ideas. I learned to "pull" ideas from the group and ways to reflect them back for further analysis. I continue to grapple with the balance between taking an active role in the discussion process, sharing authority with the group, and maintaining my neutrality toward the ideas brought up.

Although Barnett is an experienced professional developer, her comments reflect the need for continual growth and refinement of skills and abilities, no matter how experienced the professional developer.

Developing professional developers has been critical to the success of CSIN. A statewide network for elementary teachers, CSIN's 12 regional directors and more than 200 staff developers have assisted more than 1,700 elementary schools in planning and implementing quality science programs.

CSIN's regional directors each work with 8 to 12 science staff developers, who in turn work with clusters of three to five schools represented by their implementation team (lead teacher, administrator, and parent). The regional directors and science staff developers, along with the teaching cadre (a university or industry scientist, a high school science teacher, and an elementary science teacher who team teach the content and pedagogy), provide intensive professional development to the implementation team. With the support of the staff developer, regional director, and teaching cadre, the lead teacher and implementation team deliver professional development to the entire faculty.

CSIN "develops professional developers" at many levels of its infrastructure. First, the lead teachers are a critical link between CSIN and schoolwide change. They represent both experienced and novice teacher leaders—and the majority participate because they like science, want to do a better job in their classrooms, and want to assist their schools in schoolwide implementation of science. Lead teachers are selected by the school or district and are given 5 release days during the school year and a stipend at district discretion. Lead teachers attend 21 institute days throughout the year to experience and learn science content and pedagogy, explore instructional materials, and develop their leadership skills for systemic reform. They also provide, with extensive support from the staff developer, regional director, and cadres, 50 hours of professional development to their school staffs. In this process, they are mentored, they practice leadership skills, and they address content and pedagogy issues and school issues.

The development of the science staff developers offers another glimpse into the effort CSIN exerts in supporting leadership within the network. Through the years, the staff developers have proven to be one of the most critical pieces in the statewide reform because of their numbers and the fact that many were already recognized leaders (e.g., mentors) or had district positions. Staff developers are selected by their districts. Many are classroom teachers who are released 25 days a year to work with their five schools. They also receive a modest stipend to provide the 21-day Lead Teacher Program. In addition, they participate in 10 days of professional development for themselves. The Staff Developer Program provides 5 days of intensive content and science experience and 5 days of intensive leadership development. The content is taught by the scientist cadres; the leadership is provided by regional directors and recognized experts. A unique part of the program is the "CSIN Manual," which is a guide for the Lead Teacher Program. This manual represents hours of discussion, planning, and reflection about issues and how they might be addressed. The time spent developing the manual prepares the staff developers to facilitate the in-depth discussions that take place in the lead teacher institutes.

Developing a cadre of teacher professional developers to work with other teachers is also a strategy supported by the Systemic Initiative for Montana Mathematics and Science (SIMMS). The SIMMS project has nine major objectives, including the redesign of Grades 9 through 12 mathematics curriculum using an integrated mathematics program that emphasizes the relationship among topics within mathematics and between mathematics and other disciplines. The curriculum is written, revised, and reviewed by high school teachers of mathematics and science and is designed as a complete curriculum to replace existing courses. The materials are divided into 16 modules, each addressing the integration of mathematics topics.

A significant component of the SIMMS project is professional development. Teachers attend one of three intense, weeklong summer institutes that are offered nationally: mathematics as a lab discipline, assessment, and one based on the T3 model (Teachers Teaching with Technology). SIMMS leadership has worked with more than 35 high school master teachers to prepare them for facilitating the summer institutes. These teachers are themselves users of the SIMMS curriculum and have attended seminars focused on enhancing their leadership and facilitation skills. Maurice Burke (personal communication, April 1997), the project codirector of SIMMS, strongly believes in and supports the development of the master teachers as institute facilitators:

> We have found the experience of teaching the curriculum lends credibility to the master teachers. They are intimately familiar with the curriculum and the teaching strategies and have developed effective facilitation skills. These all add up to enhance the quality of the institutes and the learning on the part of the participating teachers.

Another initiative that focuses on developing teachers as professional development leaders is the Leadership for Urban Mathematics Reform (LUMR) project, developed by the Education Development Center in collaboration with the UMC and their local school districts. LUMR is developing teacher leaders in urban communities at six UMC sites throughout the country in an effort to move forward systemic reform in mathematics education. The project provides leadership training for teams of middle and high school teachers from these sites. Teachers attend 3-week summer leadership institutes, receive follow-up leadership training and support throughout the year, and receive technical assistance in their outreach efforts. A critical component of LUMR is the inclusion of district administrators on the leadership teams. Each team develops a plan that promotes reform of mathematics education, provides district support, and facilitates teacher leadership.

Commentary

Becoming a professional developer is a process that includes developing expertise as a teacher, then as a trainer or coach or both in a particular content area or program, and finally as a leader, facilitator, evaluator, and negotiator. Effective professional developers, like effective teachers, are continuous learners who are constantly seeking out new ideas, trying them, and making adjustments to meet the needs of their clients and colleagues. They require time and a commitment to ongoing learning. This combination is often hard to find in schools. Teachers are busy people who face many demands and pressures. Some people believe that professional development would be better left to consultants and outside experts. They argue that teachers should focus on good teaching and that professional developers require a different set of skills from those of good teachers. Because teachers are expected to align their practices with one another and collaborate on new initiatives, however, they need the skills of good professional developers. Schools and districts must create the opportunity for them to become professional developers—to learn over time and help them assess their performance and reflect on their work.

Quality control is a key concern as schools and projects develop professional developers from among the teaching staff. New professional developers are unlikely to be as effective as the expert consultant who has been honing skills for years. They need encouragement, observation, and coaching as they take on their new roles. At the same time, the professional development provided must be of the highest quality. Pairing a developing professional developer with a veteran is one strategy for ensuring quality. Engaging professional developers in debriefing sessions after they conduct workshops, model lessons, or work with a team helps professional developers learn from their experience and increase their effectiveness. Feedback from participants in professional development activities can be used to assess program quality and make continuous improvements in the professional developers' offerings and approaches.

As teachers and others become professional developers, they also must establish their "credentials" so that they have the respect and support of their colleagues. It is said that it is difficult to be a prophet in your own land. Effective professional developers demonstrate their skills, are a source of useful information and resources, and value and respect the contributions of their colleagues. They share the credit for the programs they support. Their success comes from building support among their colleagues and sharing the credit when they reach key milestones.

The role of professional developer is demanding and often thankless. The professional developer must juggle schedules, encourage resistant staff members, negotiate with school administrators and the community for resources and support, and stay current in areas of expertise. These demands, coupled with a teaching or administrative position, can lead to the professional developer becoming overextended and overwhelmed. Although developing local staff who have the expertise and abilities of professional developers is a beneficial strategy, these individuals need support to balance their multiple roles.

Additional Resources

Flora, V. R., & Applegate, J. (1982). Concerns and continuing education interests of staff developers. *Journal of Staff Development, 3*(2), 29-37.

Koll, P., & Anderson, J. (1982). Cooking and staff development: A blend of training and experience. *Journal of Staff Development, 3*(2), 45-53.

Leadership for Urban Mathematics Reform (LUMR), Education Development Center, Newton, MA. (Phone: 617-969-7100)

Loucks-Horsley, S., Harding, C. K., Arbuckle, M. A., Murray, L. B., Dubea, C., & Williams, M. K. (1987). *Continuing to learn: A guidebook for teacher development.* Andover, MA/Oxford, OH: The Regional Laboratory for Educational Improvement of the Northeast and Islands/The National Staff Development Council.

Sparks, D. (1982). Staff developers: Where have they come from? And what do they know? *Journal of Staff Development, 3*(2), 38-44.

Systemic Initiative for Montana Mathematics and Science (SIMMS) (Maurice Burke, Codirector), Montana State University, Bozeman.

Teacher Enhancement Electronic Communications Hall (TEECH) (NSF-funded electronic community), TERC, Cambridge, MA. (Phone: 617-547-0430)

Teachers Teaching with Technology (T3), University of Texas at Arlington. (Phone: 817-272-5828)

Technology for Professional Learning

Technology could be considered everything from paper and pencil to elaborate communication devices. For our purposes, we define *technology for professional development* as an electronic means of either supporting the "in-person" professional developer or of providing professional development opportunities without a face-to-face facilitator. Furthermore, we choose to focus on technologies that have emerged in the past 20 years rather than the more traditional ones, such as overhead and slide projectors.

What may immediately come to mind for the reader is the Internet and electronic mail systems. In this section, we expand on these two systems and, in addition, present ways in which a variety of other technologies can be used to provide effective professional development experiences for teachers of mathematics and science. In doing so, we depart from the format used to describe other strategies. Because there is such a wide variety of technologies in use for professional development, we begin by describing features they have in common and then describe the different forms they take. We then discuss some of the many issues that have arisen in their use.

Key Features of Technologies for Professional Development

Technology presents opportunities for diverse learning experiences. Given the variety of technologies available to enhance learning, teachers, now more than ever, have opportunities to participate in diverse professional development experiences. Videotapes and laser videodiscs allow teachers to experience teaching and learning in a range of other classrooms; electronic mail and networks enable teachers to have ongoing conversations with peers and experts throughout the country and throughout the world; and CD-ROMs offer access to expertise of other teachers, science and mathematics educators, and scientists and mathematicians. These vehicles allow teachers to go well beyond the typical settings in and from which they learn.

Technology supports professional learning in individual, partnered, and networked ventures. With the variety of avenues open to teachers to pursue their own learning, they have opportunities to do so individually through electronic networks or e-mail or through participating in a telecomputing course. Groups of teachers can also become part of a larger audience of learners through teleconferences or interactive television.

Technology provides access for many people separated by great distances. For many people, this is one of the greatest advantages of using technology to enhance professional learning. Teachers in separate schools or from throughout the country now have access to each other and to resources not available locally. Teachers in isolated rural areas can enroll in courses given at a major university hundreds of miles away. Scientists and mathematicians in universities or laboratories are accessible for sharing information, and presentations given in one city can be viewed in another. Technology has given teachers access to information and people that were previously unavailable to them.

Descriptions of Different Technologies

Although technology in the classroom, for numerous purposes and within almost every subject area, is becoming more commonplace, taking advantage of technology to provide or enhance professional learning for science and mathematics teachers is a relatively recent development. For many years, teachers have had access to information on curriculum, programs, and science and mathematics content through the Internet, but in recent years there have been advances in using other forms of technology to provide professional development for these teachers. Described here are some of the different technologies and the ways in which they are being used in professional development as well as their advantages and disadvantages.

Teleconferencing

Teleconferences provide one-way audio or video presentations to different remote sites. A presentation is made in a television studio, "uplinked" to a live satellite, and then delivered ("downlinked") to other sites. Lectures, panel discussions, videotapes of classroom activities, or demonstrations are usually the subject matter for teleconferences. Often, written materials that accompany the presentation are made available to the downlinked sites, which are given a telephone number to call during the live presentation so that questions can be answered by the presenter during the telecast.

Teleconferences are usually one-time activities that provide information to participants, typically with some form of activity or discussion at each site following the telecast. This technology is rarely used for ongoing professional development, and its main drawback is the lack of continuous interaction between the presenter and the participants and that between participants at each site during the telecast. One of its greatest advantages, however, is that a large number of people can be reached at one time in a great number of remote sites separated by hundreds of miles. Thus, this technology can bring information to those at rural sites who might not otherwise have access to such opportunities.

This medium is very expensive to produce and send through a satellite, but the equipment required on the receiving end is less expensive. Although probably not an option for most individual teachers, some school districts already have a satellite dish and can participate in this form of professional development with only a nominal participation fee.

Television and Interactive Television

Preprogrammed television series have been produced and aired on public television for many years. Public Broadcasting Service's *Mathline* is an example. The purpose of this type of programming is to provide a very large number of teachers with an ongoing course of study. Usually, viewers register with a program, are sent instructional materials, view the program, and conduct activities in their classrooms or read assigned materials. Some programs require that written materials be submitted by viewers, and feedback is returned to them. Although extremely inexpensive (teachers need only a television), the greatest drawback is the lack of interaction not only with the presenter but also with other viewers. To counter this disadvantage, some programs have added an e-mail component so that viewers can, in fact, communicate with each other and develop on-line learning groups.

Interactive television, unlike one-way teleconferences or preprogrammed television programs, is a two-way system. Two or more remote sites are linked through cameras, and teachers can see and hear participants at other sites through a television. This allows for interaction among participants at one site and with participants at the other sites. Like teleconferences, this medium is usually used to provide a variety of remote sites with a presentation regarding one topic or issue, but it allows for more interaction than teleconferences. It is an expensive technology, and its success often depends on the quality of the equipment used at all sites.

Telecomputing Courses

This technology is more familiar to teachers and more available to individuals. Using only a computer and a modem, teachers can enroll in telecomputing courses. Most telecomputing courses provide instruction via text; activities are then conducted in the classroom and on-line discussion follows. The advantage of telecomputing is that most programs use a conferencing software that allows for individual messages to be sent between the instructor and students and between students. There are also real-time discussions among all participants. Although times are designated for these whole group discussions, the instructional component can be accessed at any time, providing a great deal of flexibility and convenience for participating teachers.

An advantage of these courses is that teachers can participate from a location and within a schedule that is convenient for them. They benefit from interacting with peers from throughout the country and personal, one-on-one interactions with experts. A disadvantage of these courses, however, is that they are often composed of self-starters and individuals who are highly motivated to pursue professional learning on their own. The medium is limited in its ability to "recruit" the vast majority of teachers. Providers of these courses also struggle with how to keep less involved participants from "falling behind," how to combat the feeling of anonymity teachers may feel, and overcoming "technophobia" that keeps many teachers from participating.

The National Teachers Enhancement Network (NTEN), at Montana State University in Bozeman, uses telecomputing to provide graduate-credit science and mathematics courses to teachers nationwide. Teachers participate for at least 3 hours a week during a semester-long course taught by teams of university scientists, engineers, mathematicians, high school teachers, and science and mathematics educators. Most courses consist of text material, exercises, and evaluation activities. Instructors and participants work through the text material together, discussing topics using both private electronic messages and group discussions.

The Mathematics Learning Forums also use telecomputing courses to provide ongoing professional development for teachers. The forums are a partnership between Bank Street College of Education and the Education Development Center's (EDC's) Center for Children and Technology in New York City. They combine computer-based communication, print materials, and videotapes to help K through eighth-grade teachers reflect on and adopt new teaching practices consistent with the goals envisioned by the NCTM standards for improving mathematics instruction. Mathematics Learning Forums address mathematics content, teaching, learning, and assessment. Video materials model teaching practices and allow teachers to analyze the learning processes of students. Print materials provide teachers with activities to try in their classrooms and are a source for discussions. Teachers share and reflect on their experiences through on-line dialogues. Forums are hosted by a faculty facilitator who raises questions, guides discussion, and provides reflective commentary (EDC, 1995).

Electronic Mail and Networking

Electronic mail allows for a variety of interactions with peers. Listserves, bulletin boards, and chat rooms are all means of communicating and sharing ideas and information among teachers, other educators, and individuals with special expertise, such as scientists and mathematicians. Teachers can conduct conversations regarding a myriad of topics with others in a chat room. They can participate in ongoing conversations through listserves and bulletin boards. Also, they can access peers and other experts through personal e-mail. Each of these technologies allows teachers to form electronic networks in which they meet regularly to discuss issues of concern. The networks are usually self-directed, with the participants defining their own agendas. They provide an opportunity for teachers to communicate with peers throughout the country and to form professional alliances. They build the capacity of members to identify and solve their own problems, expand the boundaries of their work, overcome isolation, and increase their sense of being part of a learning community.

One example of an electronic network is Teacher Enhancement Electronic Communications Hall (TEECH) from TERC in Cambridge, Massachusetts. TEECH is dedicated to bringing together principal investigators and project directors of teacher enhancement projects, plus other leaders in the field of professional development, to form an electronic community.

The TEECH website provides resources in the form of papers, electronic lectures, and databases on numerous topics in teacher enhancement. The network also provides various "modes" (ways to interact with the site): participation in discussion groups, conducting searches, reading or listening to lectures, or accessing a calendar of events. Through the network, those in the field of teacher enhancement have the opportunity to interact with colleagues regarding key issues that they face.

Although electronic mail and networks provide teachers and other educators with a valuable opportunity to interact, without a competent facilitator or guided instruction they can become little more than places to converse, with limited learning taking place. The Mathematics Learning Forums discussed previously view the skilled moderator as essential in the success of the forums. Similarly, the LabNet project, offered through TERC, provides online support for K through 12th-grade science teachers by using teacher-moderators. The project is aimed at motivating and supporting teachers to teach science using a more experimental, collaborative, in-depth, project-enhanced approach through technological tools. The LabNet provides a meeting place for teachers to support each other in experimenting with new teaching strategies, reflecting on their teaching experiences, problem solving, sharing resources, and building collegial connections with their peers. Through the network, teachers have access to message boards, file libraries, on-line chat areas, and private e-mail communications (Spitzer, 1994). The teacher-moderators help initiate, contribute to, moderate, and sustain dialogues carried out on-line and assist in linking teacher reflection with practices in the classroom.

TAPPED IN is another example of using e-mail as a means of communication among teachers. The TAPPED IN project was developed by the Center for Technology in Learning at SRI International and is a "virtual meeting place" for teachers. Teachers "log into" a server and enter an artificial environment that resembles a schoolhouse. Teachers can enter rooms in the building to access information and communicate with others who are logged on at the same time. The main focus of TAPPED IN is to provide teachers with an opportunity to interact semivisually in a familiar environment and discuss topics of interest with other professionals—all from their own computer. Although TAPPED IN allows for real-time interaction, it does not provide a structure for these interactions or moderators to help facilitate the discussions.

Videotapes and Laser Videodiscs

Videotapes and laser videodiscs are most frequently used in face-to-face professional development experiences. The *Sense Making in Science* video series (TERC, 1996) provides videos that capture the experiences of 12 teachers as they work together exploring what it means to learn and teach science. Viewers watch the teachers investigating scientific ideas, experimenting with new teaching practices, and developing ways to study what their students are thinking. The videos also include classroom episodes on children's conversations and activities in science. Professional developers working with teachers use the videos and the accompanying resource book as a vehicle for guided and reflective discussion regarding science teaching and learning.

Biological Science Curriculum Study (BSCS) also produces materials for use by professional developers with science teachers. BSCS has produced laser videodiscs, titled *Decisions in Teaching Elementary School Science* (1995), consisting of four modules addressing instruction, curriculum, equity, and assessment. Each laser videodisc shows classroom case studies and is designed to be used by facilitators to guide teachers through discussion of and reflection on science teaching and learning in the classroom. Similarly, the New York State Systemic initiative produced a series of seven videotapes, titled *Just Think: Problem Solving Through Inquiry* (New York State Education Department, 1996), aimed at providing professional development for K through eighth-grade science teachers. The videos are used to stimulate discussion and are accompanied by a facilitation guide to be used by professional developers working with teachers.

CD-ROMs

This technology provides flexible access to a large amount of materials for use in teaching, learning, and designing professional development. CD-ROMs can contain print material, videotape footage, audio recordings, and other resources.

For example, a CD-ROM is being developed by teacher educators Magdalene Lampert and Deborah Ball (1995) for use with pre- and in-service teachers of mathematics. Currently, the materials, developed at Michigan State University through the Mathematics and Teaching Through HyperMedia Project, use a hypermedia system. The original project field tested a "collection of multimedia tools for exploring and constructing knowledge about mathematics teaching and learning in elementary schools" (Hatfield & Bitter, 1994, p. 109). The hypermedia system links audio and video records of mathematics lessons being taught, with written student work, interviews with students, teachers' journal entries, observers' field notes, and lesson annotations. Through the system, teachers can access various "pathways" between and among the data to explore mathematics teaching and learning. The CD-ROM that is under development will allow users to see and study examples of actual teaching over time, with the flexibility to ask endless questions (e.g.,

How does one child's experience differ over time? What are the patterns of teacher-student interaction? and How is what is being taught represented in the students' work?). Users will be able to stop and replay tapes, examine student work or assignments, and select times and materials that help them address their questions and more deeply understand the dynamics of mathematics teaching and learning.

Another CD-ROM is available to support use of the American Association for the Advancement of Science's (AAAS's) materials for science literacy. Its CD-ROM, titled *Resources for Science Literacy: Professional Development* (1997), presents a coordinated set of databases, analyses, course guides, and workshop templates that help educators use science literacy goals as they prepare for work in the classroom. For example, the CD-ROM contains the full text of *Science for All Americans,* annotations of tradebooks, cognitive research, college courses, and the *Project 2061 Workshop Guide,* including tools for developing a variety of Project 2061 workshops.

Finally, the Eisenhower Regional Consortia are developing the *Professional Development CD-ROM* (NCREL, in preparation), which will contain a wide variety of resources for science and mathematics professional development. Included are examples of staff development in action—videos, case descriptions, activities, articles, and a variety of other materials that address content as diverse as assessment, capacity building, planning for reform, and mathematics and science curriculum. The CD-ROM will be useful as a learning tool for educators at all levels.

Tools for Group Work

GroupSystems, from Ventana Corporation, provides a computer-based support tool for facilitation of same-time/same-place and same-time/different-place meetings. This technological tool can be extremely helpful in structuring and guiding discussion during professional development sessions. Participants are linked together through computers and the main *GroupSystems* program that is monitored by a facilitator. During a session, participants can switch from discussions to on-line group or individual work. *GroupSystems'* main feature is that the author of a comment can remain anonymous (even with participants in the same room), allowing the on-line discussion to focus on the comment and not on the author. The system has many features that allow a group to prioritize lists, brainstorm, build consensus, vote, outline, and work simultaneously on a document or graphic.

The Ontario Institute for Studies in Education has developed a similar computer-based system for informed group decision making within a collaborative environment that is titled *Computer Supported Intentional Learning Environments* (CSILE; Scardamalia & Bereiter, 1994). CSILE and *GroupSystems* are only two examples of this type of technology, which has not been explored to its fullest as a tool in professional development of science and mathematics teachers.

Considerations for Implementation

Given the diversity of technologies available, it is imperative that professional developers and teachers select the one(s) that will best meet their needs and goals. There are several considerations in choosing appropriate technologies to implement.

Purposes and Goals. A first step should be to clearly examine the purposes and goals for using any technology. For example, if a mathematics teacher is searching for an avenue to communicate and learn with others online, accessing one of the various electronic networks is a natural choice. If a school wants to provide an opportunity for the entire staff to participate in an awareness presentation being made off-site, investigating the possibility of linking the school to the presenter through a teleconference or interactive television may be the best choice. A small study group of elementary science teachers wanting to expand their knowledge might choose to enroll in a telecomputing course.

Desired Degree of Interaction. Each of the technologies described previously varies in the degree to which interaction can occur with a presenter, among on-site participants, and between participants at separate sites. Evaluating the extent to which interaction with others will help meet the goals of the professional development experience is an important consideration.

Skilled Facilitators and Moderators. Whether participating in an electronic network, a telecomputing course, or a face-to-face session, the skill of the moderator or facilitator can "make or break" the professional learning experience. Simply viewing and discussing videos is not necessarily a learning experience. Although "surfing the Internet" to obtain information or taking part in discussions in chat rooms can be beneficial, for many uses of technology in professional development to be effective it is often the skill and expertise of the facilitator or moderator that can lead to deeper and more reflective learning on the part of the teachers.

Cost and Availability of the Technology. This obvious consideration will strongly influence the selection of an appropriate technology. Although individual teachers probably will not be interested in investing in a satellite dish to access teleconferences, a school district might consider this as an option for providing opportunities for teachers over the long term. A related consideration is the desire to "link" remote sites that cover a great distance. For a rural school district, with individual schools spread out over hundreds of miles, investing in technology that allows each site to communicate with others may be a practical solution for providing professional development to a large number of teachers at one time. Another option would be for the school district to establish e-mail connections between the sites.

Number of Participants. As mentioned previously, the number of teachers involved plays a critical role in selecting a technology for professional development. If the purpose is to provide a large number of teachers spread out over a great distance with access to information, then teleconferencing, interactive television, or e-mail networks may be the most logical choice. If, however, a small group of teachers at one school is interested in delving more deeply into their own teaching and their students' learning, using videotapes or laser videodiscs in a facilitated session would be more appropriate.

Quality of Available Technology. If the cameras and audio equipment used during a teleconference are of poor quality, the endeavor is rarely worth the effort. Like a live but poor presenter or instructor, participants are distracted from learning. Similarly, an e-mail system that works only 50% of the time undermines the advantage of easy, anytime access and frustrates communication. For teachers to benefit from any use of technology, the available tools must be of high enough quality to ensure that the investment of both money and time is beneficial for all involved. In addition, it is important to evaluate the expertise and experience of those providing the technology to ensure a high-quality experience for users; staying "one step ahead of the students" may result in one more disappointing experience for ready learners.

Participants' Comfort Level With the Technology. Watching television to view a presentation or looking at videos of classroom activities are rarely uncomfortable. If teachers are expected to access electronic networks or mail, however, they must have time at the beginning to learn how to use the technology and become comfortable and confident with using it before they can move forward in meeting the goals of the experience. Ongoing technical assistance allows teachers who encounter difficulties to have access to help when they need it.

Commentary

The use of technology to provide or enhance professional learning for teachers has many advantages, some of which were discussed previously. Another advantage, noted repeatedly by providers of e-mail, networks, and telecomputing courses, is that technology is largely neutral in regard to race, status, age, income, disability, and gender (Schmidt & Faulkner, 1989; Smith, 1996; Taylor & Smith, 1995). When communicating on-line, the only personal characteristic that is identifiable is gender, which is typically given away by a name. Technology also meets the needs of learners who are homebound due to health, family responsibilities, or even personal preferences because it can accommodate individual schedules and time constraints.

Teachers have found that learning to use a certain technology, originally as a way of communicating with others regarding a topic of interest, acts as a catalyst to open the door to more extensive computer knowledge and use. Once teachers begin using these technologies and sustain ongoing conversations, they feel less isolated and begin to create a community of learners committed to each other's growth. Many of the technologies also help teachers move away from the traditional model of learning in which an expert presents information; instead, teachers begin to learn from each other, especially with the guidance of a skilled facilitator.

The use of technology can be effective in providing follow-up or enhancing other professional learning experiences. Workshop attendees can create an electronic network to continue discussing the ideas and information shared during the workshop. Viewing a videotape of another teacher's practices before implementing the same practices in their classrooms can help expand teachers' perspectives on their own teaching and provide an example of the practice "in action." If the video-viewing experience is offered during the school year, teachers then have the opportunity to apply what they learn in their classrooms.

Electronic communication has benefits for the professional developer as well. A facilitator or monitor of a telecomputer course or electronic network can take advantage of built-in "management functions," such as monitoring participation, collating answers, and posting assignments. Because most communication is done electronically, there is a complete record of all interactions and exchanges.

The lack of face-to-face interactions is the most commonly noted disadvantage of the use of technology. Interestingly, several programs have found that there is in fact an increase in participation when people online are anonymous (Smith, 1996; Spitzer, Wedding, & DiMauro, 1994; Taylor & Smith, 1995). Discussions often become more detailed and delve deeper into a topic. Given the nature of on-line interactions, teachers sometimes feel less competition for time to "speak" because they can share their comments electronically at any time.

An interesting and unanticipated outcome of this "leveling," or lack of inhibition on the part of those using electronic communication, is the quality control dilemma. Because all users have equal voice, their opinions and ideas take on an authority that may have little experience or evidence to support them. People with more time to communicate can appear to know more; those with more expertise but less time can get less or no attention for no apparently good reason. Furthermore, experienced moderators of telecommunications report that making critical comments or challenging ideas can often result in "shutting down" conversations rather than causing deeper thinking and rethinking of firmly held ideas—the real key to learning (J. Falk, personal communication, March 1996).

There are other real disadvantages to using technology for professional learning. Lack of appropriate hardware, software, or technology can impede teachers' access to the medium. This is an important equity issue. Although technology improves access for those who are geographically disadvantaged, such as those in rural areas, the economically disadvantaged have less access than those with technology already in their homes and schools. This is no different from non-technology-based professional development opportunities—those who have get more opportunities, whereas those who have not get fewer opportunities.

For those teachers who "fall behind" in a telecomputing course, it is often more difficult to catch up without face-to-face interactions and guidance. For some, technology is simply not an effective means of learning. They suffer from a lack of social and visual cues that normally accompany personal interactions, and this can interfere with learning.

For some forms of technology, there is a limit to the number of people that can effectively interact at any one time. For example, NTEN found that they must limit their courses to 30 participants if both the participants and the facilitators are to benefit from the interactions. This can make it difficult to scale up telecomputing courses to reach more teachers.

Technology is being touted by many, including President Clinton, as a critical ingredient in education for the future. Although it clearly holds great potential, professional developers must think carefully about when and where it is most appropriate and how it can extend the ability to create effective professional learning experiences.

Additional Resources

Bender, W. N., Clinton, G., & Hotaling, D. S. (1996). Using distance learning in staff development. *Journal of Staff Development, 17*(4), 52-55.

Boone, W. J., & Anderson, H. O. (1995). Training science teachers with fully-interactive, distance education technology. *Journal of Science Teacher Education, 6*(3), 146-152.

Cambre, M. A., Erdman, B., & Hall, L. (1996). The challenge of distance education. *Journal of Staff Development, 17*(1), 38-41.

Distance Learning Resource Network (DLRN), Technology in Education Program, WestEd, San Francisco. (Phone: 415-565-3000)

GroupSystems, Ventana Corporation, Tucson, AZ. (Phone: 520-325-8228)

LabNet Project, Technical Education Resource Centers, Cambridge, MA. (Phone: 617-547-0430)

Mathematics Learning Forums, Bank Street College of Education Mathematics Leadership Program and The Center for Children and Technology of the Education Development Center, Inc., New York. (Phone: 212-807-4207)

National Teachers Enhancement Network (NTEN), Montana State University Extended Studies, Bozeman. (Phone: 406-994-6550)

Taylor, E. F., & Smith, R. C. (1995). Teaching physics on line. *American Journal of Physics, 63,* 1090-1096.

Teacher Enhancement Electronic Communications Hall (TEECH), Technical Education Resource Centers, Cambridge, MA. (Phone: 617-547-0430)

Teacher Professional Development Institute (TAPPED IN), SRI Center for Technology in Learning, San Francisco. (Phone: 415-859-2881)

Context Factors Influencing 5
Professional Development

···

A group of science and mathematics teachers from a large urban center's Archdiocese Schools attended a 2-day professional development session on peer coaching. The session was part of a workshop series that had been arranged by an Archdiocese-funded staff development center in support of teachers who were concerned with issues of equity in science and mathematics and were examining whether their teaching practices helped all students learn or just some. The teachers had learned and were implementing new questioning, discussion, and grouping techniques. They knew that peer coaching would reinforce these new skills and help the teachers use them as well. They were excited about the peer coaching session. When it was time to attend a follow-up meeting, however, most admitted they had not tried peer coaching at all. After talking to the teachers, the staff development coordinator discovered that several factors were at play. School schedules made it extremely difficult for teachers to be released from their classrooms for observations and pre- and postconferences. Also, teachers had high anxiety about being observed by other teachers. Norms of risk taking and collegiality simply were not strong enough for teachers to overcome the obstacles to implementing peer coaching, especially when the focus was on how they treated individual students in their classes.

Professional development is not available in one size fits all. As in the previous example, an approach that is a great success in some situations may fail in others. What makes the difference is the context in which the program is operated—the specific situations in the organization that work to support or defeat the innovation. How can professional development planners know what design will work in their own context? How can they choose strategies that fit into their context? What factors need to be considered?

In this chapter, we discuss nine context factors that influence professional development design. These are (a) students; (b) teachers; (c) practice—that is, curriculum, instruction, assessment, and the learning environment; (d) policies; (e) resources; (f) organizational culture; (g) organizational structures; (h) history of professional development; and (i) parents and the community. For each of these factors, we identify some critical issues and raise questions that professional development planners should ask and answer. As input to the professional development process, additional factors may be important to consider in particular contexts, such as the role of key groups and stakeholders (e.g., teacher unions). Given the complex and variable nature of contexts, no single list will adequately capture every situation. Designers may generate their own list of context factors that need to be considered to ground their professional development plans in their own reality.

How does understanding context help planners? In some cases, merely being aware of these context factors can inform decision making about professional development. For example, in one district, a curriculum audit revealed that statistics was not being taught anywhere in the elementary grades and that teachers were not comfortable with the mathematics involved. That led to a decision to provide teachers with training and technical support to address this need. In other cases, designers may discover that some aspect of their context will so impede effective professional development that it must be addressed before professional development planning can move forward. For instance, if the only time currently available for professional development is during three districtwide inservice days, solving the time problem must occur before designers can implement a quality program.

Students

> Probably nothing within a school has more impact on students in terms of skill development, self-confidence, or classroom behavior than the personal and professional growth of their teachers. . . . When teachers stop growing, so do their students.
>
> —*Barth (1980, p. 147)*

Although students are not the primary clients of professional development, they are its ultimate beneficiaries. The goal of professional development is improved student learning. At the same time, student performance will not improve unless staff and organizational performance improves. It follows that a logical starting point for planners is gaining a clear picture of the students in the system—where they are and what results are desired for them. The following are questions to consider:

Who are the students in your context and how are they currently performing in science and mathematics? How do you know?

What do local, state, and national curriculum frameworks or standards for science and mathematics say about what students should know and be able to do? How are your students doing in relation to these?

What results for learning mathematics and science are most important to your system? Where are the most pressing gaps between students' current and desired performance?

What equity issues must be addressed to ensure mathematics and science literacy for all students? How are girls achieving relative to boys? How are African American, Latino, Anglo, or Asian students achieving relative to each other? How are English speakers versus speakers of other languages achieving? If disparities exist, why and how can they be rectified?

Are students tracked in mathematics or science classes or both? How are tracking decisions made? What is the gender and ethnic breakdown in the different tracks? How are teachers assigned to different tracks? How does teaching differ between tracks?

What must happen in your system to close the gap between where students are now and where you want them to be? How can professional development help meet your goals for students?

What are the norms for students in the classroom? What are they expected to do? What do they expect of their teachers?

Teachers

> A highly skilled and knowledgeable mathematics educator presented an elaborate group problem on reproduction rates. Her audience was an Islamic school in which men and women could not even speak to each other let alone discuss gestation periods and so on. Needless to say, it was a disaster.

Clearly, teachers have the most direct influence on student learning. If student learning is to improve, what do teachers need to know and be able to do and what kind of support do they need to be successful? As planners consider tailoring professional development to their context, no factor is more important to consider than the teachers themselves.

Teachers are the primary clients of professional development. Knowing the client can clinch the success of a staff development effort, and not knowing the client can guarantee its failure. How many professional development efforts have fallen flat, insulting and alienating teachers because they failed to honor their knowledge, skill, cultures, and experience? How many others have missed the mark by attempting to impose new ideas about mathematics or science education on teachers without considering the teachers' beliefs about teaching and learning these disciplines?

Being sensitive to teachers' needs means considering, among other things, what grade levels they teach. Teachers of students of different ages will vary in their knowledge, skills, and needs, and professional development designs should vary accordingly. For example, it is safe to say that most elementary teachers know less mathematics and science than do high school teachers; in fact, they are more likely to be uncomfortable or even anxious about how little they know of these disciplines. Middle school teachers typically do not know their disciplines as well as high school teachers but know them better than elementary teachers. This is due to the number of courses the middle school teachers have taken and because they are less likely to be teaching in their major field than are high school teachers.

There are other differences in teacher needs that may correspond to grade level. Elementary teachers may understand child development better than teachers of higher grades; they may have had opportunities to practice a wider range of teaching strategies because they have fewer students and more flexible schedules than teachers of higher grades. In addition, teachers at different levels are under different kinds of pressures: elementary and middle grade teachers to integrate their curricula, high school teachers to prepare students for college or for work, and so on. These variations in needs and demands must be served in professional development designs.

As planners assess teachers' needs, the following are some questions for consideration:

Given your goals for students at each level of schooling, what skills and knowledge do teachers need to be successful?

How are teachers doing in relation to local, state, and national standards and frameworks for science and mathematics education?

What are their strengths in pedagogy, content, assessment, and establishing appropriate learning environments? What are the most pressing areas for improvement?

At what stage in their careers are the teachers? What do they care most about? What goals do they have for themselves?

What do they believe about teaching and learning mathematics and science, about their students, and about the nature of mathematics and science?

What has been their experience with professional development?

What current support systems do teachers have? What additional supports do they need to be successful?

Taking stock of the students and teachers lays the groundwork for setting realistic and meaningful goals, gathering baseline data to assess progress toward goals, and helping to ensure that the professional development that is planned will meet their needs.

Practices: Curriculum, Instruction, Assessment, and the Learning Environment

If professional development is going to improve mathematics and science learning, then it must improve classroom practice. What is the state of practice and where are improvements needed? These questions probe another critical dimension of context to consider in planning professional development. National standards for science and mathematics education (National Council of Teachers of Mathematics [NCTM], 1989, 1991; National Research Council, 1996) and many state and local frameworks address four aspects of practice that require attention if science and mathematics education are to be transformed. They are curriculum (what is being taught), instruction (how it is taught), assessment (how learning is measured), and learning environment (the physical facilities and arrangements as well as the culture within the classroom).

Work on implementing national standards and state and local frameworks has given rise to a variety of tools for helping schools assess their current level of practice in each of these four areas, identify gaps, and set priorities for improvement. For example, the NCTM and the Association for Supervision and Curriculum Development prepared a guide for examining school mathematics programs (Blume & Nicely, 1991). The National Science Teachers Association has a similar school self-assessment. Professional developers can use guides such as these to assess schools or districts in relation to standards-based reform of science and mathematics education. At a minimum, the following must be assessed as input to the professional development design:

What are the goals of your mathematics and science programs? On what are these goals based?

What knowledge and skills are expected of students at each grade level and how well is the curriculum aligned to these expectations?

To what extent do teachers use strategies that engage students in active learning and inquiry, in communicating mathematical and scientific ideas, and in developing higher-order thinking, reasoning, and problem solving?

How do teachers recognize the varied needs of students and match teaching strategies to these needs?

How do teachers coordinate across and within grade levels or classes?

What instructional materials (e.g., texts, units, and manipulatives) are used? How are they selected? What criteria are used?

What assessment strategies are used? How do teachers assess learning over time? What are the criteria for high achievement? To what extent are assessments aligned with curriculum goals, frameworks, and standards?

What are the learning environments like in the school? What resources, equipment, and materials do teachers and students have and what else do they need? What opportunities do they have to take students "beyond the classroom walls"? What is the climate in the classroom? Are students and teachers respectful of one another?

No matter how school and district leaders assess the state of their practice, the results have direct implications for professional development. Such analysis reveals areas on which professional development might focus. For instance, if the analysis of a school's context indicates that the teachers are not confident in their own abilities in science or mathematics or both, they might choose to focus on professional development activities that will immerse teachers in learning these disciplines. Alternatively, teachers who know science and mathematics content but who have not developed strategies for engaging students and listening to and respecting their ideas might benefit from activities that help them learn how to establish more effective learning environments. (Chapter 7 describes how experienced professional developers decide on priority needs and select strategies to address them.)

State and Local Policies

> Most plans for systemic reform or restructuring underestimate the sustained impact of long-standing policy and practice.
>
> *—Little (1993, p. 140)*

Professional development swims in a stream of school, district, state, and national policies. Sometimes, professional developers end up paddling against the current as they attempt to implement plans in opposition to prevailing policies. A classic example of this is when teachers and districts attempt to implement new methods of teaching science and mathematics only to discover that state policy still requires their students to achieve on standardized tests that measure students' ability to recall facts and perform calculations. Another example is when the district policy dictates that professional development occurs on a voluntary and individual basis in the district even though everyone knows that change in science and mathematics education requires the involvement of a whole system. Sometimes, designers collide head on with a policy barrier such as "We were considering implementing a kit-based science curriculum, but the district had a policy requiring a textbook adoption." In the best of circumstances, policies flow with professional development, enabling planners to capitalize on the current and move more swiftly and easily toward their goals, such as in the following example: "Our state has a new grant program for teachers who want to organize study groups around the state curriculum frameworks in mathematics and science. This is going to enable us to do exactly what we wanted to do anyway." Also, a particular policy may provide a new tributary toward their destination, such as in the following example: "We wanted to use state aid to support a teacher study group, which isn't spelled out in the regulations as an eligible activity. We learned that we could get a waiver and proceed with our plans."

Policies can limit or broaden options and impede or support progress. In any case, effectively navigating the stream requires professional developers to carefully examine local, state, and national policies, which exert a strong, if not always readily apparent, influence on professional development design.

Unfortunately, more often than not, prevailing local, state, and national policies are inconsistent with the vision of professional development described in this book. In many places, professional development is not even acknowledged as a legitimate activity for teachers; policies reflect the attitude that teachers are doing their jobs only when they are in the classroom teaching. Where professional development is legitimized, it is often viewed as a way of helping teachers acquire knowledge and skills they are lacking by participating in training provided by external experts. Rarely are teachers given the opportunity to learn as a part of their daily experience, engage in inquiry with their colleagues, or actively shape the content and context of their own learning experiences (Little, 1993; McDiarmid, 1995).

When professional development planners consider their context, they need to assess the policies at work that will affect the success of their professional development plans. What policies influence professional development in your organization? What policies provide opportunities? What policies impede learning? Consider the following additional questions:

How do policies support professional development focused on core problems of teaching and learning and provide opportunities for teachers to learn over time in supportive environments, especially for those teachers who serve diverse students?

How is professional development defined by local and state policies? Does the definition focus on workshop hours, designate who will "deliver" professional development, and allocate or restrict time for professional development?

What are state and local policies for recertification and for supporting beginning teachers? Are salary increases tied to professional development or the taking on of new roles?

What incentives are provided for professional development? How well do they balance the interests of individual teachers with the overall organizational interests?

Who makes decisions about professional development—for example, about how Eisenhower funds are allocated and spent?

How do policies impede or support collegial activities such as mentoring, peer coaching, and time for teachers to get together to share, discuss, and play leadership roles and reflect on their practice?

See Corcoran (1995) for an extensive framework for reviewing professional development policies and practices.

Available Resources

We want to revamp our science curriculum, but we can't afford to purchase the hands-on materials required.

No one who plans professional development needs to be reminded about the need for adequate resources, especially time, money, and materials. More often than not, these resources are scarce and limit the scope and depth of professional development. The problem becomes even more serious as the nature of professional development changes. Long-term, sustained, "results-driven," and "job-embedded" approaches place even more demands on time and money. If professional learning is to become embedded into the fabric of the school day, educators must rethink the "three annual release days" model for professional development. Teachers need significant chunks of pupil-free time—up to 20% of a teacher's time according to Shanker (1993) and the National Staff Development Council (1994)—for ongoing, collegial learning. (See the discussion of time as a critical issue in Chapter 6.) One of the major insights for U.S. educators from the Third International Mathematics and Science Study (TIMSS) (U.S. Department of Education, National Center for Educational Statistics, 1996) is the substantial amount of time spent in professional development by teachers in countries (e.g., Japan) whose students demonstrate high levels of science and mathematics learning. Their well-supported early years and keen attention to carefully honing teaching skills during their careers are possible only with significant resources dedicated to teacher learning.

Time is not the only resource that is important to the success of professional development. Teachers often learn important content and teaching strategies from materials, equipment, and facilities other than their classrooms. New teaching units and their corresponding materials, science equipment, calculators, manipulatives, technological instruments, computers, and scientific laboratories are all important learning tools, depending on professional development goals. Furthermore, expertise is a valuable resource, and it can be found in many places. University and community college faculty, scientists and mathematicians from industry, government agencies (e.g., geological surveys and agricultural extension offices), and even gardening and environmental clubs can provide critical subject matter expertise. Experienced teachers are a rich source of "pedagogical content knowledge." When they are conscious of and can articulate what they know, these teachers bring critical understandings about how students learn specific mathematical and science concepts; what particular strategies, examples, and activities can help students at what points in their developing understanding; and how to help them demonstrate what they know and can do. Other resources, such as a video library and new technology-based professional development programs, can support teacher growth. One example is Biological Sciences Curriculum Study's *Decisions in Teaching Elementary School Science* (1995). For other examples, see Chapter 4.

Moreover, if professional development is to be conducted in the thoughtful way that this book advocates, designers of professional development cannot be burdened with so many responsibilities that they fail to do the analysis and planning needed to ensure effective experiences. They need time and other resources to plan, implement, monitor, and evaluate professional development as well as time for their own professional growth. Currently, there is more talk among policymakers about holding professional development accountable for improving teacher and student performance. As expectations for professional development increase, so too must the resources available to support it. Where are these resources to come from? Clearly, the answer in part lies in significant changes in policy at the national and state levels. Schools, however, need immediate and short-term solutions as well.

A beginning point is to take stock of all the resources available. Consider the following questions:

How much time is available for professional development for teachers?

What resources, including those currently designated for courses, credit reimbursements, or teacher evaluation, are allocated in the budget for professional development that could be rechanneled?

What grant funds are available in the state or district?

What community support, partnerships (such as universities or businesses), expertise, collaboratives, materials, and equipment are available?

Organizational Culture

Culture and professional development enjoy a symbiotic relationship. Professional development activities contribute to a culture of collegiality, critical inquiry, and continuous improvement; the school culture, in turn, stimulates ongoing professional development—a mutually reinforcing relationship. Attending to this aspect of context, assessing its strengths and weaknesses and planning accordingly, can yield a rich harvest both for professional and organization development.

—*Hord and Boyd (1995, p. 10)*

Scenario 1

Being chosen as her state's presidential awardee for science teaching was a mixed blessing for Maria Gomez. She loved the national ceremony, especially the opportunity to meet other awardees. It felt wonderful to be validated and appreciated for all the hard work she put into being the best science teacher she could possibly be. She, however, dreaded going back to school, where innovative teaching was not valued. She would not dare wear the pin she won in school or talk about the awards ceremony with her fellow teachers. She was afraid of becoming even more isolated from the other teachers, who already saw her as a "rate-buster."

Scenario 2

"I just can't seem to help the students understand inertia and the forces exerted on an object at rest. Here's what I've been doing. Does anyone have any ideas of how I could be more successful?" Richard shared at the weekly study group about the new science curriculum. His colleagues admitted they had encountered some of the same problems. One teacher invited Richard into her classroom to observe how she had been dealing with the same issue. They both agreed to share what they learned at the next study group meeting.

What accounts for the differences between the two scenarios described previously? The answer in part lies in the different cultures in which the two teachers found themselves. Some anthropologists define culture as patterns of behavior; others see it as a set of ideas or rules for what is acceptable in a particular group. No matter how it is defined, there is little disagreement that culture shapes behavior within organizations. Within any school, district, or other organization, culture acts as a powerful and pervasive influence on the change process in general and professional development in particular.

In the first example, Maria Gomez is exceptional both in her teaching and in her ability to maintain excellence in a school culture that does not celebrate or support innovative and outstanding teachers. Most individual teachers, no matter how talented or enthused about trying a new teaching strategy, will have a difficult time sustaining any kind of change in a culture that discourages risk taking and continuous learning. Cultures with strong norms of experimentation and growth, however, make good soil—nurturing teachers and enabling them to perform at their best, as in the second example. In the culture of this school, openly reflecting about one's teaching, admitting problems, and asking for help were valued. Richard did not have to worry about being marked as a "bad" teacher because teaching is viewed as a process of continuous improvement.

It is not difficult to see how a mismatch between school culture and a professional development strategy could be disastrous. Imagine the first school choosing to implement a teacher mentor program that recognizes outstanding teachers such as Maria and pays them stipends to mentor other teachers. Without norms of high expectations for teachers (and students) and collegiality, competitiveness and resentment would undermine such a program, setting up Maria and other mentors for failure. At Richard's school, however, introducing mentoring as a strategy has potential to succeed because teachers are already used to viewing the classroom as a laboratory, sharing observations, and analyzing results collectively.

There are likely to be differences in school culture that are attributable to the level of schooling. For example, high school teachers may be splintered by the differences in their subject matter expertise—biology teachers may not find much in common with mathematics teachers, for example. The general lack of science preparation by elementary teachers can influence school culture in different ways: by reinforcing why teachers need each other to share expertise or, conversely, by making them fear that their inadequacies will be discovered. Many middle schools have turned to interdisciplinary teaming with time and energy allotted to team building and building on each other's strengths. These and many other situations can influence, and also be influenced by, school culture.

How can organizations "test their own soil" to determine their own culture? What norms are at work in a school district or a professional network? At the beginning of planning for professional development, assess your culture on the basis of the following questions, which are taken, in part, from Saphier and King's (1985) 12 norms that affect school improvement (note that the questions can be applied to districts and other organizations as well as schools):

To what extent does the school support teachers working together and learning from one another? Do teachers appreciate one another's differences and strengths and share knowledge and learning personally and professionally? How do teachers who have had rich opportunities to increase their mathematics and science knowledge, or their abilities to teach these subjects, share what they have learned with others?

How safe is it to experiment with new ideas and approaches? What kind of encouragement and support are science and mathematics teachers given to try new instructional materials or new strategies in their classrooms? What happens when new ideas or approaches fail? To what extent is there an ongoing commitment to improvement?

What is the school's position with respect to science and mathematics reform? Are new sources of information and guidance—

standards, frameworks, and research studies—welcomed and discussed? Is the community brought into the conversation?

In what ways does the school hold teachers accountable for high performance?

How much autonomy do teachers have? In what ways does the culture demonstrate its confidence and trust in teachers?

To what extent is good teaching recognized and honored within the school and community?

How are staff included in decision-making processes, especially those decisions that affect their students? How are instructional materials selected?

To what extent does the school identify, confront, and resolve problems in productive ways? How does the school respond to parent complaints or community resistance to new ways of learning and teaching mathematics and science?

The results of a cultural assessment such as this can influence professional development planning in at least two ways. First, of course, organizations need to choose approaches to professional development that can thrive in their current culture. Second, they can develop plans to strengthen or change their culture where needed. Clearly, building a strong culture requires effective leadership as well as cooperation among staff. Professional development—in both content and approach—can also be a vehicle for strengthening culture. (Chapter 7 describes how professional developers address some of these issues of culture in designing and implementing their programs.)

Organizational Structures

> If you want to change an organization, change the people who come to meetings.
>
> —*S. Bailey (1995)*

Closely related to culture is the structure of the organization—the decision-making positions and groups that are in place, procedures for decision making, the quality of leadership, assignment of people, and scheduling of time. Each of these factors can constrain or support professional development.

Although structures for professional development decision making and implementation vary widely, many schools, districts, and other organizations share a common problem. In their effort to respond to myriad grants and mandates, they have literally dozens of professional development plans and initiatives managed by different people. Coordination across these initiatives is rare, resulting in duplicated efforts, mixed messages, and wasted resources.

Having a clear picture of who makes decisions about professional development and the infrastructure in place to support it will help designers initially to navigate the system and determine the leverage points. Eventually, structural changes may be necessary to support a professional development system that is aligned with district mission and goals, designed for results, and systemic. Loucks-Horsley and associates (1987) emphasize the importance of having the "right people" at the table making professional development decisions—those people that meet the criteria of relevance (most affected by professional development decisions), expertise, and jurisdiction (authority to carry out decisions).

Decision makers can be formal or informal leaders, such as curriculum supervisors, principals, teacher leaders, or university personnel involved in grant-supported programs. As Loucks-Horsley and associates (1987, p. 13) note, "The roles of instructional leadership are not exclusive, and the more people in the education community who can take on leadership roles, the more likely their sense of commitment and responsibility will lead to real school improvement." What leadership for professional development exists in the school or organization? How can planned efforts be linked to the structures in place?

Equally important is the quality of the leadership provided (Loucks-Horsley & Hergert, 1985). Effective leadership of professional development combines clear direction with ample support. Leaders champion professional development by articulating clear expectations, outcomes, and purposes for the program, linking development to other important goals and initiatives, modeling continuous learning themselves, delegating development responsibilities, and helping to focus the effort. Supports include rallying the resources, freeing up time, actively participating in professional development programs, and encouraging risk taking in the classroom (Loucks-Horsley et al., 1990).

Organizational structures can specifically support teacher development for science and mathematics teaching. For example, skills such as classroom management of materials and investigations, questioning, and grouping must be practiced in classrooms to truly be learned. Teachers need materials to practice, so a materials support system is as critical to teacher learning as it is to establishing an effective program for students, especially for science (St. John, Century, Tibbits, & Heenan, 1994). School schedules that support teacher practice, followed by reflection alone or with a colleague who has observed the teaching, can support deeper learning while also influencing the culture.

How well will your structure support professional learning and application of that learning? As you design your professional development program, consider the following questions:

Does the leadership in your organization provide clear direction and support for professional development? How committed to professional development is the school's formal leadership? How much does the leadership know about and how deeply committed are they to mathematics and science reform?

Who in the organization makes decisions about professional development? How are decisions made regarding Eisenhower funds? How are decisions made regarding what "counts" as professional development (e.g., does a teacher planning session receive the same support as workshop attendance?)?

What professional development efforts are currently under way in the organization? What structures are in place for coordinating these multiple efforts? How are teachers and others being helped to address multiple priorities and sometimes conflicting goals?

What infrastructure is in place to support professional development? For example, are school schedules flexible enough to allow for practice and reflection? Are teachers mentoring, coaching, or training? Do principals, curriculum coordinators, or others perform these functions? Does the school have access to content specialists in science and mathematics?

History of Professional Development

Another context factor that professional developers must consider is the history of professional development in the school or district. Teachers' past experiences with professional development will influence how they view new initiatives. If past efforts were a "waste of time," resulted in few or no changes, or failed to support teachers after initial training, professional development planners must help teachers see how new efforts will be more effective. If teachers have been "inserviced to death," they may need to experience very different professional development strategies.

Past professional development can vary greatly in its nature, scope, and who initiated it. Knowing where expertise from universities and other organizations outside of the school have contributed to teacher learning is helpful to designers of current efforts.

Planners can take a close look at the current state of professional development, mapping out the range of current professional development activities and their histories. It may be useful to identify the stage of development of each activity—for example, a brand new initiative, one just taking hold, or one that is an old friend. It is often surprising to planners how many new initiatives are under way and how few have really taken hold over the long term. Furthermore, it is difficult to map how individual science and mathematics teachers have pursued professional learning because often it is very individualistic, from college course work to internships in research institutes.

To clearly reflect both the history and the current state of professional development, the following questions must be asked:

What are the teachers' experiences with professional development? What is currently under way?

What has been tried and abandoned and why?

What was the nature and scope (who and how many involved) of past efforts, both successful and unsuccessful? Who initiated them and what was the nature of the outside relationships?

To what extent have the professional development activities in the school or district reflected the attributes of effectiveness discussed in Chapter 3?

What can be done to ensure that efforts in the future are more effective?

Parents and Community

As schools and teachers change what and how students learn, they must be careful to consider the views of parents and community members. Parents have many questions about new approaches to education: They worry that their children will not develop basic skills, they are concerned that the school may be changing for change's sake or that innovations such as inquiry-based science education are just "fun and games," and they worry that new approaches will hurt their children when they take a college entrance or state-level achievement test.

Community members other than parents have concerns as well. They want their tax dollars to be spent wisely (or fewer of them to be spent). They worry about conflicting reports that teachers need to spend more time with students and need more time for their own learning. They worry that the reforms in science and mathematics will not provide students the rigorous skills they need to be productive citizens. At the same time, they wonder why schools have not embraced new programs that will provide students with the problem-solving, teamwork, and decision-making skills they will need for future employment. They worry about the implications of international comparisons such as the TIMSS study for students' mathematics and science learning in their community's schools. These are all legitimate issues that need to be considered as schools seek to make changes in teaching and learning. Professional development planners need to assess the following:

What are parents' and the community's interests and concerns about the science and mathematics education you provide?

To what extent do parents and community members support new visions for science and mathematics teaching and learning? What could you do to increase their support?

Do parents and community members understand why changes in teaching are necessary and are they supportive of policies and structures needed to support effective professional development?

Is the school board well informed about the needs and nature of new directions in mathematics and science teaching and learning? Are teachers, administrators, and other educators prepared to communicate and work effectively with parents and community to increase their understanding and support? Do educators have the professional development opportunities to adequately prepare them to do so?

Where in the community can you find support for mathematics and science reform and use this as a resource for professional development?

Fear and mistrust on the part of the public can thwart professional development efforts and also the directions of science and mathematics reform. Professional development planners need to work with others in the system to identify and address the concerns of the parents and community. Consider who your supporters are in the community and plan for their involvement. If parents and community members have resisted change efforts in the past, find out why and develop plans to avoid the same results.

Summary

The nine context factors provide planners with a good sense of what they need to consider in their own settings as they plan for professional development. In answering the many questions posed about the individual factors, professional developers will become aware of the constraints and the supports operating within their systems. They have seen how some context factors overlap—for example, policies and resources and time and culture. They know which aspects of their context are givens—the mountains that cannot be moved (at least for now)—and what "landscaping" needs to occur as they construct their professional development programs and initiatives. They are becoming increasingly ready to build a professional development program that is in synch with their environment.

Critical Issues in Designing Professional Development 6

....

No matter what the design for a professional development initiative or program, several issues must be addressed if learning is to occur and be maintained over the long haul. We identified nine issues from our exploration of effective professional development: ensuring equity, building a professional culture, developing leadership, building capacity for professional learning, scaling up, garnering public support, supporting standards and frameworks through professional development, evaluating professional development, and finding time for professional development.

Each of these issues is important, and lack of attention to any one of them can doom a professional development initiative from the start. Each issue is also important because as a set they strike at the core of mathematics and science reform, going well beyond the central notions of professional learning. Consequently, a full discussion of each issue is beyond the scope of this book. Instead of elaborating at length, we have chosen to briefly discuss each issue, suggest several questions for professional developers to ask themselves as they design or reflect on their programs, give one or two examples of how science and mathematics professional developers address the issue, and provide a list of resources for further study and use.

Ensuring Equity

Ensuring equity in a diverse society has become extremely important as the goal of science and mathematics reform has shifted from producing a relatively few highly skilled scientists and mathematicians to literacy in these areas for all citizens. Numerous reports document underrepresentation of women, persons of color, individuals from lower classes, and the disabled in various aspects of science and mathematics, including careers, higher-level coursework, and opportunities to learn from adequately prepared teachers. The inadequacies of curriculum materials and instructional approaches for such a diverse population are often cited as a problem, particularly with the movement to build new learning on the learner's experiences and context. Widespread strategies such as tracking have come under attack as obstructing access to mathematics and science learning for a large portion of the student population.

How does equity relate to a discussion of effective professional development? A major issue involves equity for the participants in professional development: equal access for all teachers to quality professional development. Access is only the beginning, however. Another issue is whether the programs are designed to accommodate the diverse characteristics of educators, who have a wide variety of needs, learning styles, cultural backgrounds, and so on. A final issue relates directly to the students: ensuring that what teachers learn in professional development provides them with the skills, resources, and sensitivities necessary to help a diverse student body gain literacy in science and mathematics. Thus, the issues relate to both the design and the content of professional development. Our discussion, organized around these three areas, uses questions that professional developers can ask about their programs.

Is access to the professional development experience equitable? That is, is this opportunity available to all or does it favor people in certain locations, with certain lifestyles, and from certain cultural, gender, or racial groups? Access is a simple concept, but it is often ignored by professional development designers, who are not aware of the inequities that can be created when opportunities are offered to teachers. They may think they offer the same chance to everyone to participate in professional development, but many factors, some of which are in their control, inhibit participation. Some of these factors are scheduling, distance, and resources required to use what is learned. For example, there are many opportunities for teachers to participate in research during the summer and work side by side with scientists and mathematicians. Unfortunately, these opportunities are not always accessible to all teachers. Many teachers have summer jobs, and others have family obligations that prohibit them from enrolling in an intensive professional development program that will keep them away from home for multiple days or weeks.

Inequitable policies and practices in school funding can create unequal opportunities for professional development. Just examining the variation in how Eisenhower funds are distributed and then used in different schools, districts, and states is enlightening. Resource-rich schools, which are unlikely to be those serving underrepresented groups, can better support the learning of their staff, considered by some to be a luxury or frill when lab equipment and books are in short supply. Access to professional development is restricted when teachers do not have the resources to buy the new materials that a professional development program requires or recommends.

Does the design of the professional development invite full engagement and learning by participants? Making professional development accessible is a necessary first step, but the adequacy of its design will determine if it is truly equitable. Professional development strategies should be chosen to meet the diverse needs and learning styles of participating teachers. Unfortunately, professional development planners are not always aware of the characteristics of programs that could be problematic. Cultural norms may create barriers to some professional development activities, such as modeling and giving critical feedback. Programs that require consumption of large volumes of reading materials do not serve auditory and kinesthetic learners well.

Demonstrating equity in the design of professional development programs also involves who is chosen to play leadership roles. The designation of leaders sends a strong message about the priority of equity and its role in what and how educators learn. A challenge that is not always easy to meet is to select professional development leaders who represent the diversity in both the teacher and the student population, understand and value equity and diversity, and proactively involve teachers in professional development efforts who are from underrepresented groups or teach underrepresented students.

Does the content of the professional development experience include the issues of equitable opportunity for all students to learn science and mathematics and to participate in careers in science and mathematics? The goal of equitable science and mathematics education is to equalize outcomes for students regardless of their race, ethnic heritage, gender, disability, class, or learning style. How can professional development help teachers improve their strategies for reaching all students with effective science and mathematics education? One way is to introduce tools that assess student progress and allow teachers to identify differential impact on groups of students; areas of identified weakness can be the focus of professional development. Research-based programs that show results for increasing motivation and achievement among minority youngsters and females can be included in professional development. Support groups can explore the problem of equity through reading and discussing research and evaluation reports.

Issues of equity in mathematics and science education reveal themselves in many elements of education; opportunities for educators to become aware of the current situation and ways to think about change are very appropriate as content for professional development. Exploration of how students can best learn challenging content in a second language, the impact of tracking on opportunities to learn, cooperative learning as an alternative pedagogical approach, testing, and parent and community collaboration can all be important issues for professional development for mathematics and science teachers as well as for other educators.

Weissglass's (1996) work in mathematics education is an example of addressing the issues of equity for both education in general and professional development. His work suggests the need to make equity the central focus of the reform effort. His professional development goal is to help educators understand the relationship of mathematics and culture and to increase their capacity to provide mathematical experiences that meet both the needs of a diverse students population and the National Council of Teachers of Mathematics (NCTM) standards. Through reading, discussion, and observation, educators in Weissglass's programs explore how cultural values and ways of understanding can affect mathematics learning and teaching; understand the culture of mathematics and the value of building classroom mathematics on children's own experiences; examine instructional materials through an "equity filter"; and experience the application of mathematics to understanding important social issues, such as hunger, poverty, and teen pregnancy. These kinds of experiences help educators to better understand the issues of equity as part of their own professional development.

Building Professional Culture

We noted in Chapter 5 that the culture of a school contributes to the learning of all within its walls—young people and adults alike. It is also the case that, without a supportive culture, teachers' newly gained knowledge and skills have little chance of having a lasting impact on their practice. In the new paradigm of professional development (Loucks-Horsley, 1997), the distinction is blurred between individual development and development of the organization—for example, the school or department. Teachers learn in their work settings, which support that learning and consequently become a stronger and richer source of learning for all. What can professional developers do whose goal it is to help teachers foster improved learning of science and mathematics? Especially in instances in which the professional development opportunity is neither inside the school nor connected with the school or district in any way, professional developers have special challenges for nourishing professional cultures. The first step in that direction, however, is to understand well what is known about professional culture and why it is important.

Rosenholtz (1991) aptly coined the terms *learning enriched* and *learning impoverished* to describe elementary schools in which students, teachers, and other members of the school community either learned and grew in an exciting, supportive environment or languished with none of the expectations, norms, and rich learning experiences to help them grow. Little's (1982) work on professional development pointed out differences between schools in which teachers talked continuously about their teaching and their students, experimenting with new strategies and sharing successes and failures, and those in which teachers were isolated, private, and not prone to innovation. Both researchers found student learning differences that favored schools in which teachers also learned.

Research on the context of high schools by Talbert and Perry (1994) and McLaughlin (1993) has underlined the influence of the professional community (in this case, the high school department) on the teaching and learning that occurs in classrooms. McLaughlin noted the following:

> Classroom practices and conceptions of teaching . . . emerge through a dynamic process of social definition and strategic interaction among teachers, students, and subject matter in the context of a school or a department community. The character of the professional community that exists in a school or a department—collegial or isolating, risk taking or rigidly invested in best practices, problem solving or problem hiding—plays a major role in how teachers see their work and their students and in why some teachers opt out, figuratively or literally, while many teachers persist and thrive even in exceedingly challenging teaching contexts. (p. 98)

In their studies of high school departments, McLaughlin (1993) and Talbert and Perry (1994) determined that strong professional cultures are "essential" to changing norms of practice and pedagogy. This happens when teachers examine assumptions, focus their collective experience on solutions, and support efforts on the part of everyone to grow professionally. Professional communities with norms of privacy and unchallenged sacred principles or personal beliefs breed embittered, frustrated teachers. For professional communities, what makes the difference between communities rigidly vested in one right way or in unexamined orthodoxies and those that can play this teaching function is the existence of norms of ongoing technical inquiry, reflection, problem solving, and professional growth. Interestingly, departments within a single high school can have such different professional cultures that the influence of school leadership seems much less important.

Researchers with the Qualitative Understanding: Amplifying Student Achievement and Reasoning (QUASAR) project have examined teacher development and change in middle schools through a "community of practice" framework (Stein, Silver, & Smith, in press), which was originally developed by Lave and Wenger (1991). The notion of a community of practice helps describe how teacher learning occurs in collaborative, school-based communities. For example, in looking at ways in which "newcomers" to a school were participating in the community, QUASAR found that simply being a "member of a community of practitioners provides meaning and context to newcomers' learning experiences" (Stein et al., in press). The community provided opportunities to observe teaching strategies in action, to hear stories about the process of changing, and to become immersed in the "language" of reform. Rather than teacher collaboration being simply a contextual variable that enhances individual change and growth, learning and change are tied to the social situations in which teachers participate. It is the culture of the community itself that contributes to both individual and group changes and learning.

These findings about the power of professional community cut across levels of schooling. They provide clues to what professional developers working with teachers of science and mathematics can do to foster deeper learning and development. The following paragraphs provide questions that professional developers can ask themselves to improve the impact of their programs.

What is a good starting place? Some professional development programs and initiatives work with teachers from different schools, and some work with intact groups of teachers, such as core or leadership teams, single departments, grade levels, or whole schools. Professional developers have used three strategies to understand the importance of building professional communities. First, they have increasingly required teacher participants to "bring" a bud of a professional community with them to share in learning. For example, teachers are asked to participate in pairs or teams. The extreme case is when professional development is for the whole department (as in high schools and some middle schools), whole school, or even whole district so that an entire staff learns together.

A second strategy is for professional developers to build their own professional communities outside the boundaries of departments, schools, or districts. The professional networks described in Chapter 4 provide examples. The professional developers supporting these networks take pains to build relationships among their members that lack only the physical proximity of an intact teaching staff. A critical ingredient of what some call "temporary systems" is that they continue over time, purposely nurturing the relationships between their members in an ongoing way rather than severing them after a "main event," such as an institute or immersion experience.

A third strategy that professional developers have used to nurture professional community is to work with individual participants to equip them with skills to build their own professional communities "back home." This is not the "each one, teach one" strategy that some use, largely unsuccessfully, in which teachers learn new skills and strategies and are expected to return to their schools and teach others the same skills and strategies. (See the strategy "Developing Professional Developers" in Chapter 4 and critical issues of leadership, scale up, and capacity building for why this is unlikely to work.) In the case of developing a professional community, professional developers suggest and encourage sharing of strategies for teachers to use in their schools to (a) initiate and sustain dialogues about what they have learned, (b) work with their administrators to build realistic expectations and garner support, and (c) encourage others to participate in similar, complementary learning experiences. For example, teachers may return home with study guides for examining articles or videos that engage others in what they are learning. They practice "reentry" behaviors that keep them from becoming isolated by virtue of their changing beliefs and values and enthusiasm for new ideas and approaches and that allow them to respond constructively to questions and issues raised by others. They may also learn how to work collegially with peer teachers and how to coach prospective teachers who are teamed with them for practice teaching. These kinds of strategies help teachers make inroads in building or strengthening their own professional communities.

What can professional developers specifically do to build professional communities among teachers? Research indicates that professional communities thrive where collaboration, experimentation, and challenging discourse are possible and welcome (Hord & Boyd, 1995; Little, 1993; Norris, 1994). Collaboration is fostered through finding time for it (see "Finding Time for Professional Development," pp. 224-228, this volume). Also, collaboration must meet the needs of participants, there must be something in it for each of them, and it must have a purpose that is better served by collective rather than individual work or expertise. Effective collaboration requires special skills—in communication, in decision making and problem solving, and in managing meetings. Finally, collaboration requires a genuine caring about others that can be strengthened through opportunities to do constructive work together and to share interesting and stimulating experiences. Professional developers can foster collaboration through structuring experiences of shared learning and special skill development.

It is important to note that collaboration as a vehicle for learning and community building can be a negative as well as a positive force. Fullan and Hargreaves (1991) point out that "contrived collaboration" can take teachers away from valuable time with students, and "groupthink" can stifle rather than stimulate innovation and imaginative solutions. McLaughlin's (1993) research has found that collegiality can focus on being critical of students and reinforcing norms of mediocrity. The chances of collaboration taking a more "learning-enriched" path are increased when it is accompanied by experimentation and challenging discourse.

Experimentation requires skills and dispositions toward inquiry, norms that recognize and support failure, and ideas with which to experiment. Although we do not discuss formal action research here, clues to fostering inquiry are provided in the discussion of action research as a professional development strategy in Chapter 4. Professional development programs can be sources of new ideas and practices with which to experiment and can assist teachers to do so in ways that increase their potential for learning. More difficult is the issue of making it okay to fail. Teachers, who are often perfectionists, have traditionally been expected to be the source of knowledge and thus must always have the right answers. Learning to accept and learn from failure is harder for some than others. It can be aided by having a critical mass of people who value it, a structured way to reflect on both successes and failures, and a clear picture of which situations are low stakes and which are high—that is, the ability to analyze the consequences of failure for different situations.

Finally, challenging discussions are not very common among teachers, who often equate criticism with personal inadequacies. This is why, in some schools, peer coaching cannot include feedback if it is to maintain its value for teachers (Showers & Joyce, 1996). Building professional cultures, however, by the very definition of *professional*, carries with it a commitment to effective practice in oneself and in others who share the profession. Desiring high-quality teaching for all students requires teachers to challenge their own practices and the practices of others to improve the learning opportunities for all. Teachers need skills and practice in applying standards of effectiveness to their and others' practices;

in gathering, analyzing, and explaining the evidence for their convictions; and in communicating criticisms to each other, both positive and negative. It cannot be otherwise because the science and mathematics teaching promoted by the reforms requires challenging what the learner thinks he or she knows to reorganize or deepen understanding or both. What we want for students, we should want for ourselves as learners. Often, difficult discussions are the ones we learn from most.

Professional developers can purposely build structures that promote a positive professional culture by breaking down isolation through strategies such as study groups, coaching and mentoring, networks, and case discussions. They can teach teachers skills of collaboration and inquiry. Also, they can equip teachers with tools and techniques to build and maintain supportive, professional communities in their schools.

Developing Leadership

Leadership is a critical issue in professional development for two reasons. First, leadership development is an explicit goal of a large majority of professional development initiatives in science and mathematics, but the extent to which this goal is achieved varies greatly. Second, from research on professional development and change in schools it is clear that leadership and support are required for professional development experiences to be turned into changes in teaching and learning (Bybee, 1993; Fullan, 1991). The support of leaders—both those in positions of authority such as principals and those with more expertise than teachers taking part in the professional development—legitimizes changes, provides resources, and creates expectations that changes will occur. In this section, we address leadership from both perspectives and suggest questions to attend to in designing professional development.

Is leadership development a goal of the professional development program or initiative? The answer to this question is "yes" for most professional development because it is required by many funders and also because both the mathematics and the science education professions have identified leadership development as a component of effective professional development programs. In our examination of national standards focused on professional development for science and mathematics teachers in particular (NCTM, 1991; National Research Council, 1996) and professional development in general (National Staff Development Council, 1994, 1995a, 1995b), leadership development was a component of effective professional development mentioned in all the documents

(Loucks-Horsley, Stiles, & Hewson, 1996). As Fullan (1993) notes, for change to be successful, everyone must be a leader.

If developing leaders is important, what is meant by a leader and what roles do leaders play? Professional developers define "leader" and "leadership roles" differently. Some use the predominant view of leaders in our society in which a leader has a vision of what the future should be, is strong and forceful, and knows how to motivate those around him or her to achieve it. In this view, the leader knows in which direction to lead, makes policy, ensures that decisions are followed, and disciplines subordinates who do not obey. Power and authority are concentrated in the leader. The management structure is top down and hierarchical. In the words of a prominent management consultant, Mark McCormack (1996, p. 2C), "there is room for only one person at the top."

There are aspects of this view that are essential to any concept of leadership. A leader needs to have a vision, a set of goals, and a plan; it is difficult to conceive of a leader who has little idea of where to go. Next, leadership implies that there are others to lead. Thus, a leader must have authority, whether it be vested in the position itself; in the personality, character, or expertise of the person; or in the vision that is espoused. A leader must also recognize and accept the responsibilities of leadership.

There are other aspects of this somewhat elitist, authoritarian view of leadership, however, that few professional developers would espouse. Rather, leadership for professional development comes in different forms and can be demonstrated and shared by many people who also share responsibility for outcomes. Leadership is not the sole province of administrators; teachers have leadership roles to play as well.

For example, Becerra (1996), a mathematics teacher in California, reflects on how several mathematics education projects in her state define leadership. Becerra notes that the projects

> have come to define leadership as "taking responsibility for what matters to you." This definition has helped [teachers] to view themselves as leaders. It encourages leadership that may look very different than the traditional, authoritarian model of "the boss" or "supervisor." It enables us to see ourselves as leaders as we do what our hearts motivate us to do. It will take many of us to make the changes the mathematics reform movement talks about. It will require all of us taking responsibility for what matters to us and supporting each other as we move ahead. There is plenty of work to be done and we will need many leaders with many different perspectives to do it. For me, this means taking responsibility to support, encourage, and develop new and diverse leadership. (pp. 7-8)

In July 1996, a forum titled "The Role of Leadership in Sustaining School Reform: Voices From the Field" identified the following five leadership dimensions that further explicate this new view of leadership:

Partnership and voice: Effective leaders cultivate a broad definition of community and invite every member to contribute to helping young people meet challenging standards. They listen and develop plans that reflect the influence of a variety of stakeholders, continually seeking widespread participation in important aspects of change.

Vision and values: Effective leaders are committed to the "dream" of student success generated by the community. They are careful to apply these values and vision to every decision that is made.

Knowledge and daring: Effective leaders develop knowledge bases and cultivate human resources, increasing capacity and encouraging risk taking.

Savvy and persistence: Effective leaders know how the system works and how to work within and around it. They can put up with resistance, but they eventually find ways of winning cooperation. They manage well and maintain a network of supporters they can count on.

Personal qualities: Effective leaders have a well-developed sense of humor and use language that signals their understanding, valuing, and inclusion of others.

Given these varied and expanded views of leadership for reform, those involved with professional development programs and initiatives that have leadership development as a goal need to think carefully about their definition of leadsership and implications for their programs. Leadership development is not as simple as creating better classroom teachers; it requires explicit attention, clear expectations, and resources (time and expertise) (Friel & Bright, 1997).

What specific roles of teacher leaders are we interested in developing? Roles for teachers to take in professional development include the following:

- Teacher development: Many professional development programs expect teacher participants to conduct presentations or workshops for other teachers in the new practices they themselves are learning. In addition to the role of trainer or presenter, teachers can act as coaches and facilitators of various kinds of support groups. They can plan and initiate professional development for others, even if they do not conduct it themselves.

- Curriculum, instruction, and assessment: As an offshoot of their involvement in professional development, teachers can play leadership roles in curriculum, instruction, and assessment. Teachers play key roles as members of school and district committees that plan curriculum, that adopt textbooks and other instructional materials, that select or develop assessments, and that respond to new initiatives—for example, a call to implement national and state standards for the teaching of science and mathematics. Also, they can provide leadership in the development and writing of curriculum in collaboration with their peers. Finally, teachers can use their mathematics or science expertise by being a resource teacher for their peers.

- School improvement: Teachers can play additional leadership roles beyond their classrooms by facilitating communication among teachers, serving on school leadership or management councils, and addressing political problems with their administrators and community members that relate to new ways of teaching and learning science and mathematics (Ferrini-Mundy, 1997). They can participate in or facilitate networks within or across schools, both in person and via telecommunications.

How can these and other roles be developed? Professional developers in mathematics and science have made it increasingly clear that good teachers of young people do not necessarily make good leaders of adults. Although even the business literature increasingly views effective leaders as those who can teach and coach (Senge, 1990), experienced teachers require special development opportunities to effectively take on roles of leadership (Friel & Danielson, 1997; Grady, 1997). Furthermore, professional developers must be clear about their expectations of the roles participating teachers are to play during or after their professional development experiences (Joyner, 1997). Often, teachers are surprised by the expectation that they are responsible for leading others in the new practices they are learning.

In Chapter 4, we discussed the strategy of developing professional developers. We described the skills that teachers find useful as they take responsibility for the professional development of others. We also discussed some of the issues involved with teachers playing out this role. As they take on additional leadership roles, however, teachers need more. They need an understanding of leadership, including the bases of power and different leadership styles. They also need skills in decision making, building and managing teams, conflict resolution, problem solving, vision building, communicating, and managing diversity.

Developing leadership does not stop with learning new knowledge and skills. As in any other professional development, teachers learning to be leaders require ongoing support and opportunities to learn over time and to experiment with some of their new skills and strategies, get feedback, discuss problems that arise, and make appropriate changes. Professional development project designers have found it useful to structure regular meetings of teacher leaders for these and other purposes (see especially the Mathematics Renaissance and Cambridge school district cases in Resources C and E, respectively).

Several leadership projects in mathematics education highlight the importance of teams for both supporting teacher leadership and having greater impact. Parker (1997) notes that teams of teachers representing different levels of schooling or grade levels ensure articulation when schools or districts "work to institutionalize powerful mathematics programs" (p. 244). Furthermore, because reform efforts based on the NCTM standards "are long-term, involve many unanticipated surprises, and can often be messy, uncomfortable, and frustrating" (p. 244), teacher leaders need the support of others to understand what is happening and communicate it well to their constituents so that progress can continue. Teams lend the strength of different expertise, model the importance of collaboration, and offer strength to help each other through difficult times (Friel & Danielson, 1997; Joyner, 1997; Underhill, 1997).

Are there roles other leaders must play for professional development to be successful? If so, how can they be developed? Administrator leadership is required for professional development to move from learning to changes in classroom practices. Principals, for example, support changes in elementary school mathematics and science through such roles as advocate, facilitator of curriculum selection or development, provider of funds and other resources, broker of professional development and other support, monitor of progress, and troubleshooter (Mechling & Oliver, 1983). Principals can protect teachers from competing demands and premature expectations for success. At middle and high school levels, department chairs and team leaders may take on these roles instead of or in collaboration with principals.

Because of the important roles for administrators, many professional developers pay them special attention, even though their primary "audience" is teachers. Administrators are often asked to participate in the professional development experiences: attend workshops, join support groups, and learn to be and even become coaches for teachers. Sometimes, the participation of an administrator on a team is required for teachers to attend an institute. Also, special sessions for administrators may be held during a small part of teachers' professional development (e.g., one day of a 5-day institute) or apart from teachers' experiences (e.g., a special meeting or seminar). At these sessions, administrators are introduced to the practices teachers are learning and are sometimes provided with a tool to observe classrooms in which teachers are implementing these new practices. Administrators are also introduced to their role in supporting teachers: They learn to anticipate how teachers will feel and behave as they change their practices; what help teachers are apt to need and when; what materials, other supplies, and support staff are required; and what outcomes they can expect from the changes teachers are implementing.

All these activities and experiences reinforce the importance of building a learning community around new ways of learning and teaching and of working together to change perspectives and expectations. Learning together, when it is done in an open and trusting environment, can build respect for different roles and relationships that help school staffs deal with the difficulties of significant change.

Leadership is required for professional development to make its impact felt in schools and classrooms. Professional development programs can address this by building the leadership knowledge, skills, and dispositions of participating mathematics and science teachers, as well as of administrators, at all levels of schooling.

Building Capacity for Professional Learning

Often, professional developers view their role as more than that of providing opportunities for individual teachers, or even all teachers within a school or a district, to learn and grow. Indeed, they see an important role in building the capacity of the system—whether of a school or a district or some combination of those and universities, science-rich organizations, and other members of the community—to support teacher learning and development in an ongoing way. What would it mean to build capacity? What would it look like if there was capacity to support ongoing professional learning? A conference of mathematics and science educators pondered this question (and others) in the fall of 1994. This section reflects the results of their deliberations (for the full report, see Friel & Bright, 1997).

How would you know capacity if you saw it? Components of capacity, which can be present at any system level from local to national, are the following:

- People who can work with teachers in supporting their learning and teaching

- Support systems for professional development providers

- A knowledge base of professional development theory and practice

- Supported subcultures in which professional development flourishes

- Policies, resources, and structures that make professional development a central rather than a marginal activity

These elements constitute an "infrastructure" for professional development. Without a strong infrastructure, professional development can be of uneven quality, can be of insufficient quantity, is not cost-effective, comes in the form of projects that are not sustainable, and too often is inaccessible and noninclusive. In this section, we provide some questions that professional developers can use to determine how they do or could contribute to the capacity of their systems to support ongoing professional growth.

Do you employ and develop people who can work with teachers to support their learning and teaching? In the previous section, we discussed leadership for professional development. Here, we underscore its importance as well as the dearth of skilled professionals who can provide the leadership for professional development in science and mathematics. Traditionally, most of the individuals responsible for staff development were located in higher education and mid-level school district administration. The current view of professional development calls for a much broader range of individuals who can facilitate and lead professional development work. These include teachers who are in leadership positions, science and mathematics resource teachers, staff developers within school systems, principals, and so on. Building capacity for mathematics and science reform means developing a wide range of opportunities for individuals in all these roles to expand their existing professional knowledge to work with teachers in facilitating learning.

Professional development initiatives that are employed to build the capacity of the system to maintain the gains they help teachers to make must identify individuals who are willing and able to provide leadership and must provide professional development that assists these people in understanding and taking on expanded leadership roles. The previous section and the section in Chapter 4 titled "Developing Professional Developers" discuss how this might be done.

Do you build support systems for professional development providers, including yourself and your staff? In addition to teachers, professional developers also need support. The development of a larger and more cohesive cadre of professional development providers is of critical importance to the reform movement. They need opportunities to learn, network with others in similar roles, and confront challenges and solve problems together that are too large for them as individuals. Building capacity for mathematics and science reform thus means developing and maintaining a diverse array of structures to provide this ongoing support.

Do you recognize, study, and apply the knowledge base of professional development theory and practice? Do you help others to do so as well? As described in Chapter 3, there is an emergent but substantial knowledge base for professional development theory and practice that covers a wide range of both the contexts for professional development and the kinds of professional development encounters that can occur. This knowledge base includes psychological studies of teachers in the process of changing their beliefs, mathematics and scientific knowledge, and classroom practice; research on the process of staff development itself; studies of teachers in subject matter collaboratives and networks; studies of a variety of strategies of professional development; teachers' own writing about their practice and about changed classrooms; and so on. Although this knowledge base in its current form is valuable, it is incomplete and still growing. This book, for example, attempts to expand the current knowledge base by documenting and analyzing several mathematics and science professional development programs and synthesizing these results in terms of the framework for the design of professional development learning opportunities.

Professions are defined, in part, by shared knowledge, both practical and theoretical, that becomes a common language with which to communicate and improve. Building the profession of professional development, and thus building capacity in the system to initiate and support ongoing learning, requires that the knowledge base be recognized, built on, and used.

Does your professional development program support "subcultures" in which professional development can flourish? Increasing systems' capacities to support the continuous learning and growth of teachers is not limited to increasing the number of programs in which teachers can participate for specific lengths of time. It also includes making contexts available to teachers on an ongoing basis in which they can "join" a subculture that embodies the values of high-quality teaching and inquiry about teaching. Such subcultures would provide ongoing support for teachers who have participated in a particular program and those who might join one again but currently choose a different form of learning. They would also provide "rampways" for teachers who have not previously been engaged in intensive professional development but would like to try it on a limited basis. Finally, they would provide contexts that can sustain teachers over the long term and in which continuous questioning and learning about teaching is encouraged.

The need to create subcultures for high-quality professional development is more than instrumental and has a larger significance. The nature of the reform movement that is embodied in the mathematics and science standards not only requires change and learning on the part of a large number of teachers but also implies a different intellectual culture for schools than is typical. Therefore, we must build capacity not only for each teacher to reflect on and examine his or her own teaching but also for the culture of teaching and schooling itself to change. Viewing reform as a cultural matter, as well as an individual psychological one, opens new avenues. The deliberate creation of supportive subcultures in different parts of the system would begin the process of cultural change. Furthermore, it would give us the opportunity to study and begin to understand the nature of such cultures.

Thus, building capacity means initiating, developing, and supporting teacher subcultures at social and organizational levels that will complement efforts designed to build capacity at individual levels.

Do you work to create and influence policies, resources, and structures that make professional development a central rather than a marginal activity? In addition to adding a variety of structures and activities to the currently available menu, it is clear that certain current state and local policies and financial arrangements constrain the degree to which teachers can participate thoughtfully in whatever professional development opportunities are available. This means that to increase what is available to teachers, it is necessary to identify and institute policies that increase the capacity of teachers and schools to take advantage of what is available. As long as structures and financial policies marginalize professional development, whatever capacity we can build will be underutilized.

For example, our systems are plagued by teachers' schedules that make professional development during the school day virtually impossible; lack of opportunity for teachers to work in teams or to work together; insufficient financial resources to staff schools in such a way that teachers would have the opportunity to do professional development during the school day; and lack of long-term and consistent priorities within school systems so that teachers' learning can accumulate.

Professional developers must work with policymakers at all levels to develop and institute policies that recognize that professional development for all educational personnel is an essential component of an effective school system rather than an add-on activity that can be eliminated in difficult times. Strategies such as those described in later sections on garnering public support and providing time for professional development may offer more specific direction.

Scaling Up

Scaling up is becoming a buzzword in the educational community largely because of the concern for increasing the numbers of teachers and other educators who effectively reach students. Many professional developers have had success with helping individual teachers and even whole schools change the way science and mathematics are taught and learned. That there are 115,000 schools and millions of teachers in this country, however, makes the challenge of reaching these large numbers daunting.

The particular challenge for many professional developers is how to design programs and initiatives so that they are able to reach a significant number of teachers. In the past, many have been able to work with 30 volunteer teachers in summer institutes, help a school select and get training in a new curriculum or instructional practice, or work with one or two teachers from each of several schools who then returned and helped their schools implement changes. None of these strategies has worked particularly well for reaching large numbers, except in the most superficial ways. Furthermore, funding agencies are less interested in creating "pockets of innovation" and are impatient to spread reform more broadly. For example, witness the large percentage of resources from the National Science Foundation that are currently supporting systemwide initiatives—at the district, region, and state levels. Many of these—the Local Systemic Change initiatives—are designed to provide a substantial amount of professional development to all the teachers in a school district.

How can professional developers address this need to reach large numbers—that is, to scale up from a few to many? Although there is no single answer to this question, there are several factors that can contribute to success. This section provides some questions that professional developers can ask themselves that reflect these factors.

Is there clarity and a sound foundation for what is being scaled up? The literature reflects different ways of thinking about what is being spread or scaled up. In the implementation literature, the "innovation" is a program or practice new to the setting (Fullan, 1991; Wilson & Davis, 1994). School improvement and reform efforts refer to a vision or purpose (Olson, 1994). Others refer to standards or "normative practice"

(Elmore, 1996). The common theme is that it is important to articulate what the change is supposed to look like when it is being practiced: what teachers and students are doing (and not doing) and what one would see in classrooms and schools (Hall & Hord, 1987). This does not necessarily imply a highly prescriptive set of teaching behaviors and materials, although it could; even the national standards for science and mathematics are specific enough to reveal themselves in teachers' practices and students' responses. One knows them when one sees them.

Therefore, clarity is important but so are utility and practicality because unless a change seems possible, it will not be attempted. There must be evidence that it does not require superhuman efforts, skills that few have or can develop, or exotic equipment or special classroom or school situations (e.g., small classrooms and extra staff). It does not rely on a specific teacher or a unique situation. Finally, the change must be credible and backed by evidence that if this change were to occur, clear benefits would ensue. These attributes of a change make it better able to be shared from one place to the other, to be picked up by larger numbers of people, and to be communicated to those whose support is needed for it to become common practice (Fullan, 1991).

How do you provide professional development opportunities to large numbers of people? This is a particularly difficult question to address. Rarely does professional development succeed when it is "delivered en masse" because it usually lacks attention to individual needs, person-to-person interaction, and opportunity for in-depth study and experimentation. Several strategies, however, are being used to reach large numbers. One is technology (as discussed in Chapter 4); in some applications, such as teleconferencing, there is no limit to how many people can be reached. Other applications, as noted in Chapter 4, have limitations similar to other strategies: They are limited by how many participants a single moderator, instructor, or even conferencing system can respond to.

Another strategy is to use a *multiplier*, which is referred to by many names, including *certified trainers, teacher leadership,* and so on. This strategy is discussed in Chapter 4 under "Developing Professional Developers" and in this chapter under "Developing Leadership." Here, a cadre of teachers and others learn science or mathematics content and pedagogy or both, master the new practice(s) in their own classrooms, and are prepared to work with adult learners and given time to do so. This can have a multiplier effect, enabling large numbers to be reached.

Professional development does not have to be "one size fits all" but rather can employ a variety of strategies. Teachers can learn new teaching practices through workshops, institutes, coaching, support groups, case

discussions, and immersion. Reaching large numbers is not about everyone having the same experience and having that experience in a constrained period of time. When teachers are offered a variety of strategies
from which to learn, and these are offered over an extended period of
time, many people can be reached. Here, the issue may be one of focus.
When schools or districts decide to focus their professional development resources on one particular change or area of change, teachers
have the opportunity to learn fewer new practices more in-depth
(Bennett & Green, 1995; Elmore, 1996). They can be engaged intellectually, rather than superficially, in the change (Klein, McArthur, & Stecher,
1995).

*Does each teacher have sufficient support to change his or her prac-
tice?* Klein and associates (1995) note that "economies of scale operate
only weakly in educational reform" (p. 145). Although it may be eco-
nomical to supply teachers with materials in large numbers, such as in
the use of science kits in elementary schools, it is still the case that each
teacher needs professional development, follow-up support, and time to
learn and experiment. Scale up cannot occur if teachers lack what they
need to change. Furthermore, it may take increasingly more resources,
largely in the form of time and energy on the part of "change agents," to
reach those who come to a change at the end of the line—that is, the "late
adopters." These schools or individuals may require more evidence to be
motivated, assistance to develop new knowledge and skills, and lower
assister-teacher ratios to troubleshoot during implementation (Klein
et al., 1995). These are all items that need to be anticipated in a support
plan for all those who will ultimately be involved. The support plan must
accurately estimate and ensure provision of the resources that are necessary to reach everyone.

This points out the importance of coordinating different components
of the system and multiple actors in ways that will focus support on the
change that is to become widespread. Curriculum and assessment practices, school administration and policies, school structures (including
time, materials support, and teaching assignments), and other change
initiatives must be coordinated and focused for scale up to succeed.

*Is there quality control of the professional development received by
all?* This is a particularly important issue, especially where a multiplier
strategy is being used. When a particular change has been identified that
promises certain outcomes when its critical elements, however generally
defined, are in use, it is important that all who will be involved in the
change learn those elements well. This requires professional developers
that have themselves mastered the required knowledge, practiced the
strategies, and demonstrated their abilities to work with adults to help

them do so as well. They are both competent and conscious of their competence; therefore, they are not on "automatic pilot" with no ability to communicate to others and help them change.

We previously noted the kind of preparation professional developers need to be effective. Some programs fail because they expect teachers with limited professional development to return to their schools and share what they have learned with other teachers. Quality control requires intense attention to developing professional developers, coaching them to develop their professional development skills, and supporting them over time as they work with increasing numbers of teachers and encounter different kinds of challenges and problems.

Other quality control mechanisms include clear expectations for the roles of professional developers, written guidelines for professional development activities (e.g., workshop plans and materials, cases and facilitator notes, coaching guides, and immersion activities), and tools for monitoring and evaluating the work of professional developers.

Is there a plan at each unit of implementation (department, school, district, state, etc.) for ongoing use, support, and institutionalization? Plans at each level acknowledge the fact that successful change is simultaneously top down and bottom up (Fullan, 1991). Individual progress in learning and changing can be anticipated (Loucks & Stiegelbauer, 1991), as can the management and policy moves that each unit of organization will need to make to support increasing numbers of people involved in the change. Institutionalization, the stage at which a change becomes "how we do things around here," requires attention to such items as routine professional development for new teachers or those who change grade levels; support networks; routine ordering of required materials and equipment; continuous reflection, monitoring, evaluation, and commitment to changes based on what is learned; and ensuring a line item in the budget for support of the change (Miles, 1983).

Scaling up is a challenge that many are currently taking on in an effort to provide all students with challenging science and mathematics programs. This challenge has inspired innovative, creative, and entrepreneurial approaches by many professional development initiatives (Education Commission of the States, 1995) that all stand to learn from in the coming years.

Garnering Public Support

Constantly shrinking resources are a sign of the times and nowhere is it felt more keenly than when the public (often through the eyes of school board members) scrutinizes an education budget. What stays and what goes often relates to what is valued, and professional developers like professional development to be high on the list. Public support is required if that is to happen.

Public support for professional development is needed at times other than when budgets are being determined. When substitute teachers are in classrooms, when school is out because of "inservice days," and when word is out that teachers are at a conference far from home are the times that the public needs to voice its support for the learning that teachers must do to constantly improve their practice.

Public support for professional development is intimately related to public support for science and mathematics reform. The public must value science and mathematics learning for all young people; it must understand new views of what students need to know and be able to do to be considered scientifically and mathematically literate; it must recognize the substantial amount of effort it takes to make the kinds of changes needed for that vision to become a reality (of which professional development is one kind of change); and it must acknowledge and commit to playing an ongoing role of advocacy and support for the long term.

Professional developers can address the dual purpose of garnering public support for science and mathematics education reform and for teacher professional development. They can do so by paying attention to three areas: (a) increasing awareness of the importance of effective teaching and learning of science and mathematics as well as effective professional development and what they entail; (b) involving the public in learning situations (those of both students and teachers) and in various roles; and (c) gathering and publicizing the results of teaching and professional development.

How can professional developers build awareness of the importance of mathematics and science education reform and of effective professional development? The first step is to help clarify why reform and the public's support for it are essential. There are several reasons, of which many relate directly to parents, who are an important segment of "the public." The reasons include the following:

Parents and the general public can benefit from a better understanding of science and mathematics—for example, they can see how it is used to understand and propose solutions to everyday problems.

Parents can help by supporting their children to learn in new ways—for example, parents can help their children use inquiry by asking and investigating questions that arise in everyday life.

Schools can benefit from the contributions of committed parents and community members, such as scientists and mathematicians. They may have expertise to lend. In addition, generating their interest could increase the resources available to the school.

An informed public will be more skeptical about and able to address misinformation about science and mathematics education—for example, issues regarding teaching evolution versus creationism and teaching problem solving and computation.

Mathematics and science educators are clear about the need for public engagement in the current reforms. For example, in its charge to groups writing the *National Science Education Standards,* the National Research Council (1996) stated the following:

> The traditions and values of science and the history of science curriculum reforms . . . argue for a large critique and consensus effort. Science is tested knowledge; therefore, no matter how broadly based the perspective of the developers, their judgment must be informed by others' responses . . . particularly teachers, policymakers, and the customers of education systems— students, parents, business, employers, taxpayers. One of several reasons for the limited impact of past reform efforts was the weakness of their consensus building activities. (p. 2)

Professional developers can help teachers and other educators understand the importance of reform and, more important, become articulate about it. They can help educators formulate clear answers to questions such as "what's in it for me? us? the community? the country?" that are often heard from the public.

They can also help teachers and schools formulate strategies for communicating these messages. One way is to follow the "why it is important" message with a clear picture of what the reform will entail. Fortunately, the mathematics and science community is gaining access to videos that depict the kinds of teaching and learning promoted by the reforms as well as "kits" for use in addressing various audiences.

Mathematics and science educators have found that parent education is essential in their reform initiatives. As Parker (1997) notes, "parents become strong advocates for change if they are kept informed of the need to change and the nature of the change needed in mathematics education" (p. 240). She further explains that the California Mathematics Leadership Program found that teachers could not be expected to communicate the need for reform until they had had opportunities to experience new practices for themselves. In such cases, outside experts were often better sources of information and inspiration for parents and other community members (and sometimes they actually were parents or community members).

The University of Washington's professional development project for elementary school teachers directly addressed the issue of garnering public support for science education through a 3-day mini-institute for teachers. During that time, teachers learned how to craft messages to address the questions and concerns of various audiences, including parents, principals, business executives, and city council members. They interacted with a panel representing these groups regarding the question, "What would motivate you to support science education?" They identified the common threads and the unique needs of the various groups (C. Kubota, personal communication, July 1996).

In addition to awareness of effective mathematics and science education, the public must have awareness of the importance and nature of effective professional development. It helps to state how little education systems pay to "retrain" their employees compared with corporations. Again, clear articulation of what professional development is for, what it entails, and what its benefits are can help to increase the public's support.

How can professional developers engage the public in improving mathematics and science teaching and learning? Another strategy for garnering public support is by actually engaging them in mathematics and science education—the education of both young people and professional development. This can be done in several ways. First, parents and community members can be invited into the learning settings as learners; for example, they may join teams from schools or districts for professional development, which often occurs in summer institutes. Second, they can be invited in as "teachers," working with students in classrooms and teachers in professional development settings. This is of particular benefit when they have science or mathematics expertise and experiences or both to share (see Chapter 4 for a discussion of appropriate roles). Finally, parents and community members can relieve teachers so that they have time for their own learning. Examples of how this can and does happen are provided later in this chapter in our discussion of finding time for professional development. Support for professional development will increase as members of the community become actively engaged in it and in schools and classrooms in which its benefits reach students.

How can professional developers help justify the investment in improved mathematics and science teaching and professional development? Professional developers can assist educators in learning skills and devising strategies to measure and share the results of professional development and new ways of teaching and learning. Such information is critically important when budget and support decisions are being made. Later in this chapter, we discuss various ways of thinking about evaluation of professional development, many of which provide compelling evidence of the impact of various learning experiences on teachers and, consequently, on their students. These data not only need to be gathered but also need to be reported in such a way that questions from different audiences of the public are answered in convincing ways. Anecdotes and news stories work for some; hard data on teacher and student change are required for others. Professional development can prepare mathematics and science educators with knowledge and skills of public relations so that they can bolster the support of the public for their new directions.

Supporting Standards and Frameworks Through Professional Development

The 1990s are certain to be known as the decade in which standards became commonplace among educators and policymakers in the United States. Voluntary national mathematics and science standards developed through professional consensus have emerged from the NCTM (1989, 1991, 1995), the National Academy of Science's National Research Council (NRC, 1996), the American Association for the Advancement of Science (AAAS, 1993), and other professional organizations. State and school district standards and frameworks, some voluntary and some required, continue to emerge as well.

The most common purpose of standards documents is to identify what students need to know and be able to do. Some standards, notably the *National Science Education Standards* (NRC, 1996) and the NCTM mathematics standards, go beyond specifications for student learning to delineate what teaching and assessment should entail for such learning to occur. These standards also include specifications for professional development, programs, and systems that are of critical importance to support standards in other areas.

States and districts have made different choices about how to engage in the standards movement, including adopting the national standards in their whole form, adapting them, or creating new standards. Some have in addition or instead developed curriculum frameworks, which again differ one from another, especially in specificity. Some are as general as the national standards and allow for broad local interpretation; other, more specific curriculum frameworks include grade-level expectations and courses of study (e.g., what third graders should know and topics to be covered in high school biology) (Council of Chief State School Officers, 1997).

Rarely are standards and frameworks discussed without a reference to professional development. As Loucks-Horsley (1996) notes,

> Educators need to know *about* the standards; they need to *know* the standards; they need *to act upon* the standards as they influence the science learning of young people. All of these learning goals present an enormous challenge to the entire science education community, and particularly to those responsible for creating opportunities for professional learning. (p. 83)

This section suggests questions for professional developers to ask themselves with regard to their usage of the various standards that influence their work: how their designs reflect standards for professional development and how their content helps teachers learn what they need to know to help their students achieve the standards. Some specific questions include the following:

- In what ways is the design for professional development guided by standards for professional development? Are standards for professional development used as criteria to judge program quality and guide improvement?

- In what ways do standards define and guide decisions about the content of professional development—the science and mathematics as well as teaching, assessment, and curriculum development?

- In what ways are standards the focus of professional development?

How can standards for professional development be used? We noted in Chapter 3 that a synthesis of national standards in mathematics, science, and professional development suggested a great deal of consensus and a set of criteria that should apply to design and improvement of all professional development programs and initiatives (Loucks-Horsley, Stiles, & Hewson, 1996). According to the synthesis, programs and initiatives meeting the standards have the following criteria:

- A clear, articulated vision for the classroom that reflects the standards for teaching and learning

- Rich and rigorous content in science, mathematics, teaching, and learning

- Learning experiences designed on sound principles of learning that model the strategies teachers are expected to use with their students

- Attention to building a learning community for participants that supports their ongoing development while they learn and sustains it in their work

- A component that focuses on the development of dispositions and abilities for a variety of leadership roles

- Strong links to other parts of the education system, such as assessment and curriculum, and to other initiatives at the school or other level

- Continuous assessment for improvement and for judging the impact of the program or initiative on participants, their organizations, and their students

Several states (e.g., Michigan, Louisiana, and Colorado) have developed similar standards for professional development. They can be used by professional developers in designing and improving programs, by policymakers in selecting programs for funding and other support, by district and school leadership in selecting programs to bring to the school or to which teachers will be sent, and by evaluators to determine program quality.

How can standards guide selection of content for professional development? What do teachers and other educators need to know and be able to do? This question guides the content of professional development programs and is addressed directly by standards. The mathematics and science in the national and most state and local standards is demanding. It requires teachers to know the discipline(s) in-depth as opposed to "staying one chapter ahead of the kids" or learning along with them. Professional development focused on science and mathematics encourages exploration of the "big ideas" of the disciplines—the fundamental understandings represented in the standards. There is full acknowledgment that the rapidly expanding fields of science and mathematics preclude teachers knowing everything, but there are fundamentals without which teachers will be unable to acquire new knowledge in a meaningful way. National standards, and many state standards, go beyond traditional subject matter. For example, the *National Science Education Standards* (NRC, 1996) include not only physical, life, and earth and space sciences but also the understandings and abilities of inquiry, the history and nature of science, and personal and social perspectives. For the many teachers with only subject matter expertise, these and other areas are ones that require attention from professional development programs.

Learning the mathematics and science required to teach to standards is complicated at the elementary and middle school levels. Professional development programs that target elementary and middle school teachers must address the difficult issue of how to deepen their content knowledge when their curricula require them to know many subject areas or science disciplines or both. Given limited resources, including time, this requires creative solutions that do not water down or eliminate the science and mathematics (as do many attempts at "interdisciplinary programs" in which students merely read and write about science or use mathematics only in the service of another subject) or eliminate the possibility for teachers to connect science or mathematics to other learning by using specialist teachers who teach only these areas.

In addition to requiring in-depth content understanding, standards underline the importance of teachers knowing how to teach their disciplines. This requires not only subject matter knowledge but also an understanding of how students learn the subject. This special knowledge—pedagogical content knowledge (Shulman, 1987)—sets expert teachers apart from scientists and mathematicians in that they know how students learn different concepts, what is hard and what is easy for them, and what examples, representations, and processes are apt to help them learn. Standards emphasize that this specialized knowledge is required for effective teaching. Many of the kinds of learning strategies described in this book focus on the development of pedagogical content knowledge, especially those that connect the learner with a more experienced teacher or images of expert teaching.

How can standards be the focus of professional development? How can teachers and other educators learn about and come to understand the various standards documents? Professional development activities can help in a variety of ways for a number of different purposes. First, they can build awareness of standards, addressing questions such as "What are they?" "Why are they important?" and "What do they mean for me?" Awareness materials produced through the Annenberg Foundation and NCTM can be used with teacher, administrator, parent, or community groups to overview the national standards. The *Private Universe* video, produced by the Harvard-Smithsonian Center for Astrophysics (1995), demonstrates the general lack of understanding of science and mathematics among even our most educated citizens and the difficulty of developing in-depth understanding of fundamental concepts with traditional teaching methods. The video is a highly visual "call to arms" for higher standards and their development through new ways of teaching and learning.

Second, professional development activities can increase understanding of components of standards. For example, focusing discussion on the role of inquiry in the *National Science Education Standards* (NRC, 1996) through viewing a video and studying the actual statement in the book makes teachers aware of the emphasis given to inquiry as a set of abilities and understandings that students need to develop and a way of teaching and learning science. Likewise, study of ideas such as equity, mathematical power, and the role of technology in standards increases understanding and can lead directly to implications for practice.

Another way that professional development can lead to better understanding of standards is in helping teachers and others develop images of standards-based science and mathematics education. Analyzing videos in which teachers are teaching important content in the ways described in the standards can illuminate standards-based teaching; studying instructional materials and assessments can illustrate standards-based curriculum and assessment; and examining student work can better define what it means to demonstrate the understandings and abilities in content standards. A useful set of inservice materials is one developed by Biological Sciences Curriculum Study, titled *Decisions in Teaching Elementary School Science* (1995), that translate the national science standards into understandable, practical language. Three videodiscs provide opportunities for teachers to analyze a variety of classroom scenes through the lenses of curriculum, teaching, assessment, and equity. Other videos of teaching that can help do the same and include *Just Think: Problem Solving Through Inquiry* (New York State Education Department, 1996), a kindergarten through eighth-grade science video series; the *Private Universe* teacher workshop series (Harvard-Smithsonian Center for Astrophysics, 1995); *Sense Making in Science* series (Technical Education Resource Centers, 1996); *Science Images* videos (North Central Regional Educational Laboratory, 1996); and the *Teacher to Teacher With Mr. Wizard* (Mr. Wizard Foundation, 1994-1996) staff development video series. Another example that relates to curriculum is the following: The Project 2061 staff of AAAS helps people use the *Benchmarks for Science Literacy* (1993) through an activity in which they carefully examine lessons from a set of curriculum materials and search for various benchmarks that students are apt to be able to demonstrate once they have experienced the lessons. Using standards documents with a clear purpose in mind helps people understand them and how they can be used as a reference in the future.

Final thoughts about standards and professional development. One role standards play is to provide a common language and understanding across and within groups critical for the partnerships, networks, and other collaborations that are required by systemic change. This is particularly important if the United States is serious about reforming science and mathematics in ways consistent with the findings of the Third International Mathematics and Science Study (TIMSS) (United States Department of Education, National Center for Educational Statistics,

1996). That study suggests that one reason the United States is at or below the average in the world in science and mathematics achievement is because of the incoherence of the education system: the lack of a shared and clear vision and the vehicles for achieving it. What students learn and teachers teach is influenced variously by national, state, and local policies; textbooks and other instructional materials; the teachers' preparation and experience; and the multiple demands placed on teachers for what and how to teach. The result is a "mile wide and inch deep" curriculum. Standards offer a coherent vision. With appropriate professional development and support, they can go a long way to guiding teaching, curriculum choices, assessment, and the nature and organization of schools and other system components toward reaching that vision.

Evaluating Professional Development

Professional development opportunities are designed for a wide variety of purposes, and it is the role of evaluation to determine whether and in what ways they are successful. Fulfilling that role, however, is rarely easy for several reasons. First, regardless of the purpose of a given program, people typically jump to measure what is easiest to measure: satisfaction of participants in events. Because of this norm, it is difficult to get people to think more broadly about outcomes and measures. Second, there is increasing demand to assess the value of professional development by the achievement of students of those who participate. This demand is well-founded given the large investment of resources that has been made in professional development; it is based, however, on the assumption, often challenged (see Hein, 1997), that what and how much students learn can be attributed to an experience of their teachers. Again, broadening what is considered a valued outcome of professional development is a difficult challenge for professional developers. Finally, evaluation is a critical issue because it in and of itself is underutilized as a valuable learning experience for professional developers, participants, and others. Reflection on evaluation results, as they are being gathered and when synthesized, is an important contributor to continuous improvement.

The following are several questions that professional developers can ask themselves to help them address the challenges of evaluating their programs and initiatives:

- What are their goals or desired outcomes?
- What are the most important outcomes to assess and why?
- How can these important outcomes best be measured?
- How can evaluation contribute to continuous improvement?

What are the goals or desired outcomes of the program or initiative?
Professional developers typically have a wide range of goals, but they are
often not skilled at articulating them as outcomes. What would you see
if you were successful? What would have changed for whom? It is easier
to think of activities than accomplishments—for example, conducting a
summer institute and a series of follow-up problem-solving sessions is
often cited as a goal rather than teachers using inquiry-based strategies
in their classrooms. The range of possible outcomes is quite large: development of new abilities (knowledge, skills, strategies, and dispositions)
by a variety of people (teachers, students, and administrators) and organizations (departments, teams, schools, and districts) in a variety of areas
(teaching, leadership, and change management). Being clear about desired outcomes, articulating what they would look like if they were present, not only lays important groundwork for evaluation but also causes
the program to be more focused and purposeful.

How do you assess the accomplishment of the program's outcomes?
Evaluation helps collect evidence of the extent to which a program's aims
have been met. Although paper and pencil in the hands of the participants in professional development have traditionally been the tools of
choice in evaluation, a wide range of instruments and sources of information are preferable. Evidence from interviews, observations, product
(e.g., lesson plan) analysis, performance tasks, and focus groups can all
contribute evidence. Teachers, students, colleagues, administrators, scientists, and mathematicians can all be sources of information about the
outcomes of a professional learning experience. Obviously, there are
trade-offs for every instrument and source of information—for example,
in cost, time, degree of self-report, and amount of inference required.
These are all considered in designing an evaluation keyed to a particular
purpose, audience, and budget.

A resource for evaluators and professional developers who want to
broaden the outcomes assessed, instruments used, and sources probed
is available from Horizon Research, Inc. The National Science Foundation has been funding local projects that aim to reform the teaching of
mathematics and science across whole school systems through professional development. Horizon has developed and is supporting the use of
quality evaluation instruments so that each project does not have to
create its own and so that data can be aggregated across projects. The
framework for data collection includes such outcomes as the quality of
the professional development activities; extent of teacher involvement in
the activities; changes in teacher attitudes and beliefs; changes in science
and mathematics curriculum, instruction, and assessment; the nature of
the culture or context for teaching; and the sustainability of the professional development system (Horizon Research, Inc., 1997).

How do you acknowledge and then evaluate how a professional development initiative and its participants change over time? The impact of professional learning activities appears to be different at different times. This is why it is foolhardy to either expect or focus on measuring student learning when teachers have just begun to learn and experiment with new ideas and strategies. Well-designed evaluations unfold with expectations for change. For example, one might focus on participant satisfaction and developing basic understanding early in a program, change in classroom behavior and in the professional culture midway through the program, and on various kinds of student change, beginning with attitudes and evolving to demonstrating new, increased understandings, at the end of the program.

To address this issue, evaluators have used concepts and tools of the Concerns-Based Adoption Model to answer questions about the implementation of changes in mathematics and science education (Driscoll & Bryant, in press; Loucks-Horsley et al., 1990; Pratt & Loucks-Horsley, 1993). The following kinds of questions can be asked: How do teachers' concerns about the new program or teaching strategy change over time? How does their use of the new program or teaching strategy change over time? To what extent do teachers implement the critical components of the new program or teaching strategy over time? Two developmental scales—Stages of Concern (assessed using paper and pencil instruments) and Levels of Use (assessed through a focused interview procedure)—provide criteria for assessing progress along the change process. Components of the program or strategy can also be defined and assessed using a combination of interview and observation; the different "configurations" that the program components take on in different classrooms can then be represented and monitored over time.

After sufficient time has elapsed for teacher change to result in improvement in student learning, students are an appropriate focus for professional development evaluation. A unique evaluation scheme was used by the Mathematics Renaissance (see description in Resource C) in its fifth and final year to evaluate the impact on students of the professional development it provided to middle school teachers throughout the state of California. As part of TIMSS, hundreds of hours of classroom instruction have been videotaped in mathematics classrooms throughout the United States (United States Department of Education, National Center for Educational Statistics, 1996) and have been compared with those of classrooms in Japan and Germany using a very sophisticated coding and analysis procedure. Videotapes of classrooms of teachers participating in Mathematics Renaissance professional development were made and similarly coded and analyzed. They were compared with a sample of the TIMSS tapes of U.S. classrooms to address the question, "Do students of Mathematics Renaissance teachers have a greater opportunity to develop the kinds of mathematical understandings, skills, and attitudes called for in the NCTM standards and the California Mathematics Framework than students of teachers not involved in Mathematics Renaissance?"

How do you take advantage of evaluation as a learning experience in and of itself? Increasingly, evaluators are becoming partners with professional developers in a commitment to continuous improvement of programs and their results. Involvement through such activities as the following is important:

- Engaging program staff and participants in specifying and discussing desired outcomes as well as identifying and prioritizing evaluation questions

- Involving staff and participants in the design or review of instruments or procedures for assessing outcomes

- Sharing responsibility with staff and participants for collecting data

- Engaging staff in analyzing and interpreting data

- Sharing responsibility for reporting learnings from evaluation with a variety of audiences using a variety of formats

Each of these activities can contribute to staff and participant understanding of their own learning and that of others, of a variety of methods to assess important learning outcomes and interpret information gathered, of ways to specify and then to investigate the answers to important questions, and of how to communicate to a variety of audiences and develop arguments for new ways of acting.

An example of evaluation as a powerful learning tool comes from an elementary science program evaluation. The California Science Implementation Network (CSIN) seeks to assist elementary schools and their teachers in transforming the science learning experiences of students. In a multiyear series of professional development activities, teachers design a science program for their school, use the California Science framework to select appropriate instructional materials, and learn and practice a variety of teaching and assessment strategies to build conceptual understanding in their students. To evaluate the success of this focus on classroom and school reform, evaluators from WestEd collaborated with CSIN regional directors to develop a set of questions regarding what would be occurring in the classrooms and the school that would indicate success. A school profiling instrument, adapted from one designed by Inverness Associates, captured the nature of classroom instruction and the status of a number of factors demonstrated to support successful implementation of change in elementary school science, including leadership, school-based planning, materials support, professional development, and external support. Schools conducted self-studies using the instrument, which was followed by a 1-day site visit by an evaluator-CSIN regional director team. Discussions with the school teams and follow-up letters describing observations of the site visit team provided opportunities for inquiry and reflection by teachers and administrators. Data from a sample of 18 schools that varied in years in CSIN, designation as successful or unsuccessful by CSIN regional directors, student ethnicity and socioeconomic status, and geographic location were arrayed in data matrices by evaluators and reflected on in meetings with regional directors. This collaboration resulted in rich interpretations of the results of reform-based professional development, immediate plans for change, and additional questions to ask over time.

Finding Time for Professional Development

It is clear that, for professional development to be effective, experiences for teachers must occur over a long period of time, provide ample time for in-depth investigations and reflection, and incorporate opportunities for continuous learning (Little, 1993; Loucks-Horsley et al., 1987, 1996; Sparks, 1994). Finding the right amount of quality time to effectively carry out professional development programs or initiatives is a challenge faced by every professional developer. In fact, time has emerged as the key issue in every analysis of school change in the past decade (Fullan & Miles, 1992).

The reforms in science and mathematics education are being heralded by national standards; understanding and using these standards to inform new ways of teaching and learning takes time. It cannot happen in one-shot workshops, during three professional development inservice days a year, or by attending several seminars that are disconnected from each other in their content and focus. As discussed in Chapter 3, the idea of building new understandings through active engagement in a variety of experiences over time, and doing so with others in supportive learning environments, is critical for effective professional development.

National standards are not the only impetus for moving the reform of professional development forward; the relationship between time and learning, for both teachers and students, was reviewed in-depth by a nine-member commission of the National Education Commission on Time and Learning. The resulting report, *Prisoners of Time*, clearly stated that time for professional development is

> Urgently needed—not as a frill or an add-on, but as a major aspect of the agreement between teachers and districts. They [teachers] need time to read professional journals, interact with

their colleagues, and watch outstanding teachers demonstrate new strategies. (p. 36)

The report reflects the changing emphasis throughout the country on the value and need for professional development for teachers.

Although changes are under way, professional developers still face challenges in finding time for professional development. One of the barriers to changing the kinds of professional development experiences that teachers of mathematics and science need is the perception of what constitutes "teachers' work." The public and policymakers continue to believe that teachers are working only when they are with their students. This belief results in little support for policies that capitalize on the messages in the national standards. Castle and Watts (1992) explain that

> The traditional view of teachers' work is governed by the idea that time with students is of singular value, that teachers are primarily deliverers of content, that curricular planning and decision making rest at higher levels of authority, and that professional development is unrelated to improving instruction. (p. 2)

With this perception firmly in place, there is little room for teachers' time out of their classrooms to be spent on their own professional development.

Another barrier is the current structure of schools. Teachers typically have only their lunch time, planning period, or both, designated as time away from their students. Rarely are teachers able to use this time to collaborate or consult with their peers, reflect on either their teaching or their students' learning, or connect with others outside of the school environment. Implied in this statement is that teachers' own time is "designated" for them; rarely, however, are teachers empowered, or trusted, to "use their noninstructional time wisely and [historically they] have had virtually no control over the structure or use of their time" (Castle & Watts, 1992, p. 2).

Given the organizational structure of schools and the perception of how teachers should spend their working hours, what can professional developers do? How do professional developers design programs and initiatives that overcome the obstacles and incorporate the necessary time needed to create continuous learning opportunities for teachers of science and mathematics? The following sections suggest questions for professional developers to ask themselves as they tackle the issues surrounding time for professional development.

How do you find ways to make more effective use of time currently available within the school calendar? Even given the current structure and organization of schools, professional developers have been able to find ways to "creatively restructure" the time that is already available to teachers within the school day and the calendar year. Although some of the solutions may be "temporary and ad hoc" (Castle & Watts, 1992, p. 3), they are still realizable options for professional developers. A review of the research finds that the solutions being implemented fall into several categories: freed-up time, restructured or rescheduled time, common time, better-used time, and purchased time (Castle & Watts, 1992).

- *Freed-up time:* This strategy entails freeing teachers from their regular instructional time. The most obvious plan is to provide substitute teachers so that teachers can participate in professional development. Some schools have recruited principals and other administrators, parents, and volunteers to serve as substitute teachers; other schools use specialist teachers, such as art, music, or part-time teachers. Other options include team teaching and instituting community-based learning experiences or library research for students that free individual teachers from instructional responsibilities. Although all these solutions result in time available for professional development, they are typically only small blocks of time sporadically dispersed throughout the year.

- *Restructured or rescheduled time:* This solution requires formally altering overall instructional time—the school day, the school calendar year, or teaching schedules. For example, many schools are using schedules in which students attend school 1 hour longer on 4 days and are released early on the fifth day or in which students arrive 1 hour later in the morning and stay 1 hour longer at the end of day, providing time in the morning for teachers to meet with one another. Other schools have begun grouping students and teachers, using a team teaching approach, so that groups of teachers have scheduled time outside of the classroom. Still other schools are moving to year-round scheduling, with larger blocks of time (e.g., 3 or 4 weeks) available for professional development, whereas others (mostly middle and high schools) are increasing class size, which results in fewer classes to teach and more time for professional development. Obviously, this type of restructuring requires the support and input of administrators, but it can result in larger blocks of time consistently scheduled throughout the year.

- *Common time:* To move teachers out of individual preparation time, schools are reorganizing time so that teachers have "common" times together. Common planning or preparation times can enable teachers to meet by grade level or by discipline or subject areas or as interdisciplinary teams. Although this can often result in only 1 hour each day, many schools are organizing planning time to follow or precede lunch time, giving teachers 90 minutes to work together. This results in an uninterrupted block of time instead of divided time throughout the day—

something that is needed for teachers to engage in meaningful and in-depth professional development experiences.

• *Better-used time:* Often, teachers' time outside of the classroom during the school day is consumed by faculty meetings and administrative tasks that limit their opportunities for collaborating with peers. Schools are finding ways to reduce the administrative nature of this time, allowing teachers to focus on their own professional development. For example, using electronic mail for routine communication between teachers and administrators can save time typically spent in faculty or management council meetings discussing administrative issues. A unique solution has been to move "nonessential" student-oriented activities, such as assemblies and club meetings, to after-school time or to recruit staff other than teachers to participate in activities, thus providing time for teachers to meet together. In addition, professional developers can closely examine the days that are formally scheduled for professional development (often only 3 or 4 days a year) and reassess whether they are being used to best meet the teachers' needs and are designed around a comprehensive plan.

• *Purchased time:* Even in the face of limited funds, many professional developers have found ways to reallocate existing funds to provide time for professional development. Some schools and districts have established a "pool" of permanent substitutes or provide stipends for teachers to attend professional development activities outside of the school day, usually in the evenings and on weekends. Although paying teachers for time outside of their workday does send the message that their time is valuable, it also sends the message that professional development is not valued enough to be incorporated into the professional life of teachers.

How can you work toward influencing state policies and public perceptions that support professional development? The suggestions described previously primarily focus on implementing solutions at the school or district level. Inherent in those solutions is the assumption that schools and districts do in fact have control over their own programs, have budgets for professional development, and can institute the kinds of restructuring identified—reorganizing school days and calendar years. Many professional developers, however, are faced with policies and perceptions that further impede their efforts to create meaningful learning opportunities for teachers, such as a limited numbers of days allocated by state boards of education for professional development or public concern about teachers' time out of classrooms.

Professional developers can do much toward moving the reform of professional development forward. One step, as noted previously in the discussion of public support, is convincing key stakeholders and policymakers that new forms of professional development are essential to effectively support changes that teachers are making in their classrooms and that providing time for professional development is critical (Corcoran, 1995). To accomplish this, professional developers must identify and define what is meant by professional development. Often, schools and districts that investigate activities currently under way that are called professional development find that what is defined as professional development (inservice days, Saturday workshops, and after-school presentations) does not meet their teachers' needs for growth and learning. By simply redefining professional development to include time for participation in strategies such as case discussions, summer months spent in a scientific research lab, or action research conducted in the classroom, funds and time have been reallocated to support these strategies (Aronson, 1995; Bull, Buechler, Didley, & Krehbiel, 1994; National Education Commission on Time and Learning, 1994; Richardson, 1997).

Increasing public awareness of and support for teachers' professional development includes conveying the importance of teachers' spending time outside of the classroom and emphasizing how this is not detrimental to students but rather benefits both teachers and students. Corcoran (1995) notes that "80% of existing professional development funds are controlled locally" (p. 9). Given this, it is imperative that local communities support teachers' engagement in professional learning experiences outside the classroom. Changing perceptions about what professional development "looks like" can increase parents' and communities' understanding of its importance.

For time for professional development to be valued, all involved—including teachers, administrators, policymakers, and the public—must begin to accept a reconception of school time. As Raywid (1993) stated,

> If we are to redefine teachers' responsibilities to include collaborative sessions with colleagues, then it is necessary to reconstrue teacher time. The time necessary to examine, reflect on, amend, and redesign programs is not auxiliary to teaching responsibilities—nor is it "released time" from them. It is absolutely central to such responsibilities. (p. 34)

The Design Process 7
in Action

|||||||||||||||||||||||||||||||||||||||||||||||||||||||||||||||||||||||||||||||||||||||||||||

Why did professional development designers in Cambridge, Massachusetts, decide to implement a districtwide curriculum implementation strategy while the Workshop Center staff in Harlem, New York, opted for immersion? Why did a statewide kindergarten through sixth-grade mathematics reform initiative in North Carolina choose curriculum implementation while California's middle school mathematics effort focused on curriculum replacement and networking? Why did a national high school science program go the route of curriculum development?

This chapter describes the decision-making process of five different professional development programs. It is based on writings by and interviews with program developers. These professional development designers provide us with the rare opportunity to see the "artists" at work. We learn about more than their final products—if there ever are any final products! We learn how and why they and their colleagues make their decisions. We see the design framework presented in Chapter 2 come alive as these professional developers explain how knowledge and beliefs influenced the design of their programs, how they took into consideration features of the context, and how the planning cycle unfolded from goal setting to reflecting. Also, as we unravel the process, we learn more about the complexities and realities of planning for effective professional development not just in these five unique instances but also, to

---

AUTHORS' NOTE: Unless otherwise noted, quoted material in this chapter is from personal communications to the author.

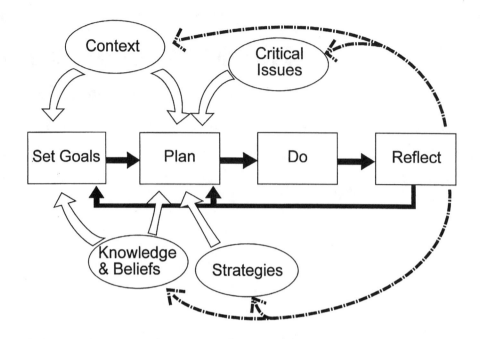

Figure 7.1. Professional Development Design Process for Mathematics and Science Education Reform

the extent that they act as mirrors, in the readers' settings. (Critical issues, which also influenced design decisions, were treated separately in Chapter 6.)

We repeat the design framework to guide our journey through professional development design and implementation (Figure 7.1).

Tapping the Knowledge Bases and Framing Beliefs: "We Stood on the Shoulders of Giants"

When asked if they consciously drew on the knowledge bases about learning, teaching, and professional development, the five designers unanimously replied, "of course." Judy Mumme of the Mathematics Renaissance Program said, "In the first year, a team of professional development leaders came together and formulated a set of principles to guide our work. We were pretty conscious of the knowledge base we were drawing on all along the way" (Table 7.1). Susan Friel of Teach-Stat echoed Mumme's sentiments: "We stood on the shoulders of giants. Our definition grew directly out of the Standards work."

TABLE 7.1 Guiding Principles of the Mathematics
Renaissance

1. Teachers must be members of a professional learning community.
2. Beliefs and behaviors are part of a reciprocal process.
3. The pedagogy of professional development must be congruent with the pedagogy desired in classrooms.
4. Equity issues must permeate the fabric of professional development.
5. Professional development must be grounded in classroom practice.
6. All teachers are capable of making the changes required by the reform.

SOURCE: Acquarelli and Mumme (1996).

Mumme's and Friel's responses were typical of the other designers. In every case, an important part of the planning process involved calling up the knowledge base and clarifying and articulating a set of beliefs, which influenced virtually every aspect of design. These professional developers could not imagine going about their design in any other way.

That did not mean that their beliefs were adhered to 100% of the time. Inevitably, compromises had to be made. The designers, however, were aware of the tensions, knew that they were making compromises, and remained committed to having their professional development program reflect, as consistently as possible, the beliefs that they held most dear.

Furthermore, as they carried out their work and reflected on it, the designers' own knowledge grew and some early beliefs gradually changed. Mumme noted, "Belief systems are not static, they have been subject to ongoing reflection and modification."

What were the particular sets of knowledge and beliefs that drove the design process for the developers and how did they influence their goals and plans? Some common themes cut across each of the five cases. All shared a similar view about the nature of mathematics and science learning, a belief that all students and all teachers can be successful learners, and a commitment to principles of effective professional development. Each of these themes and their influences on design are explored in the following sections.

Knowledge and Beliefs About the Nature of Learning and Teaching Mathematics and Science

Mumme of Mathematics Renaissance simply stated, "How did we want students to engage in mathematics and the learning process? That guided how we would go about our work with teachers." Each of the developers asked themselves the same question for mathematics or science or both. How they answered that question had a great deal to do with how their program took shape.

Susan Friel (1996) described the relationship between beliefs and program design for Teach-Stat as follows:

> We [developers] spent a number of sessions articulating our beliefs and then framing a coherent curriculum that supported teachers learning statistics in an environment that both modeled and encouraged teachers' eventual use of the key components of teaching as articulated by the *Professional Standards for Teaching Mathematics* (National Council of Teachers of Mathematics, 1991). To do this, we worked to get past the notion of putting together a set of activities that addressed selected statistical concepts because developing a list of activities did not address the process of teaching and learning that was believed central to the program. Two theoretical perspectives helped shape this direction. One was the conception of statistics as a process of statistical investigations and the articulation of the process by Graham (1987). The other was the introduction of the use of concept maps (Novak & Gowin, 1984) as a way of assessing what teachers knew about statistics prior to and following the institute. (p. 7)

For Hubert Dyasi and colleagues at the Workshop Center, a passionate belief about the nature of science as inquiry led to their focus on educating teachers to become "confident science inquirers" by immersing them in the investigation of familiar phenomena:

> At the core of the center's educational approach is the importance of experience and meaning in learning and the belief that each person is capable of inquiring and observing with meaning and understanding. . . . Concomitant with our beliefs about human capacity to learn and to create knowledge is our view that science encompasses both content and approach. Its contents are in the common materials and phenomena we encounter and the approach is inquiry built around observations and experience and around making meaning of them. Direct experience with phenomena of the world connects the content of science with children's curiosity, experiences, and observations outside the classroom. (Dyasi, 1995, p. 1)

Dyasi and colleagues believe that this approach to learning is as applicable to adults as it is to children:

Principles of human learning are not different between adults and children; they learn through direct experience and by constructing their own meanings from those experiences and from previous knowledge. . . . Teacher education must faithfully reflect the way you want teachers to teach. They must themselves experience the ways they will guide children.

This belief was shared by all the developers, who crafted professional development experiences that closely paralleled those to be used in the classroom.

"All Humans Are Educable"

> We have to select strategies that give both students and teachers the opportunities to demonstrate their educability.
>
> —*Hubert Dyasi*

Closely related to their understanding of the nature of mathematics and science learning were strong beliefs about the potential of all humans to master complex mathematical and scientific concepts and procedures. These permeated all the cases but played out in the design of professional development in different ways. For instance, at the heart of the Workshop Center's work is a commitment to the belief that "all humans are educable." Center director Hubert Dyasi commented, "The ways we were doing education in schools masked that. . . . We were using strategies that were unidimensional. We have to select strategies that give both students and teachers the opportunity to demonstrate their educability." This belief is another underpinning of the center's immersion strategy, which makes in-depth understandings of science content and process accessible to Harlem's diverse teacher and student populations.

Equity concerns influenced Melanie Barron, Director of Science in the Cambridge Public Schools, to choose a different strategy: curriculum implementation. She designed a centralized program to implement science inquiry-based units of study across the curriculum. Barron explained: "You need clear citywide goals, objectives, and curriculum for what all children are to be taught. Then you need school-based technical assistance and support to the teachers." Karen Worth, who worked with the district from Education Development Center (EDC), added, "If you don't require science from the center, not all teachers will teach it. If it is not mandated, some students won't get it." These beliefs determine Barron's decision to develop a team of science staff development teachers to provide ongoing support to teachers in every elementary school across the district. The combination of a mandate and a strong network of support, composed of both school and district-based staff developers, was Cambridge's approach to ensure that all students receive quality instruction in science. (Both Barron and Worth speak about the Cambridge program in this chapter.)

The mathematics reform programs mirrored the science programs' commitment to excellence and equity. Acquarelli and Mumme (Resource C, p. 287), from the Mathematics Renaissance, write that "None of it [reform] will matter unless it improves learning for all students, regardless of race, gender, or class." This belief strongly influenced the initial selection of the grade span for intervention because the middle grades are often where decisions about a child's future are made. Furthermore, a concern with equity influenced both what strategy was chosen—curriculum replacements units—and how it was implemented. Mumme stated,

> We used curriculum replacement units to surface issues about equity. Teachers were asked to try the units with all of their classes. We purposely asked teachers from different settings to describe their experience. They were surprised that kids from a learning disabled class and a gifted class were doing similar things.

Mumme stated that a principle of the Mathematics Renaissance program is that "issues of equity must permeate the fabric of staff development." Acquarelli and Mumme (1996) provided the following two examples of how that looked for participants at all levels of the program:

> As uncomfortable as it often makes participants, meetings of teachers [and] cluster leaders . . . tackle issues of equity head on, sharing information, data, and statistics about inequalities, confronting their own beliefs about tracking, or discussing examples of race, gender, and class discrimination in mathematics classrooms.
>
> At a March cluster meeting one teacher reported, "ESL students don't always have the words to write down but they definitely have the ideas. We let them talk about what they're going to write before they write it. Sometimes we let them dictate their words to someone else." Other teachers reacted to her comment, many nodding heads and taking notes. Teachers also learn to identify their own behaviors that can disadvantage females (e.g., calling on males more often and asking males probing questions). They may discuss the implications of the belief that "all children

can learn," and probe the inconsistencies that exist between their beliefs and actions. (p. 481)

Knowledge and Beliefs About Teachers

Developers were inspired by teachers' capacity to learn, lead, and change. Mumme stated, "We have strong beliefs that all kids are capable of engaging in quality mathematics. But, the temptation is to not believe that about teachers. We knew we could not write off any teachers."

An explicit principle of the Mathematics Renaissance program is "all teachers are capable of making the changes." As a result, the program targets all teachers, not just the most innovative or eager, at a school. It also employs strategies and structures to remove, as much as possible, obstacles to teacher change. This was, in part, the thinking behind the choice of replacement units, which provided teachers with the concrete "stuff" to take back to their classrooms that they were clamoring for but were also used as a catalyst for teachers to rethink their own practices and beliefs.

Similarly, the City College Workshop Center program was designed explicitly to contradict prevailing opinions that members of minority groups, such as residents of Harlem, lack the intellectual capacity to understand science. Through its approach of firsthand inquiry, teachers generate investigable questions, plan and conduct investigations that sharpen direct observation, and make meaning out of inquiry experiences. As a result, they become inquirers into school science as well as into their own learning and teaching. These experiences prepare them to implement new approaches in their classroom, improve their attitudes toward science, and lead professional development workshops for other teachers. Dyasi stated, "Of course, they can do this because they are humans. Teachers have been incapable only because they have not had the opportunity to do this."

A strategy that relies on teachers to develop curriculum must be rooted in respect for teachers' capabilities; this is an explicit belief of Global Systems Science (GSS). GSS brings teachers together to co-develop curriculum with staff of the Lawrence Hall of Science. Teachers field test curriculum units even before convening, and they come to a summer institute to share their experiences and feedback on the curriculum. Then they create new activities and assessment instruments. Developer Cary Sneider commented, "We have a strong belief in the importance of trusting teachers and respecting their craft knowledge. When we do that, we get the best product and the best performance from the teachers."

Although GSS relies on teachers as curriculum developers, other cases emphasize developing teachers as staff developers. Teach-Stat trained a cadre of 84 "statistics educators"—teachers who serve as resources to other teachers across North Carolina. Cambridge is nurturing school-based liaisons—teachers who have a role supporting other teachers in their building and implementing the curriculum—and district-based staff developers—former teachers released full-time to provide training and technical assistance districtwide. Mathematics Renaissance is heavily focused on developing its 70 cluster leaders who, in turn, provide support to 350 schools. Mumme stated, "Teachers are the best leaders of other teachers," which summarizes what all of the developers believe and exemplify in their goals and plans.

Knowledge of Effective Professional Development

It is not hard to see how the designers drew heavily on what is known about effective professional development. Principles of effective professional development summarized in Chapter 3 are obvious aspects of all the programs previously described. Clearly, each of the programs was driven by a well-defined image of effective classroom learning and teaching, provided teachers with opportunities to develop knowledge and skills to broaden their teaching approaches, mirrored methods to be used with their students, and prepared teachers for leadership roles. How the cases embodied the principle of continuous assessment is described later in this chapter. The two remaining principles, building and strengthening the learning community of science and mathematics teachers and providing conscious links to other parts of the educational system, were also important to our designers and came alive in interesting ways that are described throughout this chapter.

Knowledge of the Change Process

Each of the developers was well schooled in the knowledge base on change. Several reported studying and referring back to Michael Fullan's in the same manner as doctors use Gray's *Anatomy* (1989). Knowledge of the change process served as an important touchstone for these developers. It shaped their initial designs, steeled them for the chaos and complexity they faced during implementation, and informed their daily "diagnosis" and problem solving.

Because these professional developers shared a common understanding of change, their program designs had common hallmarks. They were all long-term endeavors. They were clear about the changes they were attempting to make. They addressed change at many levels, from the individual to the organizational. They had mechanisms in place for improvement. They provided different kinds of supports for learners over time as their needs evolved. Exactly how the programs embodied a particular change principle varied widely, however.

The principle that "as individuals go through a change process, their needs for support and assistance change" is an example. Each of the programs designed different learning experiences over time to address participants' changing concerns, questions, and experience. Typically, programs began with some kind of knowledge-building experience, such as the summer institutes in Teach-Stat, Mathematics Renaissance, or the Workshop Center. These were followed by opportunities for planning for implementation, classroom or clinical practice with coaching and feedback, and reflection with colleagues. (This progression through activities is discussed in more detail in Chapter 4.)

Global Systems Science, however, stood on its head the conventional wisdom about that sequence of learning experiences. Participants' introduction to the program was not in a workshop but in their own classrooms. Before ever coming to the summer curriculum development institute, teachers received the materials and taught units to their students. Then they gathered at Lawrence Hall of Science for a summer institute. The first phase of the institute was not knowledge building, as one might expect, but reflection on participants' experience teaching the program. Cary Sneider explained:

> We focused on experienced teachers and invited them to be creative, teach the material first, and then come back and talk about it. First they reflected with other teachers and gave us feedback on the units. Then, after that, they were hungry for new knowledge. That's when they were most interested in seeing what earth scientists were doing and in gathering more information. Later, teachers were given the opportunity to plan for how they would adapt materials for use in their classroom when they used them again.

While staying true to the principle that professional development is "developmental," Global Systems Science's design capitalized on the questions and concerns teachers would bring to a workshop after experiencing a change in their classroom. The change literature, discussed in Chapter 3, informs us that learners move through a sequence of developmental stages in their feelings and actions as they engage new approaches. This is predictable. This also made the designers sensitive to teachers' needs and questions as they learned. Then, based on the designers' experiences, they found that precisely what kinds of support teachers needed at each stage varied greatly depending on experience level and the nature of the professional development program itself.

Their knowledge about change influenced their initial designs as much as it served another equally important purpose during implementation: It helped designers understand, cope with, and navigate through the resistance to change and the chaos they encountered as the change process unfolded. Judy Mumme stated,

> It gave us a language for what we were observing. . . . We saw chaos in classrooms and schools. Teachers were struggling to make sense of what was happening. Change didn't come out in coherent ways. There was a lot of fumbling around. We came to understand this as our version of what Michael Fullan [1991] called "the implementation dip." I'll never forget one teacher who entered the process feeling that he was a good teacher. By all accounts, he was. But his world was being turned upside down. All that he had been doing was called into question. Before, he was clear in his mind what to do. Now it was fuzzy. He lost his sense of efficacy—his ability to say to himself, "I'm a good teacher!"

Without a framework for understanding events such as these, staff developers could easily become discouraged. For Mumme and staff (and each of the developers we interviewed), the change principles they had studied offered them perspective and reassurance. They were able to step back and look at what might seem like a setback as a natural part of the process and possibly a turning point if managed well. From initial design to daily problem solving, change theory was not "book knowledge" but a valued guide and partner in designers' work.

The knowledge bases that the professional developers brought to their programs were indeed important in their design work. Two themes, however, emerged as we heard their stories. First, their own experiences proved an important source of knowledge. Second, although they "knew" some things to be true, they were often called on to abandon that knowledge and make compromises. These themes are discussed in the following sections.

Experience as a Source of Knowledge

In addition to drawing on research and other literature, designers also tapped their own professional development experiences both as learners and as staff developers. Hubert Dyasi described the process as follows:

> You build a repertoire of experiences, which you bank. That is your database from which to select a strategy. You think, that

approach worked because of this. That one didn't because of that. That takes you beyond guesswork to a more scientific, organized way of thinking.

Teach-Stat's decision to use curriculum implementation, for example, was based, in part, on developers' analysis of why a previous effort at mathematics education reform they had been involved in had failed. Susan Friel explained this as follows:

> I had been involved in another effort where teachers were just trained in approaches to problem solving, but given no curriculum to implement. The results were that teachers went back to a very structured, didactic text book. They couldn't take what they had learned and translate it into changes in the classroom. That's why I have a bias now toward curriculum implementation. I think you can do a lot of workshops around problem solving. But if teachers don't have something to go back and work with, eventually it won't work. Teachers don't have the time to transform the curriculum.

Global Systems Science developers' experience as teachers trying to develop interdisciplinary curriculum was the impetus for the design for GSS, according to Cary Sneider (1995). He stated,

> Each of us on staff of the GSS project had considered ourselves "innovative" teachers in the past, and we had all spent many years developing hands-on activities in astronomy, physics, chemistry, and biology. But we reeled from the disorientation of our first experiences in interdisciplinary teaching. Our need to prepare new lessons would take us to unfamiliar territories in libraries and bookstores. We had to be ready to switch from physics to biology as we went from one chapter to the next, or from science to economics and politics, so that we could follow up the implications of an issue instead of going on to "cover" the next science topic. . . . If that was challenging for us in the supportive environment of a science center like the Lawrence Hall of Science, we realized it would be even more difficult for many teachers in the context of local and state school systems where the resistance to change is likely to be far greater. (p. 5)

This experience informed GSS designers about what knowledge and skills teachers would need to implement an interdisciplinary program in their own classrooms. It also led to their choice of curriculum development as a professional development strategy. Sneider stated, "We also hoped that involving teachers as codevelopers would engage their commitment to the new program, and help them acquire a deep understanding of the principles on which it is based."

Just as understanding the underlying principles of GSS was important to participating teachers, so too was understanding the underlying principles of mathematics and science teaching and learning and professional development important to each of the professional development designers. They came to their "artist's palette" with knowledge of these principles as well as their own rich experiences as learners and professional developers. These gave rise to a set of beliefs that guided the moves and choices they made. Staying true to those beliefs, however, turned out to be more of a challenge than designers anticipated.

Making Compromises

> Tensions are inherent in the work. The challenge is how to make them live comfortably together.
>
> —*Karen Worth*

The designers began with clearly articulated beliefs that influenced their goals and plans. What happened, however, when beliefs collided with reality or even with each other? The creative tensions involved with these conflicts made for some interesting dynamics.

The conflict between a belief in inquiry and the necessity to jumpstart a change effort was an important one in Cambridge. Designers settled on implementing the same commercial units districtwide not because they believed that these units represented inquiry at its purist and best but rather because they were simply a good place to start. The considerations were more practical—providing teachers with good materials, coordinating the logistics of materials support, and coordinating a support system. Science Director Melanie Barron stated,

> What was missing in Cambridge was a curriculum. We needed a way to get teachers engaged in teaching science; to get the kids learning and the teachers teaching. Many of them hadn't been doing it. We didn't have time to immerse them in inquiry. We wanted to get them familiar with a unit and then build in more reflection, interaction, and autonomy over time.

Another compromise Barron made was to focus more on leadership development rather than on broad-based teacher development. One cannot do everything at the same time—even though there was a strong belief in developing teachers. Given the constraints of time and money, the Cambridge team decided to put the bulk of the resources into building the capacity of a smaller group—not all the teachers. The goal was to develop a structure to permanently sustain the program over time.

The Cambridge team simultaneously grappled with the tension between their beliefs about teacher professionalism and their decision to mandate a curriculum. They knew the curriculum needed to be owned by the teachers. At the same time that they were telling the teachers, "we want you to own this curriculum," they were telling the teachers that they had to do these three units.

Furthermore, Cambridge professional developers felt that the system needed to have a centralized system to handle logistics and to maintain the quality and rigor of science for all students. There was a definite tension between the two beliefs of teacher autonomy and centralized decision making. Barron was trying to balance them by supporting teacher initiative, encouraging their creativity, and providing professional development for teachers to develop their own strand of the curriculum. They were not mutually exclusive, but they were difficult to reconcile.

Similar conflicts characterized the design of the Mathematics Renaissance program. Regional director Kris Acquarelli and Renaissance director Judy Mumme (1996) describe the planning as a process of balancing "tensions that are inherent in our work" (p. 479). For example, the belief that change needs to be systemic and fundamental often collides with teachers' needs. Acquarelli and Mumme wrote,

> "I do not want to be gone from my classroom for days where I am not taught a specific unit that I can take back and use. My students lose every time I am gone." This teacher's comment is typical of many. How do you develop a deep understanding of the issues in mathematics education when teachers have a strong desire for things to take back, to add recipes to their files? Time spent exploring constructivism may not feel like a day well spent to some participating teachers. Short-term gains often limit long-term growth opportunities. (p. 480)

The decision to use a curriculum replacement unit strategy grew out of this tension. Teachers would leave with "stuff" to try, not as an end but as a tool for their continuous learning. Like developers in Cambridge, Renaissance developers concede that they chose a strategy as a place to begin and not as their ultimate purpose.

Designers universally appear to struggle with being true to their beliefs. Karen Worth remarked, "That's just part of the design process.

Beliefs can't get played out purely. You have to decide what gets into the foreground, what into the background, and sometimes, what is the most expedient." Balancing beliefs with expediency has a great deal to do with the unique circumstances of a particular program—the community, policies, resources, culture, structure, and history that surrounds it—what we call context in our design framework.

Context

> Design always has to be tempered with reality. You want to both be realistic and push the system at the same time.
>
> —*Karen Worth*

The context of the five cases varied widely—the state of California; Harlem, New York; multiple schools in North Carolina; a national program based at the Lawrence Hall of Science; and Cambridge, Massachusetts, which has a small, urban school district. The different contexts helped to shape very different programs. Some common lessons, however, emerged from their varied experiences: (a) Pay close attention to your context as you design, (b) watch for and respond to changes in context and needs as a program proceeds, and (c) help participants consider their own context as they implement changes. Each of these lessons is discussed in the sections that follows.

Pay Close Attention to Context as You Design

Karen Worth explained that "Design always has to be tempered with reality. You want to both be realistic and push the system at the same time." For example, in Cambridge, Science Director Barron would have loved to have school-based liaisons freed up from classroom responsibilities full-time or more than five district-based science specialists. The resources just were not available. Therefore, working within the constraints of the resources available (nothing new for educators!), she settled on two liaisons per school, who received stipends for their work and professional development time but were not released from classroom responsibilities, and five full-time district specialists. "Tempering design with reality," Cambridge ended up with a structure for developing teacher leadership and supporting curriculum implementation that was not perfect but was a real advance for the district.

Context was not always constraining. In the case of Teach-Stat in North Carolina, designers were able to capitalize on preexisting infrastructure—the University of North Carolina's Mathematics and Science Education Network, which is composed of centers throughout the state housed at 10 of the state university system's campuses. Susan Friel explained how this contextual factor facilitated their design as follows:

> The fact that these 10 centers were available really influenced our design. The center's job was to be in touch with school districts in their geographic area. This was perfect for what we wanted to do—have university faculty help to prepare statistics educators who would in turn work with teachers in their districts. Using the structure of the centers, we were able to reach 450 teachers across the state and develop wonderful partnerships between teachers and university faculty.

Certain features of context were readily apparent and drove the design from the beginning. This was also true for the Mathematics Renaissance program. As a statewide systemic initiative funded in part by the National Science Foundation, the Mathematics Renaissance program had a political context that could not be ignored—the expectation of the funder. Its charge was to institute a process that would not only make a difference in schools but also have a ripple effect influencing multiple levels of the educational system, including state policy. Judy Mumme described how that charge propelled their design process as follows:

> As we thought about design, we had to consider those expectations. We had to reach a large number of schools. We had to be visible. We had to be viewed as more than a project. These considerations influenced our decision to go with a large-scale effort.
>
> The theory was that if you get a critical mass of schools heading in a particular direction, that pushes on the system, informs legislators, informs CDE [California Department of Education], and influences policy—"inside-out" systemic reform. We needed a design that had the potential for influencing policy at various levels. That affected how we solicited schools for participation, how we worked through the State Department, why we needed to remain neutral on issues around specific instructional materials and lots of other features of our design.

In other cases, designers wished they had been more attuned initially to certain aspects of their context—particularly parental and community concerns. Hubert Dyasi described how those concerns played out in Harlem as follows:

> In our context, Harlem, parents thought that anything that looked different was discriminatory. What was this funny thing we were doing—inquiry science? Why were their kids the guinea pigs? Oppressed groups often want what oppressing groups have. We

had to find ways of addressing their concerns. We had to bring parents into the discussion.

Mathematics Renaissance initiatives also met with parental objections. Mumme stated,

> We had to redesign some of the focus of professional development. We paid more attention to helping teachers become more articulate about where basic skills were in the work they were doing. We made the false assumption that people would see that basic skills were getting taken care of. We also realized that our parent outreach component needed to be strengthened. We worked with each school to design activities to engage parents, including initiating Family Math.

Although developers underscored the importance of being responsive to context, they also pointed out the danger of being too responsive. Judy Mumme offered an example from Mathematics Renaissance in which designers' and teachers' needs were in conflict. She stated,

> Sometimes we found that what the schools wanted wasn't what we thought was in their best interests. That felt uncomfortable. What we heard was "just give us more curriculum units." We felt what was needed were more philosophical underpinnings. We couldn't be slaves to context. We had to take it into consideration, but also try to reshape it.

Scanning contextual factors, such as teacher and student needs, political expectations, parental concerns, policies, structures, and organizational culture, helped designers ward off unexpected problems and take advantage of potential supports. Our developers learned that one must beware. Just when you think you understand your context, it changes!

Watch for and Respond to Changes in Context and Needs as the Program Proceeds

> Productive educational change, at its core, is not the capacity to implement the latest policy, but rather the ability to survive the vicissitudes of planned and unplanned change while growing and developing.
>
> —*Fullan (1993, p. 5)*

Context is slippery. It is constantly changing, sometimes serendipitously and sometimes as a direct result of the professional development programs we design. What was right for one moment in time may not be right for another. The successful designers we talked to found that they had to constantly monitor their context to discern changes that signaled the need for redesign. What happened with the emergence of teacher leadership in the Teach-Stat program illustrated the need to remain flexible and make changes. Friel noted,

> Originally, the pilot teachers were going to be available to help [with the workshop] but not to teach. However, by the second summer, faculty and teachers had developed such a good working relationship that the model of a "professional development team"—faculty and teachers coteaching—naturally emerged and was very successful. . . . This forced us to realize that you could back off and be flexible.

Cambridge science staff development teachers also found that teacher leaders' needs and capabilities changed over time. Melanie Barron stated,

> The more experience the liaisons had, the more they became rigorous determiners of what they do next. They became more reflective and more autonomous and were looking for different kinds of support, like small study groups. We couldn't have started there. The context wouldn't permit it. But, we had to be ready when they were.

Context could be as close to home as the individual teachers you work with or as removed as the national education scene. Hubert Dyasi noted that the momentum for mathematics and science education reform nationally had a dramatic effect on the Workshop Center's approach. As the national reform movement developed, so did the Workshop Center's approach to inquiry. Dyasi stated,

> What we are disseminating is not so strange now. Initially, we didn't want to scare people. Now we are more up-front. We have matured, too. Before, we were satisfied with having students uncover a phenomenon. We didn't push much on conceptualization. Now we are getting more to the heart of the matter . . . the real nature of doing science. People think that hands-on is science. It's not just a set of steps. Science is a great intellectual activity. Our work now is truer to that.

Other contextual changes, such as the school personnel changes encountered in the Mathematics Renaissance program, were less intentional or desirable. Mumme commented, "Superintendents left. Principals were transferred. Key people kept changing. We had to invest a lot more time in relationship building."

As California's state system discontinued its newly developed statewide assessment, the Mathematics Renaissance found itself missing one of the central elements it thought was in place to support reform. Mumme and her team were required once more to "regroup." Surviving the "vicissitudes of planned and unplanned change" was an essential skill for these designers of staff development. It was also important for their teachers, who faced the challenge of implementing change in the context of their own classrooms and schools. The programs found ways to help teachers meet this challenge, as the example in the following section illustrates.

Help Participants Consider Their Own Context as They Implement Changes

Any multischool or multidistrict effort can appreciate the design problem Global Systems Science faced. Participants in their national curriculum development institute came from all over the country. GSS literally had to consider as many different contexts as participants. How could GSS make the program as relevant as possible to a variety of contexts and help participants successfully implement the program? As Sneider (1995, p. 1) demonstrates in the following example, designers had some creative answers to that question:

Principal: Diane, I understand that you're excited about this new integrated program called Global Systems Science, but I'm concerned that some of our parents will worry that their children will do poorly on standardized tests if it replaces the usual science curriculum.

Diane: Then it's about time we educate some of our parents about the need for science literacy concerning environmental issues. National Science Education Standards and our State Science Framework say we should spend less time teaching science vocabulary, and more time helping our students relate science to the real world.

Jim: I'm not convinced that students who take integrated science will miss out on chemistry, physics, and biology. We plan to present the same concepts we taught before, but in a meaningful context. Students will still have labs, but they'll also debate the social implications of science and technology.

Principal: Now I didn't say I was against it, but I'll be the one to take the heat if our community is not convinced it's a good idea. Are you willing to present your ideas at the Parent Teacher's Association next Thursday evening?

The previous conversation did not take place in a real principal's office. It was a role play from the GSS summer institute, where teachers thought about what might actually happen when they went back to their school districts to implement the GSS curriculum. At the GSS summer institute, participants did not just learn about the curriculum. They studied principles of change and thought about how the principles would apply to their own particular school context.

As director Cary Sneider explains, the following was one of several ways that GSS honored participants' different contexts at the national institute:

> Because we had as many contexts as school districts, we had to look at commonalities. We discovered that there were four different ways in which GSS was fitting into the schools. The implementation strategy depended on which one was at play. For some schools, the first year of science was wide open and GSS easily slid in. Other schools were starting it as an experimental program with the expectation that students would like it. Students demanding the program would bring about the change. In other districts, there was enough top-down pressure to have nontrack science, and they needed a program like GSS. At the other extreme, the teachers taught in a traditional school and they would sneak GSS into a traditional course. We addressed each of these realities at the institute.

Most important, participants came to the summer institute having already implemented units from the curriculum in their own classrooms. Discussions about GSS did not happen in a vacuum but rather were grounded in the teachers' experiences. Participants gave feedback to the developers and designed their own activities and assessments based on what they knew from their experience would work best with their own students. In these ways, GSS was able to tailor its program to a diverse national audience.

The previous sections described how knowledge and beliefs and context influenced the professional development design process. Many questions about professional development design remain unanswered, however. What did that process look like? Who was sitting at the table? How much time did it take? What was the implementation of the program like and how did that fuel reflection and redesign? These questions are the focus of the next section, which takes a closer look at the four steps involved in program design as they played out in the five cases.

The Professional Development Design Process

> You've got to know what you are going to do, make a map, define end points and mileposts along the way. Then you meander toward them.
>
> —*Karen Worth*

Set Goals

Setting goals was an important launch point for the five programs but not a process that bogged designers down. They agreed that without clear goals, they would have had no place to start and no reason to get involved. Also important was the fact that goals were grounded in the expressed needs of participants and not just in the imagination of the designers. Although each of the designers engaged in some kind of process for figuring out what their vision was and then how to get from "here to there," they also warned against getting too caught up in the initial goal setting. Cary Sneider explained that "You've got to start out with some goals. But, goals evolve. The ones you start out with aren't the ones you end up with."

Plan

Although planning for each of the five programs appeared to be very different, three common themes emerged. Planning was collaborative, time-consuming and ongoing, and often involved the use of external consultants. These themes are elaborated in the following sections.

Collaborative

Each of the developers described a collaborative planning process with a small, clearly designated core group that expanded when necessary to take in more input. Developers consistently involved participants in the decision making.

At the Workshop Center, the idea for the immersion program was developed by three professors at the college. They immediately brought in school people to explore possibilities. From then on, "we shaped the program together."

The planning group for Mathematics Renaissance was the regional directors. Judy Mumme recalls,

> They came together in several meetings with staff development folks. The first year of the SSI [Statewide Systemic Initiative] we brought cluster leaders into the planning process. They put flesh on the model and advised us about what needed to happen. They were encouraged to talk to teachers about what they needed. It was an ongoing process of listening to teachers, administrators, and teacher leaders.

Melanie Barron reports that in the Cambridge public schools,

> The program began slowly. It was the decision to write a proposal that pushed the design process to the next stage. The original planning team was me, the director of science from the district, and the science staff development teachers, with assistance from consultants from EDC and others from MIT [Massachusetts Institute of Technology]. Once the proposal was funded and the liaison teachers became a reality, a number of them became involved with the ongoing planning.

Time-Consuming and Ongoing

Planning was time-consuming, sometimes painfully so. Susan Friel described the process for Teach-Stat as follows:

> The first year was a planning year. We met as a group of five to seven in long sessions—2 to 3 days. We drafted some material. I was intent on getting everyone's input. That was hard. I was criticized. People said I let things drag on too long. But it was worth it in the end, because we all "owned" the result.

Not only was planning time-consuming but also it never stopped. Even when the programs were being implemented, they were simultaneously being redesigned. Mathematics Renaissance is a good example of the iterative planning process. Mumme explained that "The regional directors went out and did the work. Then we would debrief and figure out what to do next." Similarly, in Cambridge, Barron stated, "The detailed planning was a constant back and forth among the science staff development teachers, the liaisons, the EDC consultant, and others from MIT."

Involving Outside Expertise

In Cambridge, Melanie Barron was convinced of the need for external partners. She brought to the job years of experience in collaborative work and was convinced of its importance at the institutional level, the professional level, and the personal level. She stated, "You can't do it alone. You need expertise and support internally and externally. A system cannot close its doors to the outside world. Any project is a combination of building internal capacity and injecting external expertise." In the case of Cambridge, Barron developed a relationship with nearby MIT. She also contracted with EDC for technical assistance. The resulting partnership between her and EDC has been a critical component of the program.

Involving stakeholders, taking time, and bringing in outside expertise were important aspects of developing a well-conceived plan for staff development. Although planning was an ongoing process that continued after the programs were implemented, the staff developers' focus eventually shifted from planning to doing. Designers settled on a plan and set it into motion. Their plans were now ready to meet the test of implementation.

Do

What happened to professional development plans as they were implemented, how they unfolded over time as programs matured, and what new decisions were made and why is as rich a story as the initial design process. In every case, programs looked very different 2 to 5 years (in the case of the Workshop Center, 25 years!) into their implementation than they did on the drawing board. During the 25-year history of the Workshop Center, the approach to professional development changed dramatically as staff developed and refined their immersion approach and added significant, new components to the program. In Cambridge, the basic program components remained the same but took on new qualities as the staff and program matured. Finally, as the Mathematics Renaissance scaled up from 78 to 420 schools in 5 years, some program elements stretched and grew as the program grew, whereas others, including replacement units, were abandoned as core strategies. The lives of these programs parallel survival in the natural world. Their capacity to adapt and respond to change was their greatest asset, enabling them to weather the inevitable storms of implementation. Their evolution over time is traced in the following sections as professional development designers describe key elements of their programs' implementation.

Workshop Center: Inquiring Into Inquiry

The Workshop Center actually did not begin with what is now its trademark—immersing teachers in scientific inquiry. It began in 1972 with Workshop Center staff engaging children in active learning strategies for language development in the corridors of Harlem's schools. The one condition the center staff put on their work was that teachers keep the classroom doors open so other students and teachers could see what was going on in the hallways. The idea was that teachers would see change happening and want to try it themselves. It worked. Curiosity mounted as teachers heard children's busy chatter and saw the hallways cluttered with high-quality work. Many teachers were inspired and motivated to learn new strategies. Workshop Center staff, however, quickly learned that watching them work with children was not enough. Teachers needed experiences that would help them develop the capacity to do what they saw staff doing.

When the center moved into science education, the staff drew on what they had learned—good and bad—from the early corridor program. Center director Hubert Dyasi elaborated as follows:

> We knew we had to educate teachers directly to become inquirers. They would learn how to learn by using materials themselves at their own level. For a long time, that is what we did. After a while, however, we realized that teachers weren't implementing inquiry science in the ways they were experiencing it with us. They were tied to using the materials in exactly the ways we had used them. They weren't really engaging students in asking their own questions. Their mind-set hadn't changed.
>
> Then we remembered the corridor program. Teachers changed because they were following their kids. That's how they got won over. This led us to add a series of Saturday sessions during the academic year with children. Sessions were taught by teachers with support from center staff. Following that, we had the teacher study groups to talk about what was happening with their kids.

The addition of two new strategies, teachers practicing with children and study groups, helped the program in two ways. First, it offered the teachers important professional development experiences that they needed to successfully implement inquiry-based learning. They had the opportunity to practice new techniques with feedback from center staff and reflect on their practice and classroom experiences. Second, the addition of the practice and study groups gave center staff more information about what teachers were doing and thinking so that staff could become more effective at supporting teachers.

As the center's staff observed and listened to teachers, they discovered another important stumbling block to successful implementation of inquiry science, which Dyasi stated as follows:

> Teachers were often just giving the students materials and letting them go. They had difficulty raising questions that would draw children's curiosity to the important science. It seemed that the teachers weren't able to distinguish between what was valuable in the children's explorations and build upon it and what was just play. Take the example of heating up water until it boils, and then continuing to apply heat. That is trivial until you begin exploring what it really means. You keep on supplying heat but the temperature of the boiling water doesn't change. Why not? What does it mean to "supply heat"? Is it the same as providing energy? If yes, is energy then different from temperature? What else can we do to find out about heat and temperature?

Teachers themselves did not necessarily know the science content. Also, even if they did, the issue was not that they should tell it to the students but rather that they should think about whether the students were ready to learn it. This observation led Workshop Center staff to another modification in the program—not a new strategy but a change in how staff worked with teachers. Dyasi noted,

> We needed to be more overt in pulling out what we were doing with the teachers. As we were doing the science with the teachers, we needed to say out loud, "the reason this is interesting is . . ." or to talk explicitly about the strands of inquiry from first-hand experience with phenomena, from asking questions, to collecting data, to making sense out of all this.
>
> We also needed to help them see what the children were doing. For example, when children put materials in a certain way, we asked, "why did you do that that way?" and refused the answer, "I was just doing it." Then we asked "what did you see as a result?" Children often do not raise questions verbally; they act their questions out through what they do. The change for us was to be much more explicit about both the important science and the scientific process. When we did this, teachers began to open up about what their difficulties were. They started to raise questions about themselves. That's when we could open up the doors.

The Workshop Center has opened up many doors for students and teachers during its long history. Also, it is not only teachers and students who have been immersed in inquiry but also the program staff themselves, who have been engaged for the past 25 years in investigating and improving their own practice. As they learned more about what it really takes to "change mind-sets," they moved from the corridors to the classrooms and to Harlem's living laboratory, improving on their workshops and adding new strategies to their professional development program.

Cambridge: Building Capacity

The professional development program in Cambridge developed quite differently and during a much shorter period of time (5 years) than did the Workshop Center program. In contrast to the Workshop Center program, the basic strategy of the Cambridge program remained the same: the development of local leadership through a structure of district-based staff developers and school-based liaisons. As these leaders developed, however, their needs changed and so did the nature of the support provided for them. Five years into the project, EDC consultant to the project, Karen Worth, noted,

> The five district-level staff developers' skills and knowledge have increased by leaps and bounds. We still meet once a week. But those meetings look very different now. I don't lead every meeting. The staff developers are more and more in charge of their own structure. Other kinds of interactions have been very important, like their intensive e-mail conversations. They are also more and more in charge of pieces of the program as a whole—the resource center, volunteers, the national gardening program, the bilingual program. And, they are doing all the staff development and training for teachers; we are using no more consultants.

It is no surprise that the character of the training for teachers changed as district-based staff developers took it over and made it their own. Worth stated,

> The summer institute has been greatly enriched. Trainers are not marching straight through the units now. As units are becoming more a part of the science program, staff developers are more interested in embellishing them. Every unit now has a field trip to a local resource. All the professional development is now delivered on site.

The school-based leaders, the liaisons, also moved in the direction of taking more control over the design of their own learning experiences. They wanted less whole-group activity and more small, diversified groups based on their emerging interests and expertise. By Year 4, they were pursuing an area of focus through four active study groups on assessment, how to pilot units, "Cambridgizing" the units through use of local resources, and peer coaching. The annual liaison institute was scrapped, and the time and money were reallocated to group meetings and classroom visits throughout the school year. Worth noted, "It isn't that the topics the leaders were interested in changed over time. They just moved along a continuum from novice to expert in a whole variety of topics ranging from science content and pedagogy to leadership skills."

As liaisons and district staff developers in Cambridge moved along that continuum, structures for their own learning changed to accommodate them, offering them increasingly more autonomy and choice.

Scaling Up With the Mathematics Renaissance

Scaling up from 78 to 420 California schools during a 5-year period brought about inevitable changes in strategy for the Mathematics Renaissance. For example, teacher academies, the initial foundation for the work, disappeared after the first year despite their apparent success. The academies brought teachers together from across the state to work with students in the morning and debrief the experience in the afternoon. The teachers involved were enthusiastic about the opportunity to experience new curriculum with their own students and receive direct support in the process. Therefore, why were they dropped? Judy Mumme explained as follows:

> They were a nightmare to administer. The first year, we involved 78 schools in 8 to 10 academies. The negotiations for stipends, time, locations were monumental. When we grew to 210 schools, we knew that we couldn't pull it off. We continued to have academies whenever we could, but they were dropped as a primary strategy. Instead, we relied on 2-week summer institutes and 1- to 2-day workshops during the school year.

Growing from 78 to 210 schools in 1 year resulted in other changes as well. The original support structure of 7 regional directors (1 for every 11 of the first cohort of schools) could not possibly meet the needs of an additional 132 schools. Three more regional directors were added in Year 2. Even 10 regional directors, however, could not make enough visits to all the schools and build the necessary personal relationships with the teachers. Therefore, a whole new structure was instituted—the cluster leaders. Mumme stated,

> Out of the initial 78 schools, we took 57 promising teachers who showed leadership potential and created a cadre of cluster lead-

ers. They were released from the classroom for 35 days to provide direct support for other teachers. That meant one cluster leader for every 5 schools. This move was based on the belief that personal relationships were critical.

With the emergence of cluster leaders and the expansion of regional directors, another need arose that helped to shape the program for the next 4 years. Acquarelli and Mumme (1996) noted,

> The need for ongoing professional development for leaders cannot be understated. This is perhaps one of the central lessons we have learned thus far. Leaders must have opportunities to reflect on their work, learning from one another the crucial lessons of leadership for reform. They constantly need to be challenged as learners, expanding their own understanding of mathematics, teaching, and learning. The initial design of the Renaissance failed to take this into account and much of the statewide professional growth opportunities have been funded catch-as-catch-can. (p. 480)

In Year 3, the project did not grow in numbers of schools (although the number of teachers involved doubled). It was an opportunity to further refine the work and respond to problems that emerged. Mumme stated,

> One of the problems we observed was that much of teachers' time and attention was focused on management issues. This distracted from getting at meatier issues about how kids were learning and experiencing mathematics. So, we developed workshops on setting up classroom environment, cooperative learning, managing extended tasks, and writing in mathematics. We asked all continuing teachers, instead of doing new replacement units, to do the same unit, only this time to focus more on kids' learning. There was a lot of resistance to this. They wanted more replacement units. They wanted to cobble together a whole curriculum. Their intent was to permanently replace their curriculum. Our intent was to provide more in-depth professional development experiences.

In Year 4, the project grew in breadth and depth. As more schools were added and new teachers joined from participating schools, project staff had a pleasant surprise, as Mumme noted:

> We thought new schools and new teachers from old schools were going to be less sophisticated and require more intensive work.

That didn't bear out. The new teachers were quite sophisticated partly because of the spreading effect of our work beyond those who directly experienced it.

By Year 5, the Renaissance faced the monumental challenge of maintaining the quality of an effort that had grown to 420 schools but that had approximately the same number of cluster leaders and regional directors as in Year 2. A key strategy was continuing to emphasize the professional development of the cluster leaders despite their limited time on the project. Mumme stated,

> The professional development of the cluster leaders grew more important over time. It was critical that they had professional growth opportunities, which we continually had to balance with their classroom teacher role. They were now only released from their classrooms for 30 days because of concerns that they were away too much. We also realized that the coaching role was an important one, and provided more professional development for them in cognitive coaching. We asked the cluster leaders to play a coaching role with each other. Here again time got in the way. Because of that, it was the least uniformly effective strategy—one we wished we could have done better. Despite the difficulties of their role, over the life of the project, the cluster leaders grew into a remarkable group of people.

Year 5 brought another major challenge to the project. The state of California adopted instructional materials, rendering the Renaissance's central strategy—the use of replacement units—irrelevant for adopting schools. In response to schools' changing and diverse needs, the Renaissance provided three choices for participation. Schools that adopted instructional materials were clustered and provided with professional development in how to use them effectively. Schools that were still interested in replacement units continued with professional development related to their use. In schools that were interested in more site-based activities, cluster leaders focused on supporting a site-based facilitator, who took over some of the functions of the cluster leader.

During the life of the Renaissance, the project made several shifts in strategy. Due to the sheer logistics of scaling up, intensive summer teacher academies gave way to a focus on developing cluster leaders. As context and school needs changed, even the core strategy of the project—the use of replacement units—was replaced with a more flexible, multi-dimensional approach.

None of the changes in the programs described previously would have occurred without reflection. Although absorbed in the "doing," these staff developers were simultaneously able to step back, gather data, and learn from their experience. How some of them did so is the subject of the next section.

Reflect

Each of the programs had multiple mechanisms—formal and informal—for gathering data about how well the program was working that fueled a process of continuous reflection and redesign. Formal mechanisms included evaluations of events, teacher surveys, and case studies. Some of the programs had a project evaluator to carry out some of this work.

It was often the less formal, more frequent means of collecting data—the one-legged chats in the hallway, the conversations in the teachers' room, or the visits to the classroom—that had the biggest influence on program redesign. Many of the programs had structures in place that allowed for a steady flow of information between the leadership and participating teachers. Karen Worth reported on how that worked in the Cambridge public schools. She stated,

> Melanie relied on collective observation and the wisdom of the staff development team. She regularly went to the liaisons and asked them what they wanted, what they liked, what their impressions of the staff response were. The staff development teachers were quite rigorous in collecting information from the liaison teachers, who had regular conversations with teachers and were in their classrooms. There was a constant back and forth between the teachers and the liaisons and between the liaisons and the staff development team.

The Mathematics Renaissance's system of 70 cluster leaders helped to ensure that regional directors stayed in close touch with what was happening in the 420 participating schools. Cluster leaders are classroom teachers with experience and credibility among other teachers. They were released from the classroom for 35 days during the academic year and worked for 5 weeks during the summer to carry out their role as professional developers. Close to the schools and teachers, these leaders provided regular input to the regional directors about how the work was progressing. In turn, regional directors used their input to reflect and redesign as needed. Mumme stated,

> Regional directors meet monthly. Part of that meeting is an assessment of how things are going. We don't look at things at a

macro level every time. But we do have an annual retreat for our cluster leaders, where we take stock. And, we have a retreat just for regional directors. We also visit classrooms on a regular basis and debrief among ourselves.

The Mathematics Renaissance also relied on outside reading to help regional directors reflect about their work. Mumme stated,

> We focused mostly on reading about change and the change process. A lot of what we read was validating of what we were observing, but gave us a language to talk about it. For example, Fullan's work on the implementation dip was reassuring. But we also made changes in our program as a result of outside reading. The literature was clear that peer coaching was important, but that was not part of our original design. We have now attempted to institute a cognitive coaching program.

Reflection often spurred developers to go back and redesign. This happened with the Teach-Stat workshops, as Susan Friel explained:

> The first year, we led people through the curriculum. But, our experience was that participants had very diverse understandings of statistics. The second year, we decided to do something different. We got a big problem from one of the modules. We found out what teachers' prior knowledge was of the mathematics involved. Then we designed the workshop experience to build on that knowledge. We had to find out more about where people were coming from first.

None of the programs discussed in this chapter moved neatly through the design process. They inevitably met up with the "vicissitudes of planned and unplanned change," discovered design flaws, were temporarily out of synch with teachers' needs, or underestimated what it took to manage change. Two factors, however, led to their eventual success. Because they went about the process systematically, they left the starting gate with good designs—programs that were grounded in sound principles of teaching, learning, and professional development; crafted from combinations of traditional and unconventional strategies; and tailored to their own unique contexts. Also, they never stopped trying to get better. They were able to "treat problems as their friends" (Fullan, 1993, p. 25), use data to inform decision making, learn from their mistakes, and improve on their initial design. They put the decision-making framework described in this book to work—not as a prescription but as a map to help them navigate the chaos of the real world.

Voices From the Field 8

....

Professional development is a critical component of science and mathematics reform and the education system in general. It must be embedded securely into the overall operation of the education profession to produce ongoing learning and improvement. Teachers, school administrators, parents, policymakers, and students all have a stake in encouraging schools, districts, universities, and others to initiate and support continuous learning for all teachers. As one first grader told us, "it's important for my teacher to keep learning new things so that us kids can learn more stuff."

This student reminds us that student learning is linked with teachers' learning. As the education system learns to continuously grow and improve, it is essential for professional developers to consider the views and voices of students such as the first grader as well as education's many stakeholders. For this concluding chapter, we surveyed some of these stakeholders and asked them what they believe are the most important ideas and messages that should guide professional development initiatives in the future. Their voices reinforce many of the messages in this book.

We heard from teachers of science and mathematics, professional developers (including university faculty), and policymakers that professional learning must be lifelong and relevant to student learning. Parents, teachers, and funders of professional development stated that we need accountability for professional development. Schools must stop counting hours or programs that a teacher participates in professional development and start measuring what happens as a result of their participation. Teachers want to stop getting one-shot workshops—often disconnected from their goals and their realities in the classroom—and start being active decision makers in the process of designing and choosing professional development opportunities. Professional developers reflected with us on the changes they are making in how they think about and provide development experiences. They are seeing the need to shift from focusing on the "program" they are implementing to focusing more on the various contexts in which the program will be implemented.

In this chapter, we share the voices of these many stakeholders in science and mathematics professional development. We outline their perspectives and advice related to three stages of professional development—planning, implementation, and follow-up.

Stakeholders' Views About Planning Professional Development

Teachers, administrators, and professional developers alike say that we need to do a better job of establishing the "big picture"—that is, investing in assessing needs and establishing a vision, goals, and plans and then connecting the professional development to this big picture. They tell us that, if science and mathematics standards are so important, they need to be the vision. As one teacher wrote, "too often we just don't know why we are attending a particular workshop or conference and what we are supposed to do with it after we attend." At the planning stage, those responsible for designing and organizing professional development should consider this and the following messages from the field.

Start with the end in mind. Participants and organizers of professional development must ask and answer several questions: What do you want to have happen? What outcomes do you envision? What do you want teachers to do differently? How can we generate a common vision? and How can science and mathematics standards, which we have all spent so much time developing, help us know where we're going?

Involve teachers in the planning for professional development. Teachers need to be both agents and objects of their own professional growth. Planners must take into account what teachers need, want, are interested in, or all three as well as what they need to know and learn to enact the broader vision of science and mathematics reform in their classrooms, school, or district.

View professional development as an ongoing, systematic strategy for enabling staff to acquire requisite knowledge and skills for teaching science and mathematics. Each district and school must have an overall professional development plan. Each teacher of science and mathematics should have professional development goals and a plan for achieving them. The school administrator's role is to support teachers to pursue development opportunities that are aligned with their interests and the school's vision and goals.

Plan to offer an array of different approaches to professional development for science and mathematics teachers. Training is only one of the many ways to provide professional development. Given the goals, needs, and context, other forms of professional development may be more appropriate and effective. Sometimes, teachers need time to work together to share what they already know and are doing with their colleagues. Bringing in outside expertise is important, but it does not always have to be in the form of a training session or workshop.

When planning professional development, take into account the larger context. Teachers told us that they are often attending multiple forms of professional development that lack coherence and seem disconnected from the school's overall focus, not to mention the science and mathematics standards they are helping their students achieve. They remind us that it is essential to ask the following: What is happening for teachers right now? What knowledge or skills do they need to have? What other change initiatives are going on in the district or school? and What is the time frame? Consider the context when pursuing professional development and watch out for creating overload among teachers.

Know what motivates teachers to change. Professional developers need to know and build on teachers' motivation to change and learn new knowledge and skills in science and mathematics teaching. If there is little or no motivation, professional developers say it will be "tough going." Raise questions about what it will take for teachers to support the new initiatives and be sure to ask them, and then address, "what's in it for them?"

The science and mathematics content of professional development must be appropriate. Teachers want to meet high national standards and teach the content that their professional associations are saying should be taught in their content areas and at their grade levels. They also want help making the content relevant for their students and support in making adaptations that will enable them to reach all students. They say they do not know all the content they are expected to teach and need to learn it themselves before they will feel comfortable teaching it. Professional development must be designed with these needs in mind.

Content alone will not do the job. The focus of the professional development must go beyond science and mathematics content to include appropriate pedagogy, leadership skills, and change theory or change agent skills. Teachers and professional developers alike say we must implement programs that not only show what to teach but also show how to teach it and how to embed it in the culture of the school.

Stakeholders' Views About Implementing Professional Development

Support, sensitivity to culture, quality of content and pedagogy, and an understanding of the change process are necessary as professional development programs for science and mathematics teachers are implemented. This section presents the messages stakeholders see as most important during this stage of professional development.

Professional development needs strong, highly visible institutional support. Professional development that results in improved science and mathematics teaching and learning has tangible support at all levels of the organization. Institutional support is given in many ways. For example, teachers are acknowledged for their participation through released time, stipends, and recognition. Administrators play an active role by participating themselves or helping teachers to plan how they will use their new learning in the classroom or both. Professional development for teachers of mathematics and science is linked to the district's or school's professional development plan. The necessary resources for implementing the program or new learning are available and teachers are accountable for their learning.

Be aware of the teachers' culture. Professional developers must know and understand the different cultures within which teachers live. The culture can dictate how much time a teacher can devote to professional development and suggest the professional development strategies that will work best. For example, strategies that require teamwork and collegiality may not work in cultures of distrust or when it is impossible for teachers to find time to get together. There must also be rapport between the professional developer and the teachers; developers need to fit in and be credible to the teachers.

Effective professional development initiatives in mathematics and science should have an appropriate level of challenge and support. Teachers need new material followed by opportunities to practice in a safe environment. Too often, teachers told us, they are asked to take on huge changes with little or no support. When this happens, they say they rarely make any lasting change in their science or mathematics teaching. Professional developers say that programs that work best are implemented over time and include varied activities that combine learning new things, trying them, and getting help and feedback.

Professional development activities should demonstrate new ways to teach and learn. Teachers want an opportunity to see how to teach mathematics and science in new ways. They want demonstrations of what the new approaches look like in action—that is, to make the teaching standards come alive. Professional developers should model the practices they are teaching or advocating and give teachers the experience of learning through inquiry and problem solving in the same ways the teacher will teach in the classroom.

Build internal capacity. Building education systems that learn continuously requires that we shift from a model of "bringing teachers to training sessions led by experts" (i.e., pull-out programs) to a model that enables and encourages teachers to assess their own professional development needs, seek out resources, coach others, and provide development experiences for themselves and their colleagues.

Whenever possible, use a team approach when implementing programs for science and mathematics teachers. If the professional development strategy is a training program, one professional developer suggests "use a team approach." She noted that it is hard for one person to attend to everything—both content and process—and that work in a team provides different voices and perspectives and encourages reflection among the team members that contribute to improvement of the training over time. Furthermore, when a teacher from the local site "teams" with the professional developer, capacity is building within the school.

Provide time for reflection. Teachers say they are often "bombarded" with new information and need an opportunity to stop and think about what they are learning and its relevance for them. Effective programs include a cycle of (1) learning, (2) practicing, and (3 reflecting.

Professional developers' most valuable asset is flexibility. One professional developer told us the following:

Even when you've done all your homework you still may find that your agenda does not address the needs, interests, or culture in the school in which you are working. Flexibility among professional developers is essential if you are to be sensitive to and address teachers' needs. Don't be afraid to change agendas or to toss away your plans when the teachers need to go in a different direction.

Evaluate the effectiveness and the impact of the professional development activity. Professional development activities for teachers of science and mathematics can be entertaining and fun, but these cannot be the only measures of success. To be successful, a development activity must result in learning, insight, a change in practice, or all three. One school principal told us that he had the same trainer come to the school every year for the past 4 years because even the most resistant teachers loved the workshops. Then he started visiting these teachers' science classrooms, however, and saw that they were not using any of the pedagogy espoused by the trainers. This principal realized that he needed different ways to assess whether the professional development was meeting its objectives. He decided that teachers should evaluate the professional development at key intervals in the process. He suggests assessing what teachers learn and, later, if and how they are using it with students. Ultimately, he says, "we should all be concerned with assessing the impact of development experiences on student science learning."

Use humor and have fun. As one teacher said, "if we should be making learning fun for our students then our professional development should be fun, too." Teachers want enriching experiences that are enjoyable. Professional developers need to be able to use humor as a means to break through the struggles that many teachers feel as they abandon comfortable patterns in their teaching and venture into new and, therefore, scary territory.

Stakeholders' Views About Follow-Up to Professional Development

We heard from many people that they believe educators need to do a much better job with follow-up to professional development. After initial professional development, teachers of science and mathematics need support, problem solving, and more in-depth learning. Specifically, stakeholders shared the following ideas and suggestions.

Provide opportunities for practice in the classroom, followed by feedback and more practice. One principal said that changing practice begins with setting clear expectations. He stated, "As the school administrator, I must communicate my expectation that the faculty will actually use what they learn. But then, I've got to make sure they have the chance to become competent with the new practices." Opportunity for practice and feedback and steady pressure to change science and mathematics teaching and learning will support improvements. Professional developers should establish support networks of teachers using new practices and provide local technical assistance to help teachers solve problems and increase their skill with the new practices.

Hold teachers accountable for their learning. School leaders say that expectations for teachers to learn new things and implement different science and mathematics curricula or teaching and assessment strategies must be an explicit part of the teachers' performance reviews. Professional development is an investment in both the teacher and the school. It is reasonable to expect a "payoff" for the investment in the form of new knowledge, improved teaching and learning, or the creation of school cultures that are open to ongoing learning for all.

Assess impact of professional development activities. One school administrator stated, "If teachers are not demonstrating new knowledge or approaches in mathematics and science, the principal or curriculum director should find out why and reassess if the professional development is working." There is an untested assumption in many schools that once teachers participate in some professional development, they will use it to make positive changes in their practice. Teachers and school administrators need structures to assess whether the development is leading to desired outcomes. They need to know if teachers exhibit new behaviors and if there is evidence of student outcomes for science and mathematics. Educators can then use the evaluation data to make adjustments in future professional development (i.e., do more of what is working and less of what is not working). Assessment should also examine whether the professional development is reaching the right people. As one principal stated, "I believe in voluntary professional development, but at some point I need to push certain people to participate or they never will."

Pay attention to institutionalizing the professional development. One seasoned professional developer wrote, "It takes time for new mathematics and science teaching practices to become part of the fabric of the school organization, but there are many things teachers and principals can do to ensure that they do." Active efforts to institutionalize reforms include allocating resources to support continued use of new science and mathematics materials or programs; getting all teachers involved; establishing clear expectations and policies that mandate the new approaches; aligning organizational structures, such as performance reviews, rewards, and recognition, with the desired changes; getting the support of parents and the public; and assessing and communicating results.

Remember: Professional development alone cannot carry a reform effort. Too many professional developers reported that their professional development program was still being viewed as "the answer" or the "silver bullet" for education reform in science and mathematics or education reform in general. Professional development is but one element of a successful reform initiative. It must be aligned and integrated with other efforts. For example, there must be adequate plans, policies, infrastructures, and community supports in place to support the reform. A state education policymaker warns that "Professional development alone won't work . . . we need a more systemic approach in which development is one strategy within the overall change effort."

* * *

These voices from the field offer evidence that beliefs about what constitutes effective professional development in mathematics, science, and all education areas are shifting. Education professionals know what needs to be done. Now they need the support and structures to enact the vision of continuous quality professional development in all schools and for all professionals. The knowledge captured in this book is intended to guide professional developers for science and mathematics teachers to design and carry out ongoing learning opportunities at all levels of education. We hope that, in time, the common knowledge about professional development will become common practice.

Resource A:
The Workshop Center at
City College of New York

HUBERT M. DYASI
Director of Workshop Center,
City College of New York

Context

The Workshop Center was founded in 1972 by Lillian Weber at the City College, City University of New York. Although the center has worked with teachers on making their classrooms better contexts for active learning, its current focus is on educating teachers to be confident science inquirers who understand the potential for science learning in the common everyday phenomena that engage children. Two corollary aspects of the focus are (a) teachers learning firsthand, under staff supervision, how children construct their knowledge of science as a result of inquiry into everyday phenomena and (b) staff helping teachers on-site to implement a science inquiry approach in their classrooms. The center also conducts workshops for school principals and for parents. Workshops for principals introduce them to constructive ways of supervising teachers who use the inquiry approach in their classrooms; those for parents familiarize them with children's roles in science inquiry so that they can better support their children's efforts.

At the core of the center's educational approach is the importance of experience and meaning in learning and the belief that each person is capable of inquiring and observing with meaning and understanding. This belief is so fundamental to all the center's work that it is easily recognizable whether working in Harlem in New York City, in suburban small towns, or in rural schools in this country and elsewhere.

In the center's view, inquiry science encompasses both content and approach: The content is derived from the common materials and phenomena we encounter; the approach is inquiry built around observations and experience and then making meaning of them. Direct experience with phenomena helps children learn to build connections among phenomena and also between their conceptions of the world and actual events in the world. They refine their knowledge by asking more and better focused questions that help them correct the limitations of their first understanding. Conceptual change and refinement on the part of children are common ingredients in elementary and middle school science practice; they must be because children's conceptions of the world undergo change as children grow and gain more direct experience with the physical world and with the worlds of symbols and ideas. The continuing search for underlying commonalties in apparently disparate phenomena and continual refinement and incremental knowledge by constructing and reconstructing are also associated closely with the development of scientific knowledge itself.

In their efforts to learn science, children need continuing support and guidance from adults. By having the most extended contact with the school-age child in organized learning situations, the teacher is the principal agent in the introduction, guidance, and maintenance of children's many-layered inquiry. To play this role well, teachers should receive a science education that is faithful to the practice of scientific inquiry and to children's ways of learning and that provides them reassurance that the physical reality we experience in the world is the subject of scientific inquiry. They need extended opportunities for sustained engagement with phenomena to see how their own inquiries unfold and to revisit earlier observations and notions in light of their ongoing explorations and growing understandings of inquiry. Furthermore, they need to conceptualize the progress of curricular inquiry and to understand the role materials, activity, interaction, and reflection play in the inquiry process. Most important, teachers themselves need to experience what they are trying to develop in children—a scientific understanding of the phenomena and an in-depth and experienced-based vision of how they themselves learn.

Center Description

The center's is a story of building the teacher's understanding of science inquiry, of how children make meaning from experience and how that process is related to the acquisition of scientific concepts, and of building the teacher's personal capacities to create contexts in which children can develop and internalize scientific knowledge. It is also a story about increasing teachers' acceptance that differences do not necessarily mean incapacity. The center has created programs to provide opportunities for teachers to view themselves as capable human beings, mobilizing their capabilities and succeeding in investigating and understanding what they had previously regarded as beyond their capacity. Teachers also learn to work directly with children, observing and recording how children learn and responding positively to their inquiries and sense making. Teachers thus leave the center's programs equipped with a rich repertoire of knowledge, practice, and resources necessary for an imaginative and educationally sound response to children's inquiry into natural phenomena. In some of the programs, teachers also acquire knowledge and strategies for providing supportive leadership to their fellow teachers, thus creating communities of inquiring teachers in their schools and in their districts. In all the programs, participants engage in science inquiry at their own level, working in small groups and sometimes individually; periodically, all participants gather to share and discuss their activities, findings, and understandings.

Each participant in the center's programs maintains a written journal of his or her experience in the program. Because the journals include notes and reflections on the teachers' experiences in the workshop sessions, they facilitate recall and reflection on participants' experiences and on special moments of the experiences that illuminate and further the teachers' investigative efforts. The journals also serve as a means of communication between each participant and the staff. They allow staff to revisit and "hold" for the teacher specific instances that illustrate their evolving understandings. As the staff learns directly from the teachers' or students' journals what they choose to recapitulate and what meanings they attach to events, staff are better able to confirm insights into what each teacher might use to further his or her efforts. With this process, they are increasingly able to identify problems that might impede growth. Participants also study, write summaries, and reflect on professional literature associated with the learner-focused approach used in the workshops. They relate the readings to possibilities of engaging children in their classes in practical science inquiry.

A very significant component of all the programs is the staff. They model what they wish the teachers to learn in science inquiry, curricular inquiry, social interaction, and classroom organization. They use instructional strategies such as engaging teachers as learners in social contexts characterized by both learning and instruction. Participants and staff together work with children and parents and examine and evaluate science curriculum resources.

Staff work as an integrated unit composed of experienced science educators, scientists, and selected public school teachers with many years of experience at various educational levels. The integrated style of work is exhibited in observable ways: Participants observe faculty relate to other faculty in planning sessions in the morning, and participants can "listen in" to faculty discussions in review sessions at the end of the day;

participants see faculty interaction in jointly led workshops and in response to a guest speaker; and participants see in action how dialogue among colleagues occurs and what issues faculty continually think about. Participants also have the opportunity to relate to and see faculty members pursuing their own inquiries, and they share in the excitement of continuing professional development and learning. How staff interact with the teachers is based on the belief that the restoration of self-worth cannot be achieved through lectures and reasoned analysis but rather through active engagement.

The Summer Institute

Open to all interested teachers and held every year since 1971, the institute's central feature is the development of the teacher to be a competent inquirer and an analytical student of his or her own process of learning through a 4-week intensive immersion in a long-term investigation of a phenomenon. Selection of a phenomenon for investigation, the design of investigative activities, collection and organization of data, and construction of meaning about the phenomenon are the responsibility of the participating teacher, who may consult the staff and other participants.

During the introductory week, staff highlight key elements that permeate successful inquiries; for example, an intense curiosity about a phenomenon, close observation and direct manipulation of the phenomenon, raising questions that increase a person's knowledge of the phenomenon and designing and carrying out ways to answer them, formulation of some tentative generalizations that lead to further questions and perceptions of patters, and generation of models. To provide participants with a general feeling for the elements of inquiry, staff use a variety of mechanisms, such as exploratory field trips on campus and in the neighboring park, visual exploration of portions of New York City from the top floor of one of the college buildings, and study of the total environment inside the Workshop Center. Homework assignments that require participants to make general and specific observations of phenomena and report on them in small group sessions are given, and assigned readings on the Workshop Center's approach to inquiry in education are discussed. The last 2 hours of the week are devoted to cultural activities—for example, stage performances organized and performed by the participants.

During the second week, participants select their areas of investigation, raise questions they wish to pursue, and proceed to design their individual activities. Two or 3-hour blocks of time are devoted to these activities. Many selected areas of investigation are predictable—for example, leaves, sound, water, and so on—but others are more unusual—

for example, chewing gum, cracks on sidewalks, and so on. In addition to carrying out individual investigations, participants meet with staff in small groups to share and discuss their work and to receive feedback from the staff on their journals and progress. Whole-group sessions are organized when specialists make presentations and when films on specific aspects of science inquiry are shown and discussed. During this week, the center organizes a panel presentation by participants from previous summer institutes—an activity that goes a long way to alleviate anxiety. Once again, cultural activities conclude the week.

The third week is devoted mostly to more intensive individual investigations. During the first 2 days of the fourth and final week, each participant makes an oral presentation of his or her work during the institute. The rest of the participants contribute to the oral presentations by raising questions and quite often by providing additional observations and data related to the investigations. Staff also raise questions and make comments that highlight the scientific and educational significance of the investigation. At the end of the institute, each participant writes a reflective account of his or her institute experience.

Development of Teachers as Science Inquirers

The teacher development model adopted by the Workshop Center follows a form of reflective teaching applied in a cyclical process in which staff and teachers continually examine, adapt, and evaluate their practice. A 3-year collaborative project with Community School Districts 5 and 8 in New York City, funded by the United States Department of Education under the Dwight D. Eisenhower National Mathematics and Science Program, provides a context for this process. Each participant is in the program for two semesters and earns 6 graduate credits. The program seeks to deepen and increase participants' investigation skills, such as their ability to formulate researchable questions, carry out investigations directly, and collect, organize, and interpret data, while pursuing answers to their own questions about natural phenomena. An additional objective is to create a critical mass of teachers in selected schools in Districts 5 and 8 who are educated in the implementation of inquiry approaches to the teaching of science in the elementary school and to help parents support their children's inquiry activities at home.

To aid reflection on learning and teaching, each participant reads and summarizes prescribed science education readings that deal with children's learning. The readings also provide guidelines for helping children to develop their capacities in planning investigations, in developing observation skills, and in constructing knowledge. Some of the readings also deal with the role of questions in stimulating children's thought and action, resources to encourage and engage children's inquiry, and the importance of children's communication in the learning process. In addition to the readings, each teacher keeps a journal on workshop investigations, class discussions, and implementation of activities.

The program staff includes a science educator, a scientist, a teacher who assists the science educator, a parent education specialist, a program evaluator, and on-site staff. The staff plans together, team teaches, and reviews students' work collaboratively. A steering committee of university scientists, social scientists, science educators, public school personnel, and representatives of professional agencies provides advice and occasional reviews of the program activities.

Saturday practica with children facilitate and support teachers' direct practice of skills acquired during the workshop sessions. Saturday workshops for parents run concurrently with the teacher-children practica to improve communication between parents and teachers and show parents how they can be helpful to their children at home.

School-Based Science Restructuring

In July 1992, Community School District 6 received a National Science Foundation grant to restructure science teaching and learning in grades kindergarten through eighth. The district in turn asked the Workshop Center and the Education Development Center (Massachusetts) to implement major parts of the program. The Workshop Center is responsible for the education of lead teachers and supervisors in science inquiry and for the education of other teachers. Each lead teacher undergoes a 2-year program (inclusive of summers). The model for teacher development follows the usual Workshop Center pattern previously described. In this program, the Saturday practicum, however, is replaced by Saturday field trips that help lead teachers generate inquiry ideas for their classrooms and for their work with other teachers. Other aspects of the program include workshops for school principals and development of on-site instructional teams.

Another two-semester program, In-Service Science Inquiry Program for Middle-School Teachers, serves middle school teachers of science in eight New York City community school districts in Central and East Harlem, Inwood, and Washington Heights in Manhattan and the entire borough of the Bronx. It is a logical extension of many years of work the Workshop Center has performed with elementary schools in the same eight community school districts. Funding is provided mostly by the New York State Education Department.

Integrating Science Inquiry With Mathematics and Technology

Community School District 4 (East Harlem) has been selected to test a New York State Mathematics, Science and Technology Curriculum Frameworks program. The state has asked the Workshop Center to develop and implement a science program collaboratively with the district. The program is divided into four phases: (a) development of teachers as learners; (b) teachers' implementation of inquiry learning, first in a clinical setting and later in their own classrooms; (c) planning, implementation, and documentation of classroom inquiry experiences to be used by teachers and administrators; and (d) dissemination of program outcomes throughout the school district.

Each phase of the program was planned in collaboration with district supervisory staff, building administrators, and teachers. The program's continued planning, teaching, and learning are implemented jointly by staff from the school district and from the center; thus, there is a built-in element for enabling the school district to maintain the program eventually with minimum outside assistance.

The first phase, developing teachers as inquirers, familiarizes teachers with local community resources and explores their use as contexts for learning. Teachers participate in several field experiences in the neighborhood near their school building and in parks, playgrounds, and city streets. An after-school enrichment program established in the school will be a vehicle for teachers to apply what they have learned at the center. Working in groups of four or five, participating teachers will plan activities for the children in this program—children will be divided into groups of 10. They will implement their plans, make observations, analyze the results, adjust their plans, and work with the children again. Program staff will be present throughout this process to observe and assist teachers as they grapple with the transition to teaching through inquiry. Activities in this phase serve the double purpose of convincing teachers that children are capable of independent, active learning, and that they themselves are capable of supporting this type of learning.

In the third phase, teachers will introduce inquiry learning in their own classrooms. Undergraduate students who have shown a particular understanding of the learning and teaching of science inquiry in other Workshop Center programs will be placed in the teachers' classrooms as student teachers. This arrangement should benefit the teachers, the student teachers, and the children. In the final phase of the program, the teachers will conduct demonstrations and workshops for teachers in other schools in the district.

Courses

A mandatory 6-hour introductory course on inquiry in education for all undergraduate majors in education at City College was introduced in 1992. The course is conducted at the center and integrates faculty in science and mathematics education, foundations in education, early childhood education, and bilingual education. All students must complete this course prior to registering for methods courses.

The course introduces students to firsthand inquiry in scientific, mathematical, engineering, and sociocultural domains and provides them with opportunities for framing questions, designing investigations and collecting data, and generating testable models. Students work collaboratively in "research" teams of three or four on topics that are suggested by instructors and later present and defend their work to the whole class. As a result of these experiences, students learn how to use physical and intellectual tools of inquiry.

During the second half of the course, individual students select topics of interest and carry out long-term investigations to answer their own questions. In the course of these investigations, they consult with the instructors and classmates, use available material and intellectual resources, and, at the end, prepare a detailed descriptive and reflective report.

Throughout the course, students also read scholarly publications that discuss the process of inquiry and provide case studies of firsthand accounts of original inquiries in the various domains. They study videotapes of professional and amateur inquirers at work and learn directly how inquiries are conducted. They write reports and reaction papers on the readings and on the inquiries conducted in the course.

All elementary and early childhood education majors also enroll in a 3-credit science education course conducted at the center.

Summary

The Workshop Center is a resource for preservice and inservice professional development for New York City and, less so, for other locations throughout the world. Its philosophy and practice are based squarely on a commitment to inquiry and to connecting to the lives of children.

Resource B: Teach-Stat: A Model for Professional Development in Data Analysis and Statistics for Teachers of Grades Kindergarten Through 6

SUSAN N. FRIEL
School of Education,
University of North Carolina at Chapel Hill

The *Curriculum and Evaluation Standards for School Mathematics* (National Council of Teachers of Mathematics [NCTM], 1989) identifies statistics and probability as a major strand across all grade levels. Since 1989, there has been growing interest in what to teach and how to teach with respect to statistics. It is only in the past few years that appropriate curricula (e.g., *Used Numbers*[1] and *Quantitative Literacy* series[2]) have become available for use at the kindergarten (K) through 12th-grade levels.

At the elementary level, available curricula are an essential ingredient in helping teachers find ways to integrate the teaching of statistics in

AUTHOR'S NOTE: This chapter is a shortened version of a chapter by S. N. Friel and G. W. Bright, "Teach-Stat: A Model for Professional Development in Data Analysis and Statistics for Teachers, K-6," in S. P. Lajoie (Ed.), *Reflections on Statistics: Agendas for Learning, Teaching, and Assessment in K-12.* Hillsdale, NJ: Lawrence Erlbaum (in press).

a coherent and comprehensive manner. Curricula for use with students are not sufficient, however; using such curricula effectively requires a reasonable knowledge of statistics to pose tasks appropriately and promote and manage classroom discourse successfully. Elementary teachers are in need of professional development opportunities that will support their learning of content and promote the use of an inquiry orientation to help their students learn and use statistical concepts.

Teach-Stat: A Key to Better Mathematics (Friel & Joyner, 1991) was a project designed to plan and implement a program of professional development for elementary teachers, Grades 1 through 6, to help them learn more about statistics and integrate teaching about and teaching with statistics in their instruction. This project included the following three components:

1. The design of professional development curricula for use with teachers and with teacher leaders (here referenced as statistics educators)

2. A large-scale implementation program to provide professional development for both teachers and statistics educators using the professional development curricula

3. A program of research and evaluation to assess the impact of the project and to surface research questions related to the agenda of the project.

Project Design

The project was funded by the National Science Foundation through the University of North Carolina Mathematics and Science Education Network (MSEN). MSEN consists of 10 centers throughout North Carolina housed at 10 of the state university system's campuses. Each center is directed by a faculty member in mathematics or science education; one of the main tasks for each center is providing professional development in mathematics or science or both for K through 12 teachers in its service region. Because of its structure, MSEN is particularly well suited for supporting the implementation of large-scale, statewide projects.

The project involved 9 of the 10 MSEN centers; one faculty member (here referenced as site faculty leader) from each of the sites served as the local coordinator of the project. The 9 site faculty leaders, with the addition of a few other university consultants, designed and implemented the Teach-Stat project. More than 450 teachers throughout North Carolina participated in the project, and, of those, 84 Teach-Stat teachers received additional professional development to prepare them to be statistics educators.

The first fall and spring (1991-1992) of the Teach-Stat project was used as a planning time to bring together the site faculty leaders and additional faculty consultants from across the state. This group met intensively for 2- or 3-day meetings several times during the first year. Their tasks were to design the draft of the professional development curriculum that would be used to teach teachers and then to jointly teach the first 3-week summer institute.

The project was designed so that during the first year, each site faculty leader selected 6 or 7 teachers as a pilot team. The 57 teachers and nine site faculty leaders participated in the 1992 3-week summer institute, which was offered as a residential program at a central site. The faculty, working in teams of 3, was responsible for various parts of the program. Throughout the following school year, each faculty site leader met with and visited the regional teacher team, jointly exploring with the teachers what it meant for them to teach statistics and integrate statistics with other subject areas.

In the second year, each of the nine sites offered a revised (nonresidential) version of the 3-week professional development program to 24 new teachers. Each site faculty leader and the pilot team of 6 or 7 teachers worked together to plan and deliver the workshop. Originally, the pilot teachers were going to be available to help but not to teach. By the second summer, however, faculty and teachers had developed such a good working relationship that the model of a "professional development team" naturally emerged and was very successful. The second-year participants were able to hear from teachers who had spent the preceding year teaching statistics and had many actual examples to show them. The first-year pilot teachers received a great deal of support, informal "how to be a staff developer" training, and coaching and mentoring from their respective site faculty leaders.

In the third year, 84 teachers from either the first or second year were selected to become statistics educators to serve as resource people throughout North Carolina to provide professional development programs in statistics education for other elementary teachers. They participated (regionally at the nine sites) in the equivalent of a 1-week seminar focused on the "how to's and the why's" of staff development. The statistics educators at each site were responsible for developing and delivering a 2-week summer institute for an additional set of 24 new teachers at their site. As a result of this program, the statistics educators were equipped to offer the Teach-Stat professional development program to other elementary teachers and to design variations of this program to meet the needs of the audience with which they happened to be dealing.

The documentation of the project includes the following various materials that permit others to replicate the program of professional development and implementation:

1. *Teach-Stat for Teachers: Professional Development Manual* (Friel & Joyner, 1997) provides a "how-to" discussion for planning and implementing a 3-week teacher education institute. It is written in a way that addresses teachers' needs for inservice education, and its audience is mainly those who provide professional development programs for elementary-grade teachers.

2. *Teach-Stat for Statistics Educators: Staff Developers Manual* (Gleason, Vesilind, Friel, & Joyner, 1996) provides a "how-to" discussion for planning and implementing a 1-week Statistics Educators Institute. This institute is designed for teachers who will serve as staff development resource people (statistics educators) and who have participated in a 3-week program in statistics education and have previously taught statistics to students.

3. *Teach-Stat Activities: Statistics Investigations for Grades 1-3* (Joyner, Pfieffer, Friel, & Vesilind, 1997a) and *Teach-Stat Activities: Statistics Investigations for Grades 3-6* (Joyner, Pfieffer, Friel, & Vesilind, 1997b) provide "how-to" discussions of the planning and implementation of activities for elementary-grade students that promote the learning of statistics using the process of statistical investigation.

Statistics Educators: Developing Leaders

The benefit of a structure such as MSEN is that it provides access to the state's school systems and assists in maintaining a consistent level of quality in the professional development programs it provides. North Carolina, however, still lacks the capacity to provide high-quality opportunities for the majority of elementary teachers to increase their subject matter knowledge and to continuously examine and modify their teaching practice. The Teach-Stat project sought to address the "capacity question" not only by providing professional development for a large number of teachers on a regional basis but also, more important, by developing teachers (statistics educators) who can work with other elementary teachers in support of their learning statistics and how to teach statistics and teach using statistics. This is one of the elements needed in building an infrastructure for professional development.

The final teams of statistics educators varied in composition: Some teams included only first-year teachers, some included a balance of first- and second-year teachers, and some included a few or no first-year teachers with a preponderance of second-year teachers. They were selected based on their interest and on their potential ability to provide professional development to their peers. In cases in which first- and second-year teachers were balanced, it was found that teaming of a first-year teacher with a second-year teacher created a mentor-coach arrangement that seemed to support the second-year teachers in their initial experiences teaching other teachers. It was assumed that, in most cases, these teachers would work in teams of two statistics educators to provide such experiences for other teachers once they "graduated" as statistics educators.

Teachers selected for this opportunity participated in an additional week's professional development program that helped them explore staff development issues and ways to conduct a workshop. The Statistics Educators Institutes included content on adult learning, the change process, and statistics pedagogical content knowledge. Statistics educators completed 3 or 4 days of work prior to the Teach-Stat workshop they taught for third-year teachers; the remainder of the work was done as part of a "looking back" effort to reflect on what happened during the workshop.

As part of their participation, approximately half the statistics educators participated in a study (Frost, 1995) to investigate the effects of classroom teachers becoming Teach-Stat workshop leaders. They responded to three different instruments, and some also participated in interviews. These were completed at three different times: at the beginning and at the end of the Statistics Educators Institute and after teaching the third-year Teach-Stat summer workshops.

Frost's (1995) study is rich with information. For purposes here, the results suggest that staff development designs built on teachers becoming workshop leaders should provide special assistance to help teachers develop in this role over time. The following are relevant:

1. Opportunities to develop and/or demonstrate strong content knowledge in mathematics before becoming a workshop leader should be an important consideration in staff development.

2. Teachers' classroom experiences are valuable assets to their work as workshop leaders. Classroom experiences using teaching activities such as those presented in workshops provide the workshop leader with "personal memory tapes" of the practical, as well as the pedagogical, issues related to the activities.

3. Teachers who become workshop leaders may need specialized assistance in conceptualizing effective staff development. The study suggests that workshop leaders progress through stages of growth in their conceptions about effective staff development; such stages can be used as "benchmarks" to assess readiness or potential of the teacher to serve as a workshop leader.

4. Teachers who become workshop leaders need opportunities to develop their own understanding of the nature of adult learners

and of creating a climate conducive for adult learning. Furthermore, there is a need to help workshop leaders explore pedagogical content knowledge related to teaching adults.

What Was Learned

When the study of statistics is framed within the context of a process of statistical investigation and involves the use of relevant hands-on applications and activities, teachers and students quickly become engaged. Unlike much of traditional elementary school mathematics, teaching statistics within this framework provides for a much more open learning environment. No longer is there "one right way" to do mathematics with "one right answer" being the norm; questioning and exploration are encouraged and promoted. Professional development experiences that model such learning environments can be successful in helping teachers bring similar excitement and engagement in learning to their students. Overall, individuals at all levels of involvement, primary grade teachers to college teachers of statistics, learned from their Teach-Stat experiences and described these experiences as having influenced change in their respective classrooms.

Notes

1. *Used Numbers: Real Data in the Classroom* is a set of six units of study for K through sixth-grade students that is published by Seymour (Palo Alto, CA).

2. The *Quantitative Literacy* series is a set of four units of study for students in Grades 8 through 12 that is published by Seymour (Palo Alto, CA).

Resource C:
The California Middle Grades
Mathematics Renaissance

JUDY MUMME
Director of Mathematics Renaissance

The Middle Grades Mathematics Renaissance has been a component of the California Alliance for Mathematics and Science, a National Science Foundation-funded State Systemic Initiative. Using professional development as its central strategy, the Renaissance was designed to help schools transform their mathematics programs so that all students, especially those historically underrepresented in mathematics, become empowered mathematically. During 1995 and 1996, 1,800 teachers from approximately 350 schools participated in the academic year and summer or off-track work that focused on professional development issues: discussing mathematics reform, experiencing hands-on mathematics, learning how to teach new state-of-the-art curriculum "replacement" units, and exploring the conditions that create opportunities for learning.

Context and Desired Outcomes

The Renaissance was developed against the backdrop of California, a state with a rich and complex environment for mathematics reform. The state has more than 5 million students, 230,000 teachers (140,000 of which teach mathematics), 7,000 schools, and 1,000 districts. Average class size is approximately 30 and per-pupil spending is $4,874, placing California 38th among states ($1,000 less than the national average). Approximately half of California's students are from Latino, African American, or Asian American backgrounds. There are more than 100 languages spoken, and 22% of the student population speak limited English. Approximately 2.2 million children live in poverty.

Several critical decisions were made early in the planning stage. First, a professional development strategy was chosen as the vehicle to achieve goals. Reaching the large numbers of California's teachers and students, however, requires resources beyond the available funding (approximately $1.1 million annually). Therefore, a second decision was made: Middle school mathematics was selected because it acts as a "gateway" to future access to higher-level mathematics courses. Moreover, curriculum at this level has traditionally been a wasteland, and this area seemed ripe for development and exploration. Third, it was decided that the program would use a school-based rather than an individual teacher focus. Collaboratively, work among faculty members can provide a support system that provides opportunities to address the school structures that promote and inhibit reform. It was believed that by working with schools as the unit of change, a process that would sustain the effort beyond program funding could be established.

Designing the Work

With middle grades as the target, schools as the focus, and professional development as the strategy, the Renaissance was born. The challenge became the creation of professional development experiences that would create the fundamental transformation of middle-grade mathematics, helping teachers meet the challenges of reform.

Leveraging Resources

Resources in education are rarely sufficient and are less so in a state the size of California. Consequently, plans were formulated to ensure that efforts not only maximize the available resources but also establish an infrastructure designed to sustain and expand the efforts throughout the system.

To maximize the leveraging of resources, the Renaissance asked schools to support their own costs. Indeed, the approximately $1.1 million in funding barely supported the statewide leadership infrastructure (one director and 10 regional directors). Schools paid a $3,000 annual participation fee to cover the costs of local teacher leadership. Establishing an expectation that schools annually allot a sizable sum for professional development increases the likelihood that the process will continue once the initiative ceases.

Large numbers of schools were enrolled statewide to take advantage of a "tip-point strategy," which suggests that systemic reform begins with a small vanguard of schools taking the lead in reform and gradually expands to include more schools. Once a critical mass of one fourth to one third of the schools is engaged in the reforms, the argument states, the system will "tip," and the majority of the other schools will follow. During the 5 years of the Renaissance, more than 500 schools participated well beyond the one third envisioned.

Teacher Engagement

At the heart of the Renaissance is the belief that such change takes time. The 8 to 12 professional development meetings a year and the summer experience allowed time to deal with a wide range of issues. Teachers discussed current research on learning and effective instructional strategies, the nature of mathematics, and the redefinition of basic skills. Teachers learned how to teach new state-of-the-art curriculum replacement units. They taught these units in their classrooms and returned to debrief their experience with other network members. The replacement strategy provided an opportunity for teachers to have direct, firsthand experience with reform curriculum. Often, teachers engaged in direct mathematical experiences as learners. It is not enough to talk about what can be. Teachers must experience a broader version of mathematics themselves to break their traditional views.

Although there is much that is common about what teachers need to learn, the Renaissance work was also responsive to regional and local demands. In a district near San Diego, the issue of algebra in middle school was a crucial discussion point, whereas another district nearby was grappling with effective methods for engaging parent and community support. Topics of interest have ranged from the place of algorithms in the middle grades to cobbling together a whole curriculum from available pieces. Agendas in one cluster have included gender bias, portfolio assessment, and the effects of tracking. Regional agendas grew to meet the interests and needs of the cluster participants.

It was also learned that two of the program's commitments—fostering fundamental change and responding to teachers' needs—are sometimes in conflict. There is often a tension between challenging teachers to consider new ideas and being responsive to what teachers want: For example, one teacher commented, "I do not want to be gone from my classroom for days where I am not taught a specific unit that I can take back and use. My students lose every time I am gone." This teacher's comment is typical of many. How does one develop an in-depth understanding of the issues in mathematics education when teachers have a strong desire for things to take back—to add recipes to their files? Time spent exploring constructivism may not feel like a day well spent to some participating teachers. Short-term gains often limit long-term growth opportunities.

Even when teachers take back curriculum units, the opportunities for reflection often begin with managerial issues. These tensions are part of the inherently paradoxical nature of constructivist teaching. How does one respect what teachers want while pushing them to reinvent themselves? Time is part of the answer. Bit by bit, discussion by discussion, clusters begin to become communities of learners, reflecting on practice in critical ways and learning to ask tough questions and to push individual and collective thinking deeper. Over time, teachers' comments shifted to "I appreciate all the time allowed for discussion."

Leadership

The two-tiered structure of the Renaissance provided both statewide and local leadership. The 10 full-time regional directors interacted as a statewide team while directing and designing the unique work of the individual regions. Selection criteria for this role was based on experience in teaching middle-grade mathematics and background in leadership for mathematics education. They played the role of a "critical friend," possessing both an understanding of the research and broad experience in schools attempting to change. Monthly 3-day regional meetings and constant communications provided an immediate feedback mechanism.

Each regional director worked with a team of teacher leaders called cluster leaders, who were classroom teachers with the personal experience and credibility to help their peers change classroom practice. Typically, a cluster leader was released from the classroom 35 days during the academic year and worked 5 weeks each summer to serve in this professional development role. The ratio of cluster leaders to teachers was kept small to allow for the crucial development of relationships with the participating teachers (Figure C.1).

Cluster leaders were key to the quality of the professional development. Their credibility stemmed from the fact that they grappled with the same issues as those of the teachers with whom they worked. It gave

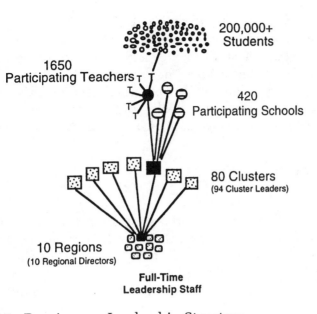

200,000+
Students

1650
Participating Teachers

420
Participating Schools

80 Clusters
(94 Cluster Leaders)

10 Regions
(10 Regional Directors)

**Full-Time
Leadership Staff**

Figure C.1. Renaissance Leadership Structure

them acceptance into the school, cluster, and regional learning communities. These cluster leaders did not simply emerge from the classroom as leaders. California has a long history of leadership development in mathematics. Many cluster leaders came from the California Mathematics Project or other reform projects. A majority of them came from the ranks of participating Renaissance teachers—many from the first schools to join.

Their work was challenging and demanding, requiring the development of skills beyond those that make one a good teacher. Therefore, another complication arises. The Renaissance design requires professional development for both teachers and the teachers who will lead those teachers. The need for ongoing professional development for leadership cannot be understated. This is perhaps one of the central lessons that has been learned thus far. Leaders must have opportunities to reflect on their work, learning from one another the crucial lessons of leadership for reform. They constantly need to be challenged as learners, expanding their own understanding of mathematics, teaching, and learning. The initial design of the Renaissance failed to account for this need, and much of the statewide professional growth opportunities have been funded catch-as-catch-can.

Cluster leaders create their own version of professional development for participating teachers, and regional directors provide guidance, inspiration, and support. Here, another tension emerged. The program's commitment to shared leadership and delegated authority does not always produce results matching its goals. Messages sometimes get distorted as individual cluster leaders construct their own understanding of the reform and the Renaissance. The program continues to struggle with the degree of control and guidance cluster leaders receive. Does one intervene and risk damaging a cluster leader's credibility and opportunity to learn? How is quality maintained while leadership develops?

Supporting Reforms

Other important elements support the Renaissance efforts. Enlisting parents as partners is one example. Schools throughout the Renaissance pilot the middle school version of Family Math with an anticipation that more than 500 parent nights would be conducted during the 1995 and 1996 school year. Administrative support offers yet another example. Principals need time with teachers and other principals, and district administrators must understand and support the reforms.

Efforts of the Renaissance have also moved beyond the middle school, in part due to conflicts that have arisen between some Renaissance middle schools and high schools they feed. Middle school teachers expressed concerns that their students went onto high school eager and excited about mathematics only to have their enthusiasm squelched by the high school placement tests and traditional course work. In many districts, these conflicts have been seized as opportunities to promote discussions between middle and high schools. As a result of these discussions, some high schools have begun to revise their programs using new innovative high school curricula.

Guiding Principles

As the Renaissance has engaged in this process, much about teacher change and professional development has been learned. Principles that guide the program's current work and future work have emerged and I elaborate on them in the following sections.

Teachers Should Be Part of a Professional Learning Community. The National Council of Teachers of Mathematics' *Professional Teaching Standards* (1991) calls for "classrooms as mathematical communities." Likewise, I believe that teachers must belong to learning communities that place inquiry at their center and focus on building capacity for further learning.

Beliefs and Behaviors Are Interdependent. Belief systems guide be-haviors. It is the examination of belief systems that encourages us to re-think our actions. Behavior, however, provides the grist for examination of beliefs. Without concrete experience, discussions of beliefs can remain empty talk untethered to practice.

The Pedagogy of Professional Development Must Be Self-Similar to the Pedagogy Desired in Classrooms. Just as students construct their under-standing of mathematics, teachers construct their understanding of the processes of teaching and learning mathematics. One's current views of teaching and learning are grounded in one's own experiences as a learner and teacher. Most teachers have learned mathematics in traditional ways. They know of no other recourse. The mold must be broken. People need ample opportunities to construct new understandings of mathe-matics, teaching, learning, and schooling. As learners, teachers must see firsthand how interaction with others increases opportunities to learn so that they can provide similar opportunities for their students. Unless effective collaborative work has been a personal experience, how can teachers be expected to establish an environment in which collaboration plays a pivotal role in increasing the quality of the classroom discourse?

Issues of Equity Must Permeate the Fabric of Professional Develop-ment. At the very heart of the reform is one simple standard. None of it will matter unless it improves learning for all students, regardless of race, gender, or class. Changing beliefs about who can do worthwhile mathe-matics must be central to the efforts.

Professional Development Must Be Grounded in Classroom Practice. The real hope for making broad-scale change is the ability to tie profes-sional discussions and examinations to what is happening in classrooms. Teachers must experience reform in their own classrooms and have opportunities to grapple with those experiences.

All Teachers Are Capable of Making the Changes. I believe that the driving force for the majority of teachers is the dream of helping children to become successful, productive adults. They want to do the best for their children. Teachers need opportunities to rethink their practices in light of new information. Given opportunities to share current profes-sional thinking and findings, teachers can begin to make shifts. These changes must occur in all classrooms, not just the classrooms of the in-novative teachers. Teachers who are new to the profession and teachers who have taught for 30 years can engage in reflective practice.

Conclusion

The Renaissance has leveraged significant resources. It has used networks of teachers and created new ones. Teachers have engaged in high-quality professional conversations about practice. The program's cadre of teacher leaders has demonstrated its capability to support school-based professional development. The Renaissance is clearly having an impact, but this is a complex agenda that will take years to assess.

Resource D:
Global Systems Science:
A Professional Development Program for High School Teachers

Lawrence Hall of Science,
University of California, Berkeley

Principal: Diane, I understand that you're excited about this new integrated program called Global Systems Science, but I'm
concerned that some of our parents will worry that their
children will do poorly on standardized tests if it replaces
the usual science curriculum.

Diane: Then its about time we educate some of our parents about
the need for science literacy concerning environmental issues. The National Science Education Standards and our
State Science Framework say we should spend less time
teaching science vocabulary and more time helping our students relate science to the real world.

Jim: I'm not concerned that students who take integrated science
will miss out on chemistry, physics, and biology. We plan to
present the same concepts we taught before, but in a meaningful context. Students will still have labs, but they'll also
debate the social implications of science and technology.

Principal: Now I didn't say I was against it, but I'll be the one to take
the heat if our community is not convinced it's a good idea.
Are you willing to present your ideas at the Parent Teacher
Association next Thursday evening?

The previous dialogue did not take place in a real principal's office.
Zooming the "camera lens" back from the small group seated around the
table, one can see at least 20 other teachers listening intently as their

colleagues role play scenes that might actually occur when they return from the 1995 Summer Institute in Global Systems Science (GSS). Previously during the institute, the participants met with colleagues from throughout the nation and compared notes with other science and mathematics teachers who field tested the student guides and laboratory activities. Later, they helped to create new activities and assessment instruments that would eventually be used in hundreds of other classrooms.

As codevelopers of this new science program, the 125 teachers who participated in the GSS programs between 1993 and 1995 increased their understanding of how studies of our planet are actually conducted and how these insights can best be communicated to diverse groups of students. They also returned to their school districts with a mission to change the current emphasis of high school science departments from preparing a small segment of the population for college to providing all of the nation's students with the skills that they will need to thrive in the modern world. The GSS program is one vehicle for accomplishing that, and the GSS professional development strategy, in which teachers learn to develop, implement, and disseminate new instructional materials, is one way to prepare them to change the course of science education as the nation enters the 21st century.

Although the professional development aspects of the GSS program took place in the 1990s, its genesis can be traced to the context of the 1980s, when the national agenda began to focus on global change and science education reform.

The Context of Global Environmental Change

The worldwide climatic disturbances of 1988 (no less than an epidemic of droughts, famines, severe storms, and forest fires) focused attention on the danger of global warming—the theory that increased carbon dioxide in the atmosphere, due to the burning of fossil fuels and other human activities, is warming the entire globe. The potential for the industrial revolution to cause global warming had been predicted more than 100 years ago, but it was not until 1988 that the prospect was finally taken seriously, although scientists were by no means in complete agreement about whether global warming was under way and, if so, what it would mean for the future.

The prospect of global climate change was not the only environmental problem on the horizon at the end of the 1980s. The ever-increasing use of the world's resources to provide energy, food, and housing for a rapidly increasing human population was clearly changing natural environments, resulting in a loss of biodiversity. Also, new developments in technology were found to be influencing the global environment in unexpected ways such as depletion of ozone gas in the stratosphere, exposing all life on the planet to higher levels of ultraviolet radiation from the sun.

Although men and women of every age probably consider themselves to exist at a unique time in history, during our lifetimes we are witness to the transformation of millions of square miles of natural habitats into farms, cities, industrial parks, and malls. The world's growing population and its tendency to become even more urbanized and industrialized is affecting the environment on a global scale. Although these changes have been under way for decades, it has only been at the end of the 20th century that a large number of people have become aware of the scope of these changes and their implications for future generations.

The Context of Science Education Reform

If the 1980s were characterized as the decade of "crisis" in science education, then the 1990s may well be characterized as the decade of "change." *Project 2061* from the American Association for the Advancement of Science (1993), the *Scope and Sequence Project* from the National Science Teachers Association (1993), and the *National Science Education Standards,* created by the National Research Council (1996), are challenging the status quo. Although each of these projects deals with a different aspect of the science education system, they all project a similar image of the ideal science classroom. All three identify similar lists of the most important scientific concepts, theories, and attitudes that should form the core of the school science curriculum. All three emphasize the need to teach fewer topics in greater depth and to teach not only what scientists have learned about the world but also how they have learned it. All three support an inquiry-based approach, recognizing that students bring their own ideas to the classroom, and that students construct new meaning from these prior ideas. Also, all three projects suggest that high school science courses might be more useful and appealing to students if they focus on interdisciplinary issues relevant to the modern world rather than on the traditional disciplines.

Responding to the call for change, many administrators directed teachers to spend the summer "writing a new course" that integrates the sciences and meets other criteria laid out by the reform documents. Global change has been a popular subject for these courses because relevant topics appear in the news almost every day. Environmental protection is of concern to high school students, and the subject lends itself to an inquiry-based approach in which depth is emphasized over breadth. Although many creative teachers have developed excellent activities and assembled useful reading materials, most of these efforts have been conducted in isolation. The problem with developing instructional materials in isolation is that the same work must be repeated by many individuals, the opportunities for testing activities with students are limited, and the potential benefit of teachers working together to share their knowledge and build on each other's ideas and strengths is entirely lost.

Development of the GSS Program

Development of the GSS materials started in 1990, when the Lawrence Hall of Science was awarded grants from the National Institute for Global Environmental Change, with funds from the U.S. Department of Energy and the National Science Foundation. The product of the 6-year effort is an interdisciplinary course for high school students that emphasizes how scientists from a wide variety of fields work together to understand significant problems of global impact. Global ideas of science are stressed, such as the concept of an interacting system, the coevolution of the atmosphere and life, the goal of a sustainable world, and the important role that individuals play in both influencing and protecting the vulnerable global environment.

The GSS course materials involve students actively in learning. Students perform experiments in the classroom and at home. They read and discuss background materials. They "meet" a wide variety of men and women who are working to understand global environmental change. They work together to dramatize their ideas for working toward solutions to worldwide environmental problems. They are challenged to make intelligent, informed decisions and to take personal actions, such as conserving energy, recycling, and preparing for their roles as voting citizens in a modern industrialized society.

The GSS Professional Development Program

The goal of the GSS professional development program was not just to implement a new course of integrated studies but also to enable teachers to actively carry out the new educational reforms. The key strategy that was selected to achieve this goal was teacher as curriculum developer. According to nearly all the teachers who attended the institutes, the experience of working intensively with colleagues for 3 weeks to discuss what to teach and how to teach, within a framework of guiding principles, was a valuable educational experience in itself. In addition, their creative work in helping to shape and improve the program increased their commitment and their understanding of the principles on which it is based. In the GSS program, this strategy played out in five distinct phases, which are discussed in the following sections.

Phase I: Pilot Testing

Unlike many professional development programs that begin with an institute or a workshop, this strategy begins by asking the teachers to help pilot test new course materials. During the 4- to 6-week period of pilot testing, the teachers do what they usually do—teach science; they substitute, however, a new unit of instructional materials in place of what they normally teach at this time of year. The materials themselves are quite different from the usual textbook, and the accompanying teacher's guide offers suggestions for teaching methods and supplementary activities. During this phase of the program, teachers become familiar with and develop opinions about the new approach.

Phase II: Summer Institute

Having pilot tested the GSS materials, teachers arrive at the summer institute with a common experience. During the first week, they share their insights about the content and process of teaching the new materials and provide critical feedback to the GSS staff. In the second and third weeks of the institute, the teachers focus their creative energies on making the course better by inventing new activities and assessment tasks. They present these to their colleagues and receive affirmation of their efforts and constructive feedback. They also visit laboratories and meet scientists involved in GSS research. Finally, they learn how the GSS program fits into the context of science education reform, and they participate in activities such as the role-play session described at the beginning of the chapter.

Phase III: Assessment of Impact on Students

For teachers to commit to an innovative approach, they need to be convinced that it is making a positive contribution to their students' learning. The teacher's guide provides several ideas for testing student understanding before and after teaching a unit so that it is possible for teachers to see what their students have learned; the guide also provides ideas for maintaining portfolios of student work. Many of the teachers also provide student test data to the GSS staff in Berkeley for analysis and publication of comprehensive evaluation studies.

Phase IV: Networking

Experiences in working with other teachers to develop innovative approaches often lead to a desire for continued contact with the growing community of teachers who share an interest in the program both to find out about new activities developed by others and to share their own innovations. Electronic bulletin boards, newsletters, and reunions at teachers' conferences are ways that are currently being used to support the network of teachers using the GSS materials.

Phase V: Dissemination

It is hoped that the teacher-as-curriculum developer strategy will be maintained as new teachers learn about the program and adapt it for use by their own students.

The strategy of teacher as curriculum developer is by no means a new approach to professional development. Federally funded curriculum development projects have traditionally involved teachers both in the early brainstorm phases of materials development and in trial testing experimental activities. Teachers have contributed very important ideas to many of the science programs used in today's schools, and some sets of classroom activities have been entirely developed by teachers. The focus of these programs, however, has generally been on the products of the instructional materials that were developed rather than on the value of the teachers who helped to develop them. Recognizing that teacher as curriculum developer is a strategy for professional development should make it easier to export it to new situations. This strategy is especially effective for experienced teachers who are being asked to expand their capabilities and adopt new approaches and perspectives.

Resource E:
Professional Development for Elementary School Science Curriculum Implementation: The Case of Cambridge, Massachusetts

KAREN WORTH
Senior Scientist, Education Development Center,
Center for Urban Science Education Reform,
Newton, Massachusetts
and Faculty, Wheelock College

MELANIE BARRON
Director of Science, Cambridge Public School System,
Cambridge, Massachusetts

Context

This case describes the professional development components of an effort to reform science education in a district through implementation of a districtwide core of in-depth science inquiry-based units of study. The setting is Cambridge, Massachusetts, which is a city of 72,938 people with an elementary student population of 5,725 in kindergarten (K) through sixth grade and an elementary teacher population of 300. Fifty-six percent of the children are minorities and 43% come from poor homes. The city has 15 K through eighth-grade schools and one large high school. The program described in this case is for elementary schools only; the district, however, is also implementing reform in Grades 7 through 9 with the goal of having a fully articulated K through ninth-grade program in place within the next several years.

Five years ago, the city hired a new science director who came with the charge and mission of reforming science education throughout the district. At the start, she undertook four key initiatives that laid the foundation for the professional development plan that has been in place for 2 years.

The first initiative was the redeployment of science specialists who had been teaching science classes in the elementary grades. The role of teaching science specialist was eliminated. To support the district reform effort at the classroom and school level, 5 teachers were selected to become science staff development teachers. Each works in up to three schools with approximately 50 teachers and provides a wide range of support to individual teachers, groups of teachers, and school-level planning teams.

A second initiative was the development of a conceptual framework for science in the elementary years. This framework, based on a new state framework, the *National Science Education Standards* (National Research Council, 1996), and the *Project 2061: Benchmarks for Science Literacy* (American Association for the Advancement of Science, 1993), was brief and to the point, providing an outline of basic concepts that students were to have studied by the second and sixth grades. This framework is providing the necessary guidance for the gradual selection of hands-on, inquiry-based science units at every grade level—the curriculum itself.

A third initiative was the decision to require all teachers at each grade level to teach four units of science per year, with three to be determined by the district and the fourth to be selected at the school or classroom level. A plan was set into place in which a wide variety of curriculum units were to be piloted in classrooms throughout the district. Out of this process would come a set of criteria for selecting units and information that would lead to the list of required units at each grade level. Teachers would be asked to begin with one unit and then, during a period of 3 to 5 years, incorporate all four. This process is currently ongoing.

Finally, a plan for a centralized resource center was initiated to provide teachers with the necessary materials for teaching the science units.

As these efforts were proceeding, the district science director prepared and submitted a proposal to the National Science Foundation for an intensive multiyear teacher enhancement program to support the entire elementary teaching staff in the implementation of this modular, inquiry-based science program. The following were the goals of the plan:

- To improve science learning for all elementary students in the Cambridge public schools

- To implement an inquiry-based, modular science curriculum across the district

- To build teacher leadership and expertise within the system

- To develop a structure that would permanently sustain the science program

The following assumptions were made as the program was designed:

- Districtwide reform of science education must be systemic with strong support structures at the central and school levels, real support for classroom teachers, and support and engagement from the community.

- District-mandated reform reduces the risk for teachers and administrators at the school level.

- Professional development must support different tiers of teachers, different levels of expertise among teachers, and different areas of interest among teachers.

- Implementation of materials-rich, inquiry-based curricula is often a staged process during which teachers move from awareness to mechanical use, to inquiry teaching, and to ownership and adaptation.

- Building capacity for growth and renewal within a system is critical to sustainability

The professional development plan that was funded followed a structure that, in various guises, is quite common throughout the country where systems are attempting to put into place a centrally determined modular curriculum. It is a three-tiered approach with five science staff development teachers, two liaison teachers acting as point people at each school but with full classroom responsibilities, and the remaining staff teaching in their classrooms. The professional development program had to address the needs of these three different groups of professionals. In addition, the program had to consider the reality that teachers in the district and in each category were very diverse. For some, teaching from an inquiry perspective was unfamiliar; others were already skilled in the instructional strategies of inquiry teaching but did not apply them in science; still others, although fewer in number, were skilled in teaching inquiry-based science.

Program Description

The following sections present a brief description of each group of teachers, the professional development program for each group, and some of the reasoning behind the design.

The Science Staff Development Teachers

It was clear from the start that the staff development teachers were critical to the success of the reform effort. The district had to develop a cadre of experts from within who could lead the implementation process. The science staff development teachers were the frontline professional support people; their skills and knowledge would be critical in helping the district, schools, and teachers implement the district plan. It was important to build an intensive professional development program with and for them from the start so that they would be supported on a continual basis.

The science staff development teachers all came from classroom teaching. All but one had been a science specialist within the district's more traditionally structured program. Each was chosen for his or her experience and interest in teaching science. All were interested in moving from working directly with children to playing a role supporting other teachers.

The professional development program for the staff development teachers needed to address several areas. It had to systematically and continuously enhance their knowledge of inquiry-based science and science teaching. It had to develop their knowledge of the curriculum materials that were under consideration and those being used in the system. It had to provide them with skills in working with others, both individually and in groups; skills in leading workshops, institutes, and presentations; and skills in taking responsibility for the design and implementation of a variety of activities within the district.

The following four professional strategies were selected:

- Weekly meetings: These 3-hour meetings provide the opportunity for reflection, communication, sharing, and problem solving. They are facilitated by one of the program consultants.

- Ten professional days: The professional development days provide an opportunity for intensive work in science inquiry and curriculum, peer support and mentoring, and group leadership. These days are facilitated by individual experts but are structured and designed by the five science staff development teachers.

- Apprenticeships and mentoring: Learning to be a staff development teacher also requires clinical experience. Working with more experienced facilitators and workshop leaders allows the staff development teachers to develop the skills they need before assuming the full responsibility for such activities themselves.

- Access to individual professional growth opportunities: The local community offers many opportunities for individual professional growth, including courses, workshops, and conferences. Making the science staff development teachers aware of these and assisting with access and, at times, cost is an important component of this program.

Liaison Teachers

The reform effort in the district could not rely on the work of just five people to support the implementation in every school and every classroom; therefore, school-based liaison teachers were critical. With limited resources, it was impossible to provide release time for the liaison teachers. Therefore, the program planners felt it was critical at the start that the liaison teachers focus their time and development on their own science teaching so as to create exciting science classrooms within each building. At the same time, this plan would begin the process of developing a cadre of classroom experts within the system.

There are two liaison teachers in each building who work with the science staff development teacher to support schoolwide implementation of the reform. They are not released from their classrooms but receive stipends for their work and for their professional development time. To become a liaison teacher, teachers must submit an application. Some do so because of their particular skill and interest in science teaching, some apply because of their interest in something new and in working in a new way, and some apply because they were asked to do so by a building administrator.

The professional development program for this group needed to address the skills of good science teaching. The liaison teachers needed experiences with the concept of inquiry, the teaching of inquiry-based science, and the curriculum units that were being identified by the district. In the long run, they also needed the skills to work as a liaison within the building, supporting colleagues and supporting school-level planning.

The following four professional development strategies were selected:

- Four-day institute: A 4-day institute each summer, jointly led by the staff development teachers and selected external consultants, provides the opportunity for the liaison teachers to engage in inquiry, discuss and share ideas about teaching and learning science, and study the Cambridge frameworks and the modules that are under consideration for the Cambridge curriculum.

These 4 days also bring the group together to discuss and reflect on the many demands of their role as liaison.

- Unit workshops: All liaison teachers are given the opportunity to participate in two types of unit workshops: (a) after-school meetings and (b) mentoring and coaching.

  Six after-school meetings take place during the academic year. These maintain the networking and communication among the members of the group and provide opportunities to familiarize the liaisons with a range of resources for their buildings and particular aspects of science teaching, such as assessment and adaptation of units.

  The staff development teachers provide mentoring and coaching to support the liaison teachers in their growth and development. They coach the liaisons in their classrooms, meet with them to discuss school issues, and cofacilitate activities at the school with other teachers.

- Apprenticeships: Some liaisons have begun to apprentice themselves to workshop leaders, engage in leadership in other science projects in the district, and take advantage of resources made available through the district.

- Study groups: During the second year, small study groups of 6 to 10 liaison teachers were formed to allow liaisons to pursue issues of particular interest and to become experts in a particular domain.

Regular Classroom Teachers

For the reform effort in the district to reach the classroom level, support was necessary for every teacher.

All the classroom teachers are being asked to eventually teach four units of study per year. They are, as in any system, a diverse group of people with many different levels of expertise and experience. Some are very knowledgeable in the teaching and learning of inquiry-based science; some are less comfortable with science but teach from a child-centered, inquiry-based philosophy; and some teach from a more traditional belief system.

Because of limited resources, it is not possible to provide intensive professional development experiences for everyone. The decision was made to provide the intensive development support to the leadership cadre—to build the leadership capacity within the district—and limit the program for the rest of the teachers. The program planners, however, feel it is essential to provide teachers with a significant introduction to each of the units. Once familiar with a unit, teachers can turn to the staff development teachers, the liaisons, and one another for ongoing in-school support.

The following professional development strategies were selected:

- Two-day institute: A 2-day summer institute was developed for each unit selected for the district. These 2-day institutes are designed to take teachers through an entire unit, exploring the materials themselves, the science content, the nature of the inquiry, and the teaching strategies required. In addition, time is spent exploring ways in which each unit might be enriched by local resources and connected to other areas of the curriculum. The institutes are led by the science staff development teachers and external consultants and include scientists from the community for each unit.

- Individual school-based support: This support is available to all teachers through the science staff development teachers who are present in each school at least one day a week. The support they provide varies in response to teacher and school needs and includes model teaching, classroom assistance, leading grade-level discussions, being members on schoolwide science action committees, and helping to access community resources. The liaison teachers are not freed from classroom responsibilities, so they have a limited role in direct classroom support. They are, however, available for such things as answering questions, providing resources, and coordinating meetings.

Neither the overall program in Cambridge nor the individual components have remained static during the 2 years of operation. As the groups have matured, a number of interesting developments have occurred. This growth and development is a powerful sign of success. As each group changes and becomes more diversified in strengths, needs, and interests, however, the program leaders must reexamine the design and make new decisions to meet a new set of strengths, needs, and interests in a changing context.

Status of the Program in Its Third Year

The staff developers have begun to broaden their activities, engaging in grant writing and program management. One coordinates the volunteer students from two local universities, one wrote a successful grant to the National Gardening Association and is coordinating the infusion of this program into the system, and another is responsible for a program of minisabbaticals at the local science museum. Their work in the schools has become increasingly sophisticated. Weekly meetings and professional development days for the science staff development teachers now focus on in-depth issues of teacher change, school reform, and the role of a staff developer. They have become leaders of institutes and workshops and cofacilitators of liaison study groups. There is a trade-off in this change. As they take on new tasks and their roles change, the staff development teachers spend less time in their schools and in classrooms providing the site-based support for reform. Care needs to be taken so that the shift away from direct classroom support does not move more quickly than the building of capacity of liaison teachers and the overall capacity of the teaching staff.

The liaison teachers have become more comfortable in the classroom and in their roles, and many have begun to develop interests in different areas as well as interest in becoming more involved with the design of their own professional development activities. A uniform professional development plan for them is no longer possible. The study groups described previously reflect one adaptation to their request. In addition, opportunities such as the museum fellowships, courses at local institutions, and intensive institutes provide additional possibilities. Full group meetings still occur, although less frequently, to maintain the sense of community deemed critical by the liaisons themselves.

The K through sixth-grade teachers have been introduced to many of the kits. The individualized and small group support they receive at the school is, of course, constantly changing to meet their needs and as the science staff development teachers become increasingly skilled in their roles. Some teachers are considering the adaptation and enrichment of the kits; others are looking forward to a second institute with the materials to increase their understanding of a particular unit. A number are becoming involved in new initiatives within the district and growing professionally through these. This development is powerful and a sign of success, but it requires that program designers reexamine decisions and realign the components to meet a new set of needs and groups within groups.

Many questions confront the Cambridge team as it moves forward. Much has been accomplished. There is now a foundation that includes a framework and a curriculum, a materials center, a growing cadre of teacher leaders, a powerful relationship with the Massachusetts Institute of Technology, and a partnership with several key consultants at the Education Development Center. Every Cambridge school and teacher at the elementary level has been influenced by the work in science. To no one's surprise, however, true inquiry-based science teaching and learning in every classroom is not yet a reality.

The team must reexamine the progress made, what needs to be done, and the resources available. Is the decision to focus on leadership development still a good one? What is needed now for the liaison teachers in their work at the school level? Should the balance of efforts be shifted to the classroom teachers? What is the nature of professional development for classroom teachers once the kits are in use? Should building administrators be the target of some of the professional development efforts? Are the efforts at the seventh- through ninth-grade level moving forward so as to support the students as they emerge from the elementary years?

The team must also begin to look to the future. What is the long-term picture after the Teacher Enhancement grant is over? How will the progress be sustained? Who will pay for the efforts needed to sustain the work? What will those efforts look like?

Both sets of questions are the focus of discussion of the Cambridge design team as they plan for Year 4 and beyond.

References

Acquarelli, K., & Mumme, J. (1996). A renaissance in mathematics education reform. *Phi Delta Kappan, 77*(7), 478-484.

American Association for the Advancement of Science. (1993). *Project 2061: Benchmarks for science literacy.* New York: Oxford University Press.

American Association for the Advancement of Science. (1997). *Resources for science literacy: Professional development* [CD-ROM]. Washington, DC: Author.

Aronson, J. Z. (1995). *Stop the clock: Ending the tyranny of time in education, policy perspective on time and learning.* San Francisco: Far West Laboratory.

Badders, B., Klamar, L., Saunders, G., Miller, R., Berger, M., Byrd, C., Ricketts, R., Zeigler-Nizer, Y., Fanning, C., & Brown, R. (1996). *Journeys: A collegial study group of Cleveland teachers.* Paper presented at the annual meeting of the National Science Teachers Association, St. Louis, MO.

Bailey, S. (1995, December). *Managing reform efforts—Detecting & "gardening" multiple change initiatives.* Speech presented at the annual conference of the National Staff Development Council, Chicago.

Ball, D. L. (1996). Teacher learning and the mathematics reforms: What we think we know and what we need to learn. *Phi Delta Kappan, 77*(7), 500-508.

Ball, D. L., & Cohen, D. (1995). *Developing practice, developing practitioners: Toward a practice-based theory of professional education.* Paper presented at the National Commission on Teaching and America's Future, New York.

Barnett, C. (1991). Building a case-based curriculum to enhance the pedagogical content knowledge of mathematics teachers. *Journal of Teacher Education, 42*(4), 263-272.

Barnett, C., & Friedman, S. (in press). Mathematics case discussions: Nothing is sacred. In E. Fennema & B. Scott-Nelson (Eds.), *Mathematics teachers in transition.* Hillsdale, NJ: Lawrence Erlbaum.

Barnett, C., & Sather, S. (1992). *Using case discussions to promote changes in beliefs among mathematics teachers.* Paper presented at the annual meeting of the American Education Research Association, San Francisco.

Barth, R. (1980). *Run school run.* Cambridge, MA: Harvard University Press.

Becerra, A. M. (1996). Developing and supporting diverse leadership. *Open MIC: A Journal of the California Subject Matter Projects, 3*(2), 6-8.

Beeth, M. E. (1993). *Dynamic aspects of conceptual change instruction* (pp. 126-132). Unpublished doctoral dissertation, University of Wisconsin at Madison.

Bell, B., & Gilbert, J. (1996). *Teacher development: A model from science education.* London: Falmer.

Bennett, B., & Green, N. (1995). Effect of the learning consortium: One district's journey. *School Effectiveness and School Improvement, 6*(3), 247-264.

Biological Science Curriculum Study. (1995). *Decisions in teaching elementary school science* [videodisc]. Colorado Springs, CO: Author.

Blume, G. W., & Nicely, R. S. (1991). *A guide for reviewing school mathematics programs.* Reston, VA: National Council of Teachers of Mathematics.

Brown, C. A., & Smith, M. S. (1997). Supporting the development of mathematical pedagogy. *The Mathematics Teacher, 90*(2), 138-143.

Bull, B., Buechler, M., Didley, S., & Krehbiel, L. (1994). *Professional development and teacher time: Principles, guidelines, and policy options for Indiana.* Report prepared for the Indiana Department of Education. Indianapolis: Indiana University, School of Education Office, Indiana Education Policy Center.

Burns, M. (1994). *Replacement units: A direction for changing math instruction.* Sausalito, CA: Math Solutions Publications, Marilyn Burns Education Associates.

Bush, S. S. (1997). The Kentucky K-4 mathematics specialist program. In S. N. Friel & G. W. Bright (Eds.), *Reflecting on our work: NSF teacher enhancement in K-6 mathematics* (pp. 173-178). Lanham, MD: University Press of America.

Bybee, R. (1993). *Reforming science education: Social perspectives and personal reflections.* New York: Teachers College Press.

Campbell, P. F., & Robles, J. (1997). Project IMPACT: Increasing the Mathematical Power of All Children and Teachers. In S. N. Friel & G. W. Bright (Eds.), *Reflecting on our work: NSF teacher enhancement in K-6 mathematics* (pp. 179-186). Lanham, MD: University Press of America.

Castle, S., & Watts, G. D. (1992). The tyranny of time. *A Forum on School Transformation from the NEA National Center for Innovation, 7*(2), 1-4.

Center for Children and Technology, Education Development Center, Inc. (1995). On-line learning, on-line communities. *CCT Notes, 3*(1), 1-6.

Clarke, D. (1994). Ten key principles for research for the professional development of mathematics teachers. In D. B. Aichele & F. Coxford (Eds.), *Professional development for teachers of mathematics: 1994 yearbook* (pp. 37-48). Reston, VA: National Council of Teachers of Mathematics.

Cobb, P. (1994). Where is the mind? Constructivist and sociocultural perspectives on mathematical development. *Educational Researcher, 23*(7), 13-20.

Coble, C. R., & Koballa, T. R., Jr. (1996). Science education. In J. Sikula, T. J. Buttery, & E. Guyton (Eds.), *Handbook of research on teacher education* (pp. 459-484). New York: Simon & Schuster/Macmillan.

Corcoran, T. B. (1995, June). *Helping teachers teach well: Transforming professional development* (Policy Brief No. RB-16). New Brunswick: Rutgers, the State University of New Jersey, Consortium for Policy Research in Education.

Corwin, R. B. (1997). Talking mathematics: Supporting discourse in elementary school classrooms. In S. N. Friel & G. W. Bright (Eds.), *Reflecting on our work: NSF teacher enhancement in K-6 mathematics* (pp. 187-192). Lanham, MD: University Press of America.

Costa, A., & Kallick, B. (1993). Through the lens of a critical friend. *Educational Leadership, 51*(3), 49-51.

Council of Chief State School Officers. (1997). *Mathematics and science content standards and curriculum frameworks: States' progress on development and implementation.* Washington, DC: Author.

Davenport, L. R., & Sassi, A. (1995). Transforming mathematics teaching in Grades K-8: How narrative structures in resource materials help support teacher change. In B. S. Nelson (Ed.), *Inquiry and the development of teaching: Issues in the transformation of mathematics teaching* (pp. 37-46). Newton, MA: Center for the Development of Teaching Paper Series, Education Development Center.

Deal, T. A., & Kennedy, A. A. (1982). *Corporate cultures: The rites and rituals of corporate life.* Reading, MA: Addison-Wesley.

DiRanna, K., Osterfeld, M., Cerwin, K., Topps, J., & Tucker, D. (1995, Spring). *Facilitator's guide to science assessment.* California Department of Education, California Science Implementation Network, California Science Project, Scope, Sequence, & Coordination Project, & Santa Barbara County Office of Education Region 8.

Driscoll, M., & Bryant, D. (in press). *Getting started with teachers.* Washington, DC: National Research Council, Mathematical Sciences Education Board.

Driver, R., Asoko, H., Leach, J., Mortimer, E., & Scott, P. (1994). Constructing scientific knowledge in the classroom. *Educational Researcher, 23*(7), 5-12.

Duckworth, E. (1986). Teaching as research. *Harvard Educational Review, 56*(4), 481-495.

Duschl, R. A. (1990). *Restructuring science education: The importance of theories and their development.* New York: Teachers College Press.

Dyasi, H. (1996). *The Workshop Center at City College of New York.* Paper presented at the Professional Development Project of the National Institute for Education.

Dyasi, H. M. (1995). *The City College Workshop Center program for reculturing teachers to teach inquiry-based science in the elementary school.* Unpublished manuscript.

Education Commission of the States. (1995). *Scaling-up math, science and technology education reform: Strategies from the National Science Foundation's statewide systemic initiatives.* Denver: Author.

Elmore, R. F. (1996). Getting to scale with good educational practice. *Harvard Educational Review, 66*(1), 1-26.

Evans, C. S. (1993). When teachers look at student work. *Educational Leadership, 50*(5), 71-72.

Far West Laboratory. (1990, Summer). *Case methods: A knowledge brief on effective teaching.* San Francisco: Author.

Farrell, A. M. (1994). Industry internships and professional development. In D. B. Aichele & A. F. Coxford (Eds.), *Professional development for teachers of mathematics, 1994 yearbook* (pp. 276-285). Reston, VA: The National Council of Teachers of Mathematics.

Fennema, E., Carpenter, T. P., & Franke, M. L. (1997). Cognitively guided instruction (CGI). In S. N. Friel & G. W. Bright (Eds.), *Reflecting on our work: NSF teacher enhancement in K-6 mathematics* (pp. 193-196). Langham, MD: University Press of America.

Fenstermacher, G. D. (1986). Philosophy of research on teaching: Three aspects. In M. C. Wittrock (Ed.), *Handbook of research on teaching, 3rd edition* (pp. 37-49). New York: Macmillan.

Ferrini-Mundy, J. (1997). Reform efforts in mathematics education: Reckoning with the realities. In S. N. Friel & G. W. Bright (Eds.), *Reflecting on our work: NSF teacher enhancement in K-6 mathematics* (pp. 113-132). Lanham, MD: University Press of America.

Filby, N. N. (1995, November 30). *Analysis of reflective professional development models.* San Francisco: WestEd.

Friel, S. N. (1996). *Teach-Stat: A model for professional development in data analysis and statistics for teachers K-6.* Paper presented at the Professional Development Project of the National Institute for Science Education, Madison, WI.

Friel, S. N., & Bright, G. W. (Eds.). (1997). *Reflecting on our work: NSF teacher enhancement in K-6 mathematics.* Lanham, MD: University Press of America.

Friel, S. N., & Bright, G. W. (in press). Teach-Stat: A model for professional development in data analysis and statistics for teachers, K-6. In S. P. Lajoie (Ed.), *Reflections on statistics: Agendas for learning, teaching, and assessment in K-12.* Hillsdale, NJ: Lawrence Erlbaum.

Friel, S. N., & Danielson, M. L. (1997). Teach-Stat: A key to better mathematics. In S. N. Friel & G. W. Bright (Eds.), *Reflecting on our work: NSF teacher enhancement in K-6 mathematics* (pp. 197-206). Lanham, MD: University Press of America.

Friel, S. N., & Joyner, J. M. (Principal Investigators) (1991). *Project Teach-Stat: A key to better mathematics* (Grant No. TPE-9153779). Arlington, VA: National Science Foundation.

Friel, S. N., & Joyner, J. (Eds.). (1997). *Teach-Stat for teachers: Professional development manual.* Palo Alto, CA: Seymour.

Frost, D. L. (1995). *Elementary teachers' conceptions of mathematics staff development and their roles as workshop leaders.* Unpublished doctoral dissertation, University of North Carolina at Greensboro.

Fullan, M. G. (1991). *The new meanings of educational change.* New York: Teachers College Press.

Fullan, M. G. (1993). *Change forces: Probing the depths of educational reform.* Bristol, PA: Falmer.

Fullan, M. G., & Hargreaves, A. (1991). *What's worth fighting for? Working together for your school.* Andover, MA: The Regional Laboratory for Educational Improvement of the Northeast and Islands.

Fullan, M. G., & Miles, M. (1992). Getting reform right: What works and what doesn't. *Phi Delta Kappan, 73*(10), 745-752.

Garmston, R. (1987). How administrators support peer coaching. *Educational Leadership, 44*(5), 18-28.

Gleason, J., Vesilind, E., Friel, S., & Joyner, J. (Eds.). (1996). *Teach-Stat for statistics educators: Staff developers manual.* Palo Alto, CA: Seymour.

Grady, A. (1997). Elementary and middle school math and technology project. In S. N. Friel & G. W. Bright (Eds.), *Reflecting on our work: NSF teacher enhancement in K-6 mathematics* (pp. 207-214). Lanham, MD: University Press of America.

Graham, A. (1987). *Statistical investigations in the secondary school.* Cambridge, UK: Cambridge University Press.

Gray, H. (1989). *Anatomy: Descriptive and surgical.* New York: Livingstone.

Grouws, D. A., & Schultz, K. A. (1996). Mathematics teacher education. In J. Sikula, T. J. Buttery, & E. Guyton (Eds.), *Handbook of research on teacher education* (2nd ed., pp. 442-458). New York: Simon & Schuster/ Macmillan.

Guskey, T. R. (1986). Staff development and the process of teacher change. *Educational Researcher, 15*(5), 5-12.

Hall, G. E., & Hord, S. M. (1987). *Change in schools: Facilitating the process.* Albany: State University of New York Press.

Harvard-Smithsonian Center for Astrophysics. (1995). *The private universe teacher workshop videos.* Burlington, VT: The Annenberg/CPB Math and Science Collection.

Hatfield, M. M., & Bitter, G. G. (1994). A multimedia approach to the professional development of teachers: A virtual classroom. In D. B. Aichele & A. F. Coxford (Eds.), *Professional development for teachers of mathematics, 1994 yearbook* (pp. 102-115). Reston, VA: National Council of Teachers of Mathematics.

Hein, G. (1997). The logic of program evaluation: What should we evaluate in teacher enhancement projects? In S. N. Friel & G. W. Bright (Eds.), *Reflecting on our work: NSF teacher enhancement in K-6 mathematics* (pp. 151-162). Lanham, MD: University Press of America.

Hewson, P. W., & Hewson, M. G. A'B. (1988). An appropriate conception of teaching science: A view from studies of science learning. *Science Education, 72*(5), 597-614.

Hewson, P. W., & Thorley, N. R. (1989). The conditions of conceptual change in the classroom. *International Journal of Science Education, 11*(5), 541-553.

Hirst, P. H. (1971). What is teaching? *Journal of Curriculum Studies, 3*(1), 5-18.

Hixson, J., & Tinzmann, M. B. (1990). *What changes are generating new needs for professional development?* Oak Brook, IL: North Central Regional Educational Laboratory.

Holly, P. (1991). Action research: The missing link in the creation of schools as centers of inquiry. In A. Lieberman & L. Miller (Eds.), *Staff development for education in the '90s: New demands, new realities, new perspectives* (pp. 133-157). New York: Teachers College Press.

Hord, S. M., & Boyd, V. (1995). Professional development fuels a culture of continuous improvement. *Journal of Staff Development, 16*(1), 10-15.

Hord, S. M., Rutherford, W. L., Huling-Austin, L., & Hall, G. E. (1987). *Taking charge of change.* Alexandria, VA: Association for Supervision and Curriculum Development.

Horizon Research, Inc. (1997). *1997 local systemic change: Core evaluation data collection manual.* Chapel Hill, NC: Author.

Joyce, B., & Showers, B. (1987). Low cost arrangement for peer coaching. *Journal of Staff Development, 8*(1), 22-24.

Joyce, B., & Showers, B. (1988). *Student achievement through staff development.* New York: Longman.

Joyner, J. (1997). TEAM: Teaching Excellence and Mathematics. In S. N. Friel & G. W. Bright (Eds.), *Reflecting on our work: NSF teacher enhancement in K-6 mathematics* (pp. 223-228). Lanham, MD: University Press of America.

Joyner, J., Pfieffer, S., Friel, S., & Vesilind, E. (Eds.). (1997a). *Teach-Stat activities: Statistics investigations for Grades 1-3.* Palo Alto, CA: Seymour.

Joyner, J., Pfieffer, S., Friel, S., & Vesilind, E. (Eds.). (1997b). *Teach-Stat activities: Statistics investigations for Grades 3-6.* Palo Alto, CA: Seymour.

Klein, S. P., McArthur, D. J., & Stecher, B. M. (1995, February). *What are the challenges to "scaling up" reform?* Briefing paper for National Science Foundation Conference, Washington, DC.

Kleinfeld, J. (n.d.). *Ethical issues and legal liability in writing cases about teaching.* Unpublished manuscript.

LaBonte, K., Leighty, C., Mills, S. J., & True, M. L. (1995). Whole-faculty study groups: Building the capacity for change through interagency collaboration. *Journal of Staff Development, 16*(3), 45-47.

Lampert, M., & Ball, D. (1995). Using hypermedia to investigate and construct knowledge about mathematics teaching and learning. In *Mathematics and teaching through hypermedia.* Ann Arbor, MI: The Math Project.

Lave, J., & Wenger, E. (1991). *Situated learning: Legitimate peripheral participation.* Cambridge, UK: Cambridge University Press.

Leonhardt, N., & Fraser-Abder, P. (1996). Research experiences for teachers. *The Science Teacher, 63*(1), 30-33.

Lieberman, A. (1986). Collaborative research: Working with, not working on. . . . *Educational Leadership, 43*(5), 28-32.

Lieberman, A., & McLaughlin, M. W. (1992). Networks for educational change: Powerful and problematic. *Phi Delta Kappan, 73*(9), 673-677.

Little, J. W. (1982). Norms of collegiality and experimentation: Workplace conditions of school success. *American Educational Research Journal, 19*(3), 325-340.

Little, J. W. (1993). Teachers' professional development in a climate of educational reform. *Educational Evaluation and Policy Analysis, 15*(2), 129-151.

Loucks-Horsley, S. (1995). Professional development and the learner centered school. *Theory Into Practice, 34*(4), 265-271.

Loucks-Horsley, S. (1996). Professional development for science education: A critical and immediate challenge. In R. W. Bybee (Ed.), *National standards and the science curriculum: Challenges, opportunities, and recommendations* (pp. 83-95). Dubuque, IA: Kendall/Hunt.

Loucks-Horsley, S. (1997). Teacher change, staff development, and systemic change: Reflections from the eye of a paradigm shift. In S. N. Friel & G. W. Bright (Eds.), *Reflecting on our work: NSF teacher enhancement in K-6 mathematics* (pp. 133-150). Lanham, MD: University Press of America.

Loucks-Horsley, S., Harding, C. K., Arbuckle, M. A., Murray, L. B., Dubea, C., & Williams, M. K. (1987). *Continuing to learn: A guidebook for teacher development.* Andover, MA/Oxford, OH: The Regional Laboratory for Educational Improvement of the Northeast and Islands/National Staff Development Council.

Loucks-Horsley, S., & Hergert, L. (1985). *An action guide to school improvement.* Andover, MA/Alexandria, VA: The NETWORK, Inc./Association for Supervision and Curriculum Development.

Loucks-Horsley, S., Kapitan, R., Carlson, M. O., Kuerbis, P. J., Clark, R. C., Melle, G. M., Sachse, T. P., & Walton, E. (1990). *Elementary school science for the 90's.* Alexandria, VA/Andover, MA: Association for Supervision and Curriculum Development/The NETWORK, Inc.

Loucks-Horsley, S., & Stiegelbauer, S. (1991). Using knowledge of change to guide staff development. In A. Lieberman & L. Miller (Eds.), *Staff development for education in the 90's: New demands, new realities, new perspectives.* New York: Teachers College Press.

Loucks-Horsley, S., Stiles, K., & Hewson, P. (1996). *Principles of effective professional development for mathematics and science education: A synthe-*

sis of standards. Madison: University of Wisconsin at Madison, National Institute for Science Education.

Makibbin, S., & Sprague, M. (1991). *Study groups: Conduit for reform.* Paper presented at the annual meeting of the National Staff Development Council, St. Louis, MO.

McCormack, M. (1996, September 17). *The Plain Dealer,* p. 2C.

McDiarmid, G. W. (1995). *Realizing new learning for all students: A framework for the professional development of Kentucky teachers* (Special Report, pp. 1-33). East Lansing, MI: National Center for Research on Teacher Learning.

McLaughlin, M. W. (1993). What matters most in teachers' workplace context? In J. W. Little & M. W. McLaughlin (Eds.), *Teachers' work: Individuals, colleagues, and contexts* (pp. 79-103). New York: Teachers College Press.

Mechling, K. R., & Oliver, D. L. (1983). *Promoting science among elementary school principals.* Washington, DC: National Science Teachers Association.

Merseth, K. (1991). *The case for cases in teacher education.* Washington, DC: American Association of Higher Education/American Association of Colleges for Teacher Education.

Miles, M. B. (1983). Unravelling the mysteries of institutionalization. *Educational Leadership, 41*(3), 14-20.

Miller, D. M., & Pine, G. J. (1990). Advancing professional inquiry for educational improvement through action research. *Journal of Staff Development, 11*(3), 56-61.

Miller, L. D., & Hunt, N. P. (1994). Professional development through action research. In D. B. Aichele & A. F. Coxford (Eds.), *Professional development for teachers of mathematics, 1994 yearbook* (pp. 296-303). Reston, VA: National Council of Teachers of Mathematics.

Mr. Wizard Foundation. (1994-1996). *Teacher to teacher with Mr. Wizard, a staff development video series.* Plymouth, MI: Mr. Wizard Institute.

Mumme, J. (1996). *The middle grades mathematics renaissance.* Paper presented at the Professional Development Project of the National Institute for Education, Madison, WI.

Murphy, C. (1992). Study groups foster schoolwide learning. *Educational Leadership, 50*(3), 71-74.

Murphy, C. (1995). Whole-faculty study groups: Doing the seemingly undoable. *Journal of Staff Development, 16*(3), 37-44.

National Center for Improving Science Education. (1993). *Profiling teacher development programs: An approach to formative evaluation.* Washington, DC: Author.

National Commission on Teaching and America's Future. (1996). *What matters most: Teaching for America's future.* New York: Author.

National Council of Teachers of Mathematics. (1989). *Curriculum and evaluation standards for school mathematics.* Reston, VA: Author.

National Council of Teachers of Mathematics. (1991). *Professional standards for teaching mathematics.* Reston, VA: Author.

National Council of Teachers of Mathematics. (1995). *Assessment standards for school mathematics.* Reston, VA: Author.

National Education Commission on Time and Learning. (1994). *Prisoners of time.* Washington, DC: Author.

National Education Goals Panel. (1995). *National educational goals report: Executive summary.* Washington, DC: U.S. Department of Education.

National Research Council. (1996). *The national science education standards.* Washington, DC: National Academy Press.

National Research Council. (in preparation). *Guidelines for aligning instructional materials with the National Science Education Standards.* Washington, DC: National Academy Press.

National Science Resources Center. (1997). *Science for all children: A guide to improving elementary science education in your school district.* Washington, DC: National Academy Press.

National Science Teachers Association. (1993). Scope, sequence and coordination of secondary school science. In *The content core: A guide for curriculum designers.* Arlington, VA: Author.

National Staff Development Council. (1994). *Standards for staff development: Middle level.* Oxford, OH: Author.

National Staff Development Council. (1995a). *Standards for staff development: Elementary school.* Oxford, OH: Author.

National Staff Development Council. (1995b). *Standards for staff development: High school.* Oxford, OH: Author.

Nelson, B. S. (1995). Introduction. In B. S. Nelson (Ed.), *Inquiry and the development of teaching: Issues in the transformation of mathematics teaching* (pp. 1-7). Newton, MA: Center for the Development of Teaching Paper Series, Education Development Center.

The NETWORK, Inc., Continuous Assessment in Science Project. (1996). *Report to the National Science Foundation.* Unpublished document.

New York State Education Department, Office of Educational Television and Public Broadcasting and Thirteen-WNET and Educational Resources Center. (1996). *Just think: Problem solving through inquiry, a K-8 science video series and guidebook.* New York: Author.

Newton, A., Bergstrom, K., Brennan, N., Dunne, K., Gilbert, C., Ibarguen, N., Perez-Selles, M., & Thomas, E. (1994). *Mentoring: A resource and training guide for educators.* Andover, MA: Regional Laboratory for Educational Improvement of the Northeast and Islands.

Norris, J. H. (1994). What leaders need to know about school culture. *Journal of Staff Development, 15*(2), 2-5.

North Central Regional Educational Laboratory. (1996). *Science images video series.* Burlington, VT: The Annenberg/CPB Math and Science Collection.

North Central Regional Educational Laboratory (NCREL). (in preparation). *Professional development* [CD-ROM]. Oak Brook, IL: Author.

Novak, J. D., & Gowin, D. B. (1984). *Learning how to learn.* New York: Cambridge University Press.

Oja, S. N., & Smulyan, L. (1989). Collaborative action research. In *Collaborative action research: A developmental approach* (pp. 1-25). Philadelphia: Falmer.

Olson, L. (1994, November 2). Learning their lessons. *Education Week,* 43-46.

Parke, C. S., & Lane, S. (1996/1997, December/January). Learning from performance assessments in math. *Educational Leadership, 54*(4), 26-29.

Parker, R. E. (1997). Comprehensive school and district restructuring of mathematics: Principles and caveats. In S. N. Friel & G. W. Bright (Eds.), *Reflecting on our work: NSF teacher enhancement in K-6 mathematics* (pp. 237-246). Lanham, MD: University Press of America.

Patterson, J. L. (1993). *Leadership for tomorrow's schools.* Alexandria, VA: Association for Supervision and Curriculum Development.

Peters, T., & Waterman, R. (1982). *In search of excellence.* New York: Harper & Row.

Pfundt, H., & Duit, R. (Eds.). (1994). *Bibliography: Students' alternative frameworks and science education, 4th Edition.* Kiel, Germany: Institut fur die Padagogik der Naturwissenschaften.

Posner, G. J., Strike, K. A., Hewson, P. W., & Gertzog, W. A. (1982). Accommodation of a scientific conception: Toward a theory of conceptual change. *Science Education, 66*(2), 211-227.

Pratt, H., & Loucks-Horsley, S. (1993). Implementing a science curriculum for the middle grades: Progress, problems and prospects. In G. M. Madrazo & L. L. Motz (Eds.), *Sourcebook for science supervisors* (pp. 61-72). Washington, DC: National Science Teachers Association.

Raizen, S. A., & Michelsohn, A. M. (1994). *The future of science in elementary schools: Educating prospective teachers.* San Francisco: Jossey-Bass.

Raywid, M. A. (1993). Finding time for collaboration. *Educational Leadership, 51*(1), 30-34.

Regional Educational Laboratories. (1995). *Facilitating systemic change in science and mathematics education: A toolkit for professional developers.* Andover, MA: The Regional Laboratory for Educational Improvement of the Northeast and Islands.

Richardson, J. (1997). Smart use of time and money enhances staff development. *Journal of Staff Development, 18*(1), 46-50.

The role of leadership in sustaining school reform: Voices from the field. (1996). http://www.ed.gov/pubs/Leadership/

Roseman, J. E., Kesidou, S., & Stern, L. (1996, November). *Identifying curriculum materials for science literacy: A Project 2061 evaluation tool.* Paper presented at the colloquium of the National Research Council, Washington, DC.

Rosenholtz, S. J. (1991). *Teachers' workplace: The social organization of schools.* New York: Teachers College Press.

Russell, S. J., Schifter, D., Bastable, V., Yaffee, L., Lester, J. B., & Cohen, S. (1995). Learning mathematics while teaching. In B. S. Nelson (Ed.), *Inquiry and the development of teaching: Issues in the transformation of mathematics teaching* (pp. 9-16). Newton, MA: Center for the Development of Teaching Paper Series, Education Development Center.

St. John, M., Century, J. R., Tibbits, F., & Heenan, B. (1994). *Reforming elementary science evaluation in urban districts: Reflections on a conference.* Iverness, CA: Iverness Research Associates.

Saphier, J., & King, M. (1985). Good seeds grow in strong cultures. *Educational Leadership, 42*(6), 67-74.

Scardamalia, M., and Bereiter, C. (1994). Computer support for knowledge-building communities. *Journal of the Learning Sciences, 3*(3), 265-283.

Schifter, D. (1994). *Voicing the new pedagogy: Teachers write about learning and teaching mathematics.* Newton, MA: Center for the Development of Teaching, Education Development Center.

Schifter, D. (1996a). A constructivist perspective on teaching and learning mathematics. *Phi Delta Kappan, 77*(7), 492-499.

Schifter, D. (Ed.). (1996b). *What's happening in math class?* (Vols. I and II). New York: Teachers College Press.

Schifter, D., & Bastable, V. (1995, April). *From the teachers' seminar to the classroom: The relationship between doing and teaching mathematics, an example from fractions.* Paper presented at the annual meeting of the American Education Research Association, San Francisco.

Schifter, D., & Fosnot, C. T. (1993). *Reconstructing mathematics education: Stories of teachers meeting the challenges of reform.* New York: Teachers College Press.

Schifter, D., Russell, S. J., & Bastable, V. (in press). Teaching to the big ideas. In M. Solomon (Ed.), *Reinventing the classroom.* New York: Teachers College Press.

Schmidt, B. J., & Faulkner, S. L. (1989). Staff development through distance education. *Journal of Staff Development, 10*(4), 2-7.

Schön, D. A. (1983). *The reflective practitioner: How professionals think in action.* New York: Basic Books.

Schön, D. A. (1988). Educating teachers as reflective practitioners. In P. Grimmett & G. Erickson (Eds.), *Reflection in teacher education.* New York: Teachers College Press.

Senge, P. M. (1990). The leader's new work: Building learning organizations. *Sloan Management Review Report Series, 32*(11), 1-5.

Shanker, A. (1993, September). *The developer: The newsletter of the National Staff Development Council.* Oxford, OH: National Staff Development Council.

Showers, B., & Joyce, B. (1996). The evolution of peer coaching. *Educational Leadership, 53*(6), 12-16.

Shulman, J., & Kepner, D. (1994, October). *The editorial imperative: Responding to productive tensions between case writing and individual development.* Unpublished manuscript, Far West Laboratory, San Francisco.

Shulman, L. S. (1986). Those who understand: Knowledge growth in teaching. *Educational Researcher, 15*(2), 4-14.

Shulman, L. S. (1987). Knowledge and teaching: Foundations of the new reform. *Harvard Educational Review, 57,* 1-22.

Shulman, L. S. (1992). Toward a pedagogy of cases. In J. H. Shulman (Ed.), *Case methods in teacher education* (pp. 1-30). New York: Teachers College Press.

Silver, E. A., Kilpatrick, J., & Schlesinger, B. (1990). *Thinking through mathematics: Fostering inquiry and communication in mathematics classrooms.* New York: College Entrance Examination Board.

Smith, M. S., & O'Day, J. (1991). *Putting the pieces together: Systemic school reform* [Policy briefs]. New Brunswick, NJ: Consortium for Policy Research in Education.

Smith, P. S. (1996). *Report of NTEN evaluation activities and findings: January 1995-January 1996.* Durham, NC: Horizon Research.

Sneider, C. (1995). *Global systems science: A professional development program for high school science teachers.* Paper presented at the Professional Development Project of the National Institute for Education, Madison, WI.

Sneider, C. (1996, June 17). *Summative evaluation report: Astronomy and space science summer institutes for elementary and middle school teachers* (Award No. ESI-9153783). Arlington, VA: National Science Foundation.

Sparks, D. (1994, March 16). A paradigm shift in staff development. *Education Week, 42.*

Sparks, G. M., & Simmons, J. M. (1989). Inquiry-oriented staff development: Using research as a source of tools, not rules. In S. D. Caldwell (Ed.), *Staff development: A handbook of effective practices* (pp. 126-139). Oxford, OH: National Staff Development Council.

Spitzer, W., Wedding, K., & DiMauro, V. (1994). *Fostering reflective dialogues for teacher professional development.* Cambridge, MA: Technical Education Resource Centers.

Stein, M. K., Silver, E. A., & Smith, M. S. (in press). Mathematics reform and teacher development: A community of practice perspective. In J. Greeno & S. Goldman (Eds.), *Thinking practices: A symposium on mathematics and science learning.* Hillsdale, NJ: Lawrence Erlbaum.

Strycker, J. (1995). Science first. *Science and Children, 32*(7), 26-29.

Talbert, J. E., & Perry, R. (1994, April). *How department communities mediate mathematics and science education reforms.* Paper presented at the American Educational Research Association meeting, New Orleans.

Taylor, E. F., & Smith, R. C. (1995). Teaching physics on line. *American Journal of Physics, 63,* 1090-1096.

Technical Education Resource Centers. (1996). *Sense making in science* [Video series]. Portsmouth, NH: Heinemann.

Underhill, R. G. (1997). The lead teacher program of Virginia's state systemic initiative. In S. N. Friel & G. W. Bright (Eds.), *Reflecting on our work: NSF teacher enhancement in K-6 mathematics* (pp. 263-270). Lanham, MD: University Press of America.

United States Department of Education, National Center for Educational Statistics. (1996). *Pursuing excellence* (NCES Publication No. 97-198, pp. 97-198). Washington, DC: U.S. Government Printing Office.

Wallace, M., Cederberg, J., & Allen, R. (1994). Teachers empowering teachers: A professional-enhancement model. In D. B. Aichele & A. F. Coxford (Eds.), *Professional development for teachers of mathematics, 1994 yearbook* (pp. 234-245). Reston, VA: National Council of Teachers of Mathematics.

Wandersee, J. H., Mintzes, J. J., & Novak, J. D. (1994). Research on alternative conceptions in science. In D. L. Gabel (Ed.), *Handbook of research on science teaching and learning* (pp. 177-210). New York: Macmillan.

Watkins, J. (1992, June). *Speaking of action research.* Paper adapted from a presentation to the Board of Overseers of the Regional Laboratory for Educational Improvement of the Northeast and Islands, Andover, MA.

Weissglass, J. (1996). *No compromises on equity in mathematics education: Developing an infrastructure.* Santa Barbara: University of California at Santa Barbara, Center for Educational Change in Mathematics and Science.

WestEd. (1996, Fall). Scientists and teachers working together. *SEABA Journal, 9.*

Wilson, K. G., & Davis, B. (1994). *Redesigning education.* New York: Henry Holt.

Wood, P. (1988). Action research: A field perspective. *Journal of Education for Teaching, 14*(2), 135-150.

Index

**CORWIN
PRESS**

The Corwin Press logo—a raven striding across an open book—represents the happy union of courage and learning. We are a professional-level publisher of books and journals for K–12 educators, and we are committed to creating and providing resources that embody these qualities. Corwin's motto is "Success for All Learners."